BILL'S STORY

…and it's not all
"BULLDUST"

BILL HAND

Memories of Outback Roads and Characters

Second Edition

Copyright© Bill Hand 2018 ISBN 978-0-6481075-1-4

All rights reserved.

No part of this publication may be reproduced, stored in a retrieval system, or transmitted, in any form or by any means, electronic, mechanical, photocopying, recording or otherwise, without the prior written permission of the copyright owner and the publisher.

Disclaimer.

Whilst every effort has been made to ensure that the information contained in this book was correct at the time of publication, no liability will be accepted by the author for the accuracy or completeness of the information. To the best of the author's knowledge, the material used is free of copyright, or has been acknowledged. An apology is extended for the use of any material unwittingly unacknowledged.

Published by

Mini-Publishing

www.minipublishing.com.au

CONTENTS

		Pages
Map		iv
Preface		v
1	The Beginnings of the Sundowner Story	1 - 7
2	1962/3 Redline Experiences	8 - 23
3	1964/5 Our Own Coach "Sundowner"	24 - 36
4	1965 Around Australia Tour	37 - 49
5	1966 The New Leyland	50 - 57
6	Our Holidays & Friends	58 - 76
7	1967/9 Offer of Partnership Expanding Routes to Birdsville & Oodnadatta	77 - 88
8	The Victorian Naturalists Society Water & Ted Egan	89 - 93
9	1970 New Denning Coach V6 53gm, Gunbarrel, Tanami & Dave Simpson	94 - 117
10	1971 Movies, New Zealand, Borroloola, 1974 Lake Eyre, Cyclone Tracy	118 - 131
11	1975 Fiji	132 - 140
12	1976 Obiri Rock & Missing Fingers	141 - 144
13	1977 New Domino Coach & Fire, U.S. Tour	145 - 151
14	1978/79 Marla, Craig Souter, Desert Breakdown, Coopers Creek	152 - 159
15	1980/1 New Denning Bogie Drive Coach, Fraser Island, Death	160 - 166
16	New Road Challenges, Donohue Highway & Gibb River Road	167 - 174
17	Simpson Desert Crossing	175 - 190
18	1984/87 Yulara, Kings Creek, Edith Falls, Characters	191 - 198
19	1988 Australia's Bicentennial Year Rules & Regulations, 1989 Cape York & The Gulf	199 - 203
20	1990-94 Outside Job, Sore Toe, Tasmania, Last Goodbyes & Retirement	204 - 210

Front cover photograph: 1988 Queensland Gulf Country - bulldust
Back cover photographs: 1982 Our LandCruiser at Chambers Pillar N.T.
1990 Bill & Doreen Hand on sandhill near Birdsville

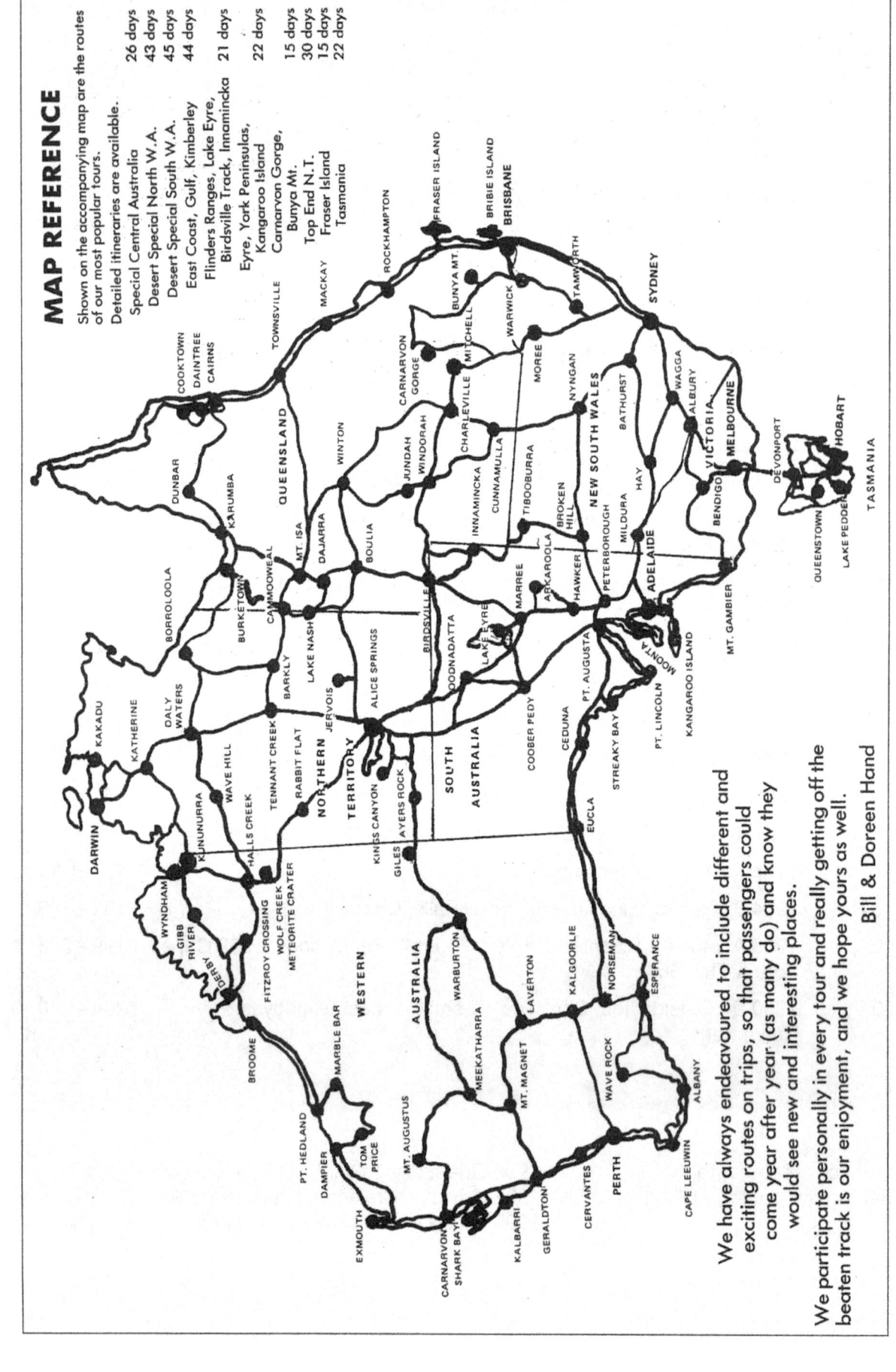

MAP REFERENCE

Shown on the accompanying map are the routes of our most popular tours.
Detailed itineraries are available.

Special Central Australia	26 days
Desert Special North W.A.	43 days
Desert Special South W.A.	45 days
East Coast, Gulf, Kimberley	44 days
Flinders Ranges, Lake Eyre, Birdsville Track, Innamincka Eyre, York Peninsulas,	21 days
Kangaroo Island	22 days
Carnarvon Gorge, Bunya Mt.	15 days
Top End N.T.	30 days
Fraser Island	15 days
Tasmania	22 days

We have always endeavoured to include different and exciting routes on trips, so that passengers could come year after year (as many do) and know they would see new and interesting places.

We participate personally in every tour and really getting off the beaten track is our enjoyment, and we hope yours as well.

Bill & Doreen Hand

PREFACE

Maybe I am wrong in having always considered a fair bit of ego was a necessary part of the desire to write one's life story, so I have worked to convince myself that this was not my reason, but rather it was a worthwhile thing to record some details of what was surely a unique period in time.

There was a time between the two World Wars when adventurous types travelled to way-out places and even entire countries that were somehow run by foreigners, but a working man simply worked and never had either the time, nor the money to indulge in those sorts of things.

The era of tourism as we know it today really started in the years following the Second World War in the 1950s and we were privileged to live through and participate in this window in time when it all began.

If my reasons seem insufficient to justify this story, then I must add that I wrote it because to do so and renew memories of old mates has given me great pleasure. Should it likewise give just some amount of enjoyment to the reader, I shall be perfectly satisfied.

Hazards for outback coach drivers – as defined in *Macquarie Dictionary* —

    bulldust   -   fine dust on outback roads
    bullshit   -   to boast, to exaggerate

I have tried to be objective in my approach to both.

(The term "bulldust" is generally regarded as a corruption of "bullocky's dust". The bullocks pulling supply wagons would churn up columns of dust that could be seen from many miles away, resulting in the waiting homesteaders saying, "They're coming, I can see the bullocky's dust".)

B.H.

NOTE

Because all our early travels were during the years of Imperial measurements, I have tended to use them, and frankly I still have some problem thinking in Metric.

The Australian Metric Conversion Board convened in 1970 and with all major programs completed, the Board disbanded in 1981.

However, I don't think many people have any difficulty understanding Imperial measurements as many are still in use today in one form or another.

To overcome any difficulty: 1 mile equals 1.6 kilometres.

I would like to gratefully acknowledge the input of two regular Sundowners, Jan Trompp and Jack Maddock. Jan for the extensive use of her diaries and Jack (who has passed away), for his articles which have been reprinted with the permission of his ex-employer, *Truck and Bus Transportation* magazine.

1

THE BEGINNINGS OF THE SUNDOWNER STORY

I was brought up during the Great Depression when times must have been incredibly hard, but as a child not having any comparisons, I can't say that I was really aware of hardship, although by today's standards we certainly lived frugally.

Both Mickey Mouse and I were launched into the world in 1928 almost at the end of a period of great post war prosperity and at the start of the Great Depression. It's interesting that Mickey rather than ageing looks better all the time, would that I could claim the same.

My dad had served in the Australian Flying Corps in the Great War and borrowed money to set up a Service Station (it was called a Garage in those days) on Pittwater Road, North Manly. At the foot of the hill from Harbord, it backed onto the Lagoon and Golf Course and out the front was the tramline where I caught the tram to the Infants School in Manly.

The cars that came to our driveway would all be collectors' items today, mostly with bathtub shaped bodies and wooden spoke wheels, and when they wanted fuel Dad had to pump it by hand. It was pumped up into a glass cylinder marked in gallons and then drained down through a hose into the car.

There was no such thing as radio, washing machines, refrigerators, air conditioning, or electric hot water, the sort of things we take for granted today, and we rejoiced the day when Dad bought an ice chest that relied on regular blocks of ice to operate.

Then when radio stations began to broadcast we even acquired an early radio set that in those days was always referred to as "the wireless".

Getting hot bath water was a bit of a chore – like most people we had a "chip heater" which required starting with newspaper and then adding chips of wood or sticks.

The business had a night bell and was literally open 24 hours a day, seven days a week and I have memories of being woken up during the night with the noise of Dad hammering tyres off rims.

For all his hard work I doubt Dad was much of a business man (a bit like myself years later) and as the Depression started to bite, it appears he was working for nothing, as people were always "Gunna pay", but never did as money dried up.

At least the people he dealt with in the Shell Oil Company must have appreciated his dedication and hard work because although work was increasingly unavailable, they found him a job as a driver in the country town of Goulburn.

I had never thought much about religion – at Manly our family had worked a seven day week, and were on call 24 hours a day. I had never thought of people taking time out for religious activities.

Goulburn was very different, although only a country town it supported two cathedrals. The huge railway workshops were the main employer with a mostly Catholic Irish workforce.

My mates next door, Pat and Eric Connelly said they were sad for me, as I was doomed, not being born a Catholic. They used to quote Brother Maloney at great length and I had no doubt that both God and the Pope sought Brother Maloney for advice. I had to attend Bourke Street Public School where all the kids were doomed as God had no time for non-Catholics.

I didn't realise then that for millions of people religious faith is simply an accident of birth. Our school was ruled with the cane - Mr Bombell our science master doled out reams of home work then asked for answers - a wrong answer brought an automatic two cuts of the cane. We learned things like "The atom is the smallest particle that may exist, and is indivisible".

At a school football game one day I was running with the ball, when one of our teachers decided to join in, I put my head down and trampled right over him, this brought six cuts of the cane. Mum was outraged when I told her, I had to talk her out of going to the school, I was afraid of copping another six.

Bourke Street school was only one mile to walk, but when I started high school it became two miles, so I became the proud owner of a second-hand bicycle. Everyone in Goulburn cycled, a bit like China, only one person in our street owned a car - Mr Harrison - they said he was very wealthy. It was a 1928 Essex, but even he mostly cycled.

Our class were mostly from railway families, so when the futuristic locomotive 3801 came through Goulburn, classes were cancelled and we all trooped down to the railway to admire this beautiful green and gold loco.

During the battle of Britain, if you asked anyone in our class what they wanted to be, there was only one answer, a Spitfire pilot, and many of us believed we would be, as the war looked like going on forever. I had a bit of an edge on the others as Dad had been in the Australian Flying Corps in the first World War, and had just enlisted in the RAAF.

I somehow managed to pass my final exams and left school just when Dad was posted to Forest Hill airforce base at Wagga, so for a short time we went to live in Wagga.

During the war people were moved around like pawns under the control of the Department of Manpower. I was told my fate was to move to Sydney and work at De Havilland Aircraft, so Mum and I moved to live with her sister, Auntie Chriss and her husband Uncle Bob in Ryde.

Their family were strict Methodists and I had to watch my Ps and Qs. I found I had lots of old maid aunts, like Auntie Nellie who cycled around to people's houses to collect the mission money to save the poor black people.

Nellie wore elastic from her skirt attached to her pedals, just in case her skirt might blow up. She also carried a pot of pepper in case some man accosted her. This seemed most unlikely to me, and I had visions of some poor fellow being blinded after asking her the time of day.

I used to think of my Catholic mates in Goulburn as being a bit obsessive about religion, but they were relaxed compared with our Methodist relatives. Among other things it appeared God worked like mad for six days creating the earth and on the seventh just collapsed and did absolutely nothing, and we had to do the same. No activity at all was allowed, well, apart from praying and going to church. Even sewing on a button meant God would catch up with you and give you a hiding to nothing for breaking his Sabbath.

It was family folk lore that during Mum and Dad's wedding reception a recording was played of a new decadent singer called Bing Crosby. Uncle Bob demanded it be stopped or he would break the record as this was a solemn occasion.

In church they assured us of "life everlasting" which I took to mean spending eternity with my uncle and aunts, so it seemed a poor bargain, although the alternative was hell. The

Methos were very big on fire and brimstone – although I never did find out what brimstone was.

De Havillands were building aircraft known as D H 98s better known as Mosquitos and initially as the boy I was sent all around the operation. The wings were made at Beales piano factory in Annandale. As the aircraft was made of balsa and plywood they were considered the top people in this field. The timber was glued together with a highly secret new product called contact cement.

With Russia being our ally during the war people had a very pro-Russian attitude, so much so that I nearly became a paid up Communist. Some of the Communist crowd at De Havilland's had literature about dear Uncle Joe Stalin and the paradise in Russia. No wonder the Russians fought so well, it was for their love of Uncle Joe. I made the mistake of telling Uncle Bob about the communist paradise, and he went through the roof, screaming that Stalin was the great Satan. It needed Mum on bended knees to prevent us being thrown out into the street, and I had to swear off becoming a communist.

In 1945 the war finally ended, but peace meant the end of war plane production, then luckily, I continued with an apprenticeship at a kitchenware manufacturer. With the war over Dad returned from the air force and at last we put a deposit on a house in Ryde.

Public transport was adequate, a tram service from Ryde to the city, a bus service to work, but like all young folk I wanted personal transport. After the Second World War cars were almost unobtainable and prices went through the roof. A new car called the Holden came onto the market and people lucky enough to get on the waiting list could resell them straight away at a huge profit. The only alternative was a motor cycle, after a couple of smaller bikes I finally achieved my ultimate, a Harley-Davidson. This opened up new friendships with like-minded bikies and we became what today might be called a gang. After more than 50 years I am still best mates with Ern McStravick, a member of that gang. These days Harley riders tend to fall into two groups, the hard-outlaw types, and affluent older people reliving their youth. Just like our dentist who rides with his Harley group when he is not driving his BMW.

Later, to further my education, I shifted work to Cockatoo Island to study marine engineering. Codock was an education all right, it was run by the unions and management deferred to the unions at all times. It was often a matter of "all-out", we rarely asked why. The work might have been easy, but the study was dreadful, perhaps I needed Mr Bombell with his cane, for I found I was slipping further behind, the maths was simply more than I could absorb.

I was feeling completely dumbed-out when a couple of mates suggest that we should go into business. This was a big decision but helped by the fact that I was very young, immortal and knew everything. Of course, it's only as you begin to age that you realise how little you really know.

At this time a company called Redex were making a fortune convincing motorists that their engines were coking up, and Redex added to their petrol was the cure. The Redex Around Australia car trials became the greatest marketing coup of the 1950s. We decided that there must be money in its "de coking" business, so we hung out our shingle and started pulling off cylinder heads and grinding in valves.

We worked in the back of Bluey Campbell's service station, we were always running out of money, but Bluey was flexible with the rent, I suppose he thought we were quite mad. With our confidence building we hung out another shingle, crash repairs and panel beating. Today's bureaucrats with their rules and regulations would never allow this, but we became quite proficient practicing on customers cars.

A friend caught polio and lost the use of his legs. Automatic cars hardly existed and were dreadfully expensive. We saw it as a relatively easy exercise to fit vacuum boosters to the foot pedals and progressive action aircraft controls at the rim of the steering wheel. It worked very well, was passed by the D. M. R., and *Wheels* magazine gave us a four-page special write up. The article was titled "Cars Modified for Cripples" - there was no political correctness in those days. Our instant fame brought sales of more units and then we were approached by some top brass from the British Motor Corporation. BMC was a big manufacturer of cars such as Austin, Morris, Wolseley, MG, Riley, etc., and were later absorbed into British Leyland.

It appeared that the Federal Government was considering supplying cars to disabled ex-servicemen if cars could be modified so that they could drive them. The BMC people wanted us to state that their Morris Minor was our top choice for the modification.

After we digested this turn of events, we decided to try for much more, like why not a car dealership. George Lloyd the big boss BMC said, "certainly no problem, but of course, ha, ha, we will need a showroom and workshop facilities".

We hadn't made much money in business, but more importantly had made many friends, particularly among local small business people. Our bank manager blamed us for his heart attacks and literally threw us out the door. So, we left his bank, and looked for a younger manager, who still had a sense of adventure. Apart from family help we had mates in electrical work, steel fabrication, glass, hardware, and the very best of all one owned a vacant double block of land on the main road, Victoria Road, Gladesville.

With a deposit on the land and a bank loan and with help from friends we built the showroom ourselves. On paper our initial car sales looked brilliant, as our friends all called in their debts. But we were in business although it was ironic that the government never did contract cars for the disabled, George Lloyd should never have believed the politicians.

The 1950s were a boom period for car sales, wartime petrol rationing had only ended in 1950, and people were rushing to buy new cars. As few people owned a car we were not troubled with many trade-ins.

A year or two after the first car had rolled out the door we were invited to join a new club to be called the Australian Racing Drivers Club, or A.R.D.C. The meeting was held in a room above a fish shop in Erskineville, and we met some real characters. No wives or girlfriends were invited maybe because it was a very blokie turnout, or perhaps it was the toilet arrangement. This meant opening the back window and peeing into the back yard of the fish shop. A dreadful smell always rose up, I would never have bought fish there.

From this small beginning the A.R.D.C. became highly successful with hundreds of new members signing up, and was able to move to quite lavish premises in Norton Street, Leichhardt.

During the Second World War at least two airfields were built on the empty plains west of Sydney, one at Castlereagh and another at Mt Druitt. After the war these were great places for car and motorcycle races and gymkhanas. Belfred Jones secured a lease on the Mt Druitt airfield. Belf extended the main strip into a racing circuit, then did a deal with the A.R.D.C. to use this circuit for weekend motor racing.

We saw some great driving from people like Don Gibson, Frank Hann, David McKay, and of course Jack Brabham who went on to become world champion. Motor racing was not only expensive fun, it was good for business, it allowed us to mix with many influential people from all walks of life.

My most unforgettable race was in May 1954 when I entered the Great Australian 24-hour Race, based on the famous Le Mans race. My mate Bill Ford and I entered a Singer roadster.

It rained heavily during the night and the track broke up into potholes. The famous British racing driver Peter Whitehead was well into the lead when he smashed the rear suspension on his Jaguar XK 120. We snapped a front stub axle, dismantled one from an enthusiastic spectator's car, fitted it and drove on into the night. We were beaten into second place in our class by a Morris Minor, and I guess I'm philosophical about these sorts of things, but Bill Ford took it quite hard, muttering "Of all things a bloody Morris Minor". Of course, all we young fellows thought we had the ability to be world champion racing drivers, but I now realise lack of fear, rather than driving ability was our main asset.

Nearly 40 years later a friend, Janet (Bin) Allport told me that she was in David Mackay's pit crew that night, and other friends John and Jill Corby showed me an album of photos they took during the meeting.

After the race we had to strip down the front axle and rebuild our spectator friend's car, and then return later and rebuild our car. Returning home in a hurry, I came on the railway gates closed at Mt Druitt, hit the brakes and went straight through the gates. It is a mistake to forget to connect the brakes when you're over-tired.

With segregated schools, girls essentially didn't exist when I was a kid, then between study and work I never had much time for girlfriends. But one night after a race meeting Belf opened his wallet and put on supper and a keg, and then I fell in love across a crowded table. She was one of the girl drivers, her name was Doreen, I thought it was like in the *Sentimental Bloke* with Bill and Doreen. But then I felt my hopes were dashed when I found she was with a fellow we knew as Sexy Rexie.

However, I found she lived in Wangee Rd., Lakemba and gathered up the courage to go on a door knock. After a few setbacks I finally had a win, though the gentleman I spoke to seemed less than impressed with a young fellow knocking in the middle of the night and asking if a girl called Doreen lived there. Things progressed well with Doreen, but I had the distinct feeling that her father believed his daughter was dating some sort of idiot. She explained it was mostly little things - like spinning my tyres and throwing gravel on the front lawn, or vaulting the front fence and loosening the fence posts, then trying to explain getting home late because our MG ran out of fuel in the middle of the Harbour Bridge - unlikely but quite true. It seems I was a slow learner, but I think I gradually improved.

Still trying to impress, one night I took Doreen out in a Packard - very smart. It stopped dead on Concord Road and I had the bonnet up when a police car pulled-in and parked ahead of us. I found the problem then convinced the cops that we weren't stealing the car. The starter refused to engage, so with Doreen behind the wheel I tried to push start it, but it was too big and heavy, so I asked the cops to help, the car fired, charged forward and missed by the merest whisker demolishing the police car.

Arnold Glass was a fellow who knew his way around the motor industry and he believed that BMC was close to collapse. He showed us a car called a Datsun (later called Nissan) that he intended to import. We weren't very impressed although it had an Austin A40 motor made in Japan. Arnold offered us the agency, but I couldn't see how this car could possibly sell, for a start everybody knew that "made in Japan" signified cheap and nasty.

At least Arnold was right about one thing, BMC or British Leyland as it had become was about to fold and about this time a friend at York Motors asked if I would test drive a car called a Toyota Tiara and fill out a comment sheet. The only serious improvement I thought was needed was a four-speed gearbox, (it had a three speed), and it appears others said the same thing.

A dealer conference was held in a flash hotel in the city where we understood dealer complaints about persistent problems and poor-quality control were to be thrashed out. Instead Lord Somebody (I forget his name) who had just arrived from England got up and abused us. It appears we were just a complaining lot of sods and we should get off our backsides and get out and sell because they were providing us with the finest cars in the world. As he raved on it was becoming obvious why the great British motor industry was dying.

In the meantime, we heard that Toyota had taken on board our comments and all future cars would have four-speed gearboxes. Fancy, a motor company that listens to what people want. So, when the first cars arrived we became Toyota dealers, it was only about 15 years since our troops had returned from fighting the Japanese in the Pacific, and a lot of people were very bitter about us promoting Japanese as opposed to British cars.

It didn't help that the Toyota handbooks were a bit of a joke, poorly printed on cheap paper and full of spelling errors. They contained advice like "never drive the car with the fuel tank empty." but the Japanese unlike the British were very quick learners.

Still, Toyota was becoming very successful, but as sales increased they became more demanding, it was carry more stock, more spare parts, bigger showroom, more staff.

More money? No problem, Toyota would arrange for loans but of course on their terms. How many big-time dealers are owned by the car makers or the finance companies? If we were to go down that road perhaps we would end up owning the only thing we started with, our shingle out the front.

Doreen and I married in 1959, we had decided to build beforehand and bought a block on a hillside in what was then bush, with a view of the Lane Cove River. When Doreen's father saw it he said, "Sell it right away you might get your money back, the foundation will cost as much as the house, get a flat block." And that was the wisdom of the 1950's.

The car showroom that we built was steel framed and welded using 4 inch galvanised steel tube and we decided to build our house the same way. This nearly sent our local council bureaucrats crazy, we had to talk to the Chief Building Inspector, Don Rutherford, who was a brilliant man and went out of his way to help and advise us. After that it was just a great deal of hard work in our limited spare time.

It was really made possible by the help of Doreen's father and her brother Rod. One of our great regrets is that when Rod was building his own home we were touring in the Outback and could be of little help.

At home we were looking for cheap secondhand furniture while at work trying to hold the Toyota people at bay.

On coming home from work one day I found Doreen in raptures over an advertisement in the Herald. At high school she had studied a book by H.H. Findlayson called "The Red Centre", written in the 1930s. It was all about exploring Central Australia by camel, seeing Ayers Rock and living with aborigines. This book was considered a classic and studied in schools, and left her with an obsession about the outback. But who ever heard of going to Central Australia.

The advertisement stated that Redline Coaches of Brisbane intended running a coach trip of three weeks duration from Sydney to Central Australia and back, taking in things of interest along the way. They claimed to have successfully run this trip from Brisbane.

Apart from the cost, 50 pounds ($100) per person, plus your own meals and expenses I couldn't see that I could spare the time. Two hundred dollars seems a paltry amount by today's standards, but in 1962 it represented nearly six weeks wages which brings home the incredible effect of inflation.

This was further complicated by a depression starting in 1961 caused by the infamous credit squeeze that brought the Menzies Government within a whisker of defeat in an election the following year.

1933. My first set of wheels

Except for our short honeymoon I hadn't had a holiday for 10 years, simply never had the time. Although Doreen had a very good job, as secretary to a company manager, she like everyone else was only entitled to two weeks holiday per year, although she assured me that her boss would be cooperative. I thought it was a bit like parachute jumping - why jump out of a perfectly good aeroplane, or out of a perfectly good house to live in a tent?

Nevertheless, the cheque made out to Redline coaches for 100 pounds was sent, and so we were committed. The itinerary described the trip as a safari, and on looking this up found it to be Swahili for a long journey, usually with hunting. This was getting a bit involved, what were we going to hunt? At least we will be going in winter, as I recalled the schoolboy who wrote "The climate in Central Australia in summer is such that the inhabitants live elsewhere".

It seems really quite remarkable to me to think that most people alive today were not alive in 1962 when we first ventured into the Outback, and so would have little understanding of the conditions at that time.

1953. Easter holidays with mates at Coolangatta. Proud owner of Singer 9 Tourer.

1962/3 REDLINE EXPERIENCES

Many people would remember 1962 as the year that Marilyn Monroe died, but to us the most important event was our first trip to Central Australia. We had to assemble at Kings Cross, it was a strange sight if anything can be called strange at the Cross. A mob of people in big hats, with billycans, blankets, sleeping bags, boxes of food, suitcases, etc. preparing to board two Redline coaches.

The driver of the first coach was Doug Fredericks, tall, dark and looking very capable and with a rifle lying across the dashboard, so it was a safari. However, we were in coach No. 2 and our driver was Brad Franklin.

I was still having doubts. I felt a bit vindicated when Brad got totally lost driving out of Sydney, he was supposed to be following Doug but lost him in the traffic.

A passenger navigated Brad from the Liverpool Highway on the way to Melbourne, and back on to the Western Highway, but it was Tennant Creek before we caught up to Doug again.

On the right-hand side of the road, about 10 miles (16 km) past Dubbo there is a stand of big gum trees, still there today. In the dark Brad eased the coach into the trees and told us to set up camp, he advised us to gather twigs and light our separate fires. We had the spectacle of 30 odd people in small groups trying to boil billies over their individual fires.

Today people expect coach companies to provide their meals, with Redline it was the reverse the passengers had to feed the driver, who was always too busy working on the vehicle to buy or cook food. The Company only provided transport and we had to provide our own food, water, tent and cooking utensils, and of course making sure the driver didn't starve. In the morning there were some sorry looking tents, it seems some people hadn't practiced putting them up, well certainly not in the dark.

After buying more supplies in Nyngan it was on to Bourke along a rough dusty road, then across the Queensland border to Cunnamulla where we saw our first Queensland houses. Brad called them Queenslanders, the houses that is, not the people. They were made of timber, with wrap-around verandas, and sitting high above the ground on wooden posts. We wondered if they were expecting to become a second Venice.

Flies caught up with us at this point - flies are like tourists they both get into a frenzy at sunrise and then settle down as the day progresses.

Brad was at home among the locals, they spoke in cliches - 'sheel be right ay', 'he's a shingle short ay', 'fair crack of the whip ay', 'we're back a Bourke ay', etc. We found that in Queensland and the Northern Territory "ay" is not "eh" - it's not a question, it's an indication that a point is being made.

Almost unbelievably the road from Charleville to Augathella was bitumen but it was narrow and broken. It was even rougher, if that was possible, than the dirt roads although it would have been a bonus in wet weather. In these Western Queensland towns, the streets were lined with bottle trees, great swollen trunked members of the kurrajong family.

Every town seemed to have some claim to fame. In Blackall it was Jackie Howe the gun shearer who set the world shearing record on nearby Alice Downs Station. As well they claimed at 7000 feet the world's deepest artesian bore. Outback Queensland is a land of bores, not the human kind who grab you and tell you about themselves, when you would rather tell them about yourself, but deep holes in the ground discharging life giving water.

Our map readers were variously quoting the next town as Bar-cal-deen, or Bar-cel-deen and Brad had to put them right with Bar-cauld-in. Those among us who were politically inclined found interest in the tree of knowledge in Barcaldine. In 1891 the striking shearers met to form the Australian Workers Union under the shade of this tree. Well-chosen too as the opposite side of the street was lined with beautiful two-storey pubs. The A.W.U. became the Australian Labor Party, and in response the local Grazier's Association formed what is today the National Party.

The road to Longreach was long, rough and dusty, had the fences been removed we would have lost the road as there was no difference between the road and the bare black soil plains stretching to the horizon on either side. This country had been drought stricken for eight to ten years and it was hard to believe that it once supported hundreds of thousands of sheep. No point in a shearer's strike now, there were no sheep left. They had been trucked out, mostly to New South Wales and were sold for as little as three pence (three cents) per head. Most never made it and were thrown off the trucks out of Cunnamulla where they were buried with bulldozers.

Brad pointed out that eventually the drought would break and with rain all these outback towns would become isolated as black soil roads are impassible in wet weather, but there was nothing to suggest that rain ever fell in this wilderness.

Longreach was the biggest town we had seen for a long time, and it was possible to climb the water tower alongside the Tropic of Capricorn and look down on the streets of the town that were all named after birds. We saw the original Qantas hangar which in 1926 became Australia's first aircraft factory producing six DH 50 biplanes that were a far cry from the DH98s that I had worked on during the war. The term aircraft factory sounds impressive but aircraft in those days were little more than sticks stuck together, covered in fabric and an imported engine bolted on the front end.

Black soil roads don't break up or pothole very much and are relatively good, the main problem was dipping down into the culverts. These were filled with rocks to prevent washing out in wet weather and were real spring breakers at more than walking speed.

I really didn't have anything against going to Central Australia providing we could return home the same night, but now I was starting to enjoy the adventure. The passengers were a completely mixed group but got on extremely well together, and now that we were in the tropics most of us even stopped bothering to put up tents.

Somebody asked Brad didn't he have a uniform, as when he did get out of overalls his clothes looked like something out of a rag bag. He laughed and said, "Only bus drivers wore uniforms, outback safari drivers wouldn't be seen dead in a uniform". Along with his appearance Brad had no airs or graces and cheerfully admitted any lack of knowledge, often his answer was "I wouldn't have a clue ay" followed with a chuckle. When I see and hear today's "Coach Captains" I have to wonder which I prefer.

We renewed our supplies in Winton, a small town with a huge general store on the right-hand side of the main street. This was Garfield and Fitzmaurice (since closed down) and it had departments selling everything imaginable. The cashier was seated a half storey above the main floor with wires radiating out to all the counters. Our money and bills were stuffed into a cylinder and at the pull of a lever it raced up the wire, then came back with the receipt and change. Okay, I know there is nothing new about this, but it reminded me of Anthony Horderns in Sydney when I was a kid, so what was this big store doing in a backwoods place like Winton?

The next town across the plains was Kynuna. On the left hand side just before town was a sign made of welded wrought iron, this pointed the way to the Diamantina River and the Combo water hole billabong that Paterson referred to in his song "Waltzing Matilda". We hear of swagmen humping their bluey, in the early days it appears that Waltzing Matilda was also in common usage, some say it had German or Austrian origins, Mathilde being a soldier's bed roll, and *auf der walz* was carrying same. Maybe Mathilde was a camp follower and the blanket was just a poor substitute. Today the new bitumen highway bypasses this, although it is possible to detour back on the old road to the water hole. Apart from the hospitable Blue Heeler Hotel there was the Kynuna store run by a fellow called "Arry Urst", and it seemed the store had been stocked a hundred years before and nothing had ever been sold. Rather tragically it has totally gone as it could have been a wonderful museum. Arry's hobby was feeding and taming the local brolgas, which tended to make them rather cheeky and demanding.

It seemed that the distance between towns averaged about a hundred miles with the next town being McKinlay - an unbelievable collection of structures of old galvanised iron. This was the town that Paul Hogan would use someday in his movie *Crocodile Dundee*. In the film McKinlay was renamed Walkabout Creek and the pub kept that name from its brush with fame. It was two blocks down a side street but to catch passing traffic has now been jazzed up and moved onto the Highway. Incidentally the original name comes from Big John McKinlay the great South Australian explorer who roamed this country looking for the lost Burke and Wills expedition.

Later we passed a car pulling a caravan and Brad commented "I hope that poor bugger doesn't think he can get to the Isa with that in one piece". The road had become more stony with regular washaways but I didn't think it was that bad. However, after passing through the old mining town of Cloncurry the road deteriorated quickly, and I started to see what he meant. In a Redex Trial only a few years earlier an ABC reporter had coined the name "Horror Stretch" for this goat track through the ranges. Jack Murray who won the trial in which 176 cars started but only 63 finished wrote later "It is the worst road I have driven on in the world

- the road dips down and rises again so steeply that at anything over 40 mph (65 kph) your bumper digs straight into the other side". From our racing days I knew what a mad driver Jack was, not the sort of bloke easily put off by your average bit of rough road.

The state of the roads almost caused the abandonment of Mt Isa in the early days, and it was saved when a rail line that skirted south of the ranges was built. Those who did use the road ensured the resident spring maker was kept busy and although I didn't know it at the time, over the next few years we would become part of his loyal customers.

The Isa as everyone called it was divided by the Leichhardt River into Mineside with the mine area and single men housing, and Townside with its shops and pubs. The main block Townside had a pub on each corner, causing an English passenger to remark, "Whole place is one bloody big poob". A mine inspection consisted of walking to the edge of a huge pit called the Black Rock open cut and watching haulage trucks climb up a spiral track from the bottom. The workforce we were told were mostly young migrants from over 40 countries including the biggest Finnish community outside Finland. There was a distinct shortage of young women in town and our girls were constantly accosted by burly young men with foreign accents. On leaving Isa we came upon an absolute miracle - a bitumen road. This road was built during the Second World War. Men and supplies were railed from Townsville and then the road had to be built west to link up with the Stuart Highway, bitumen being laid between Alice Springs and Darwin. No time had been wasted here with cuttings, the road simply went over the hills, down into the creeks and up and over the next hill. It gave a roller coaster ride, but was welcome after the horror stretch.

Further on the countryside began to look like a vast cemetery, red tombstones stretched *off* in all directions. These were ant hills or more correctly termite mounds. Unlike the termites back home that chewed through people's houses these little critters consumed grass and spinifex, and as they numbered in the millions, could be regarded as much grazing animals as the cattle they were competing with.

Camooweal came up just before the Northern Territory border where in the past great herds of cattle were driven down the Barkly stock route from as far as the Kimberley then dipped for ticks before proceeding into Queensland. Where the streets were once lined with pubs only two remained with one of these about to go.

A stop at the border showed the great Mitchell grass plains stretching out ahead and to the left of the road what almost looked like a picket fence disappearing over the horizon. We were looking along the line of poles of the overland telegraph line running from Tennant Creek.

Like the other O.T. lines this was dismantled some years later and replaced by the new technology of microwave relay towers. Further along the road we called in to Barry Caves roadhouse, built and owned by Herbie and Dorrie Harms. Herbie was a battler, he was building the place out of over-the-counter income and unless this improved drastically the place never looked like being finished.

A couple of years later Dorrie became ill and they were forced to give up and sold out to Freddie Charlton. Fred had two disabilities, a wooden leg and a flash wife who totally ruled him. Fred plastered the walls with little homilies like "Beat a hangover, stay drunk", or "I spent most of my money on women and grog, the rest I just wasted". He installed a jukebox and always wanted to dance with the young girls, but most declined probably realising that their toes might be stomped with a wooden leg. Fred's problems then started to mount up, first his wife left with a young fellow that he sacked, then one day he was wearing a beaut black eye. He said, "I had some young toughs come in here and I ordered them out, one lent over the counter, grabbed me by the shirt front, pulled me over the counter and belted me in the eye". Fred bought a gun after that, heaven help the next customer.

Another time we stopped to see a scene of devastation - half the roadhouse was burnt out and the driveway was covered in exploded beer cans. Fred explained that he had sacked an employee that he found robbing the till and when the fellow left he threw a Molotov cocktail into the fuel store and cool room. The disasters kept coming but the final straw was the meat. Freddie sold the best and cheapest meat and hamburgers anywhere, but this ultimately landed him in newspaper headlines. It appears the local station people had been aware for some time that he was taking their cattle and butchering them for his cheap meat supply. They set a trap and caught him literally red-handed. After being taken to court and heavily fined Fred had had enough adventures and placed Barry Caves on the market.

The new owner doubled the price on everything and when I chided him about this, he answered 'The suckers will pay, they have no choice. I intend to make my money and get out." I was a little bit offended at being treated as a "sucker" and never stopped there again. It appears others felt the same and the place folded up. There is simply nothing whatever to show that Barry Caves roadhouse ever existed when driving along the Barkly Highway today. It seemed a long lonely drive across the tableland and the next point of civilisation, about half way to Tennant Creek was the Wonarah overland telegraph repeater station. Two huge windmills faced due east into the prevailing wind, charging batteries to boost the telegraph signal. Wonarah closed in the early seventies along with the O.T. line.

Some distance further, a dirt road went off to the right and a faded sign said Borroloola. Today's travellers would find a bitumen road, but more importantly opposite a huge modern roadhouse called the Barkly Homestead, but for us that was years into the future.

Our next stop was Frewena, a roadhouse built on the site of a wartime staging area.

Our host was Arthur Fitzgerald, a big hearty man with a black beard and blue eyes, he and his family made us so at home we didn't want to leave. He had been the accountant on the local cattle station and some years after the war took out a lease over the army buildings and made the area into a roadhouse. Hillary, one of our English passengers so fell in love with the place she asked to return and work there for 12 months, where she was treated as one of the family. Later she wrote to us to say that she felt she could no longer fit in back in England and was returning to Australia.

A couple of years later Arthur became ill and the family moved to Melbourne to be with him, and left the business in the hands of Billie, a trusted employee. It became almost impossible to get served as Billie's mates moved in and proceeded to drink their way through the grog supply. Finally, Arthur's brother Don Fitzgerald came up with his family from Dee Why in Sydney and kicked Billie out, then spent 12 months trying to rebuild the business, but was forced to give up.

Crocodile shooting had just been stopped and a couple of out-of-work shooters took over the place. I don't know if they took drugs or were just naturally mad. An Alice Springs mate, Paddy Ethel told of coming through one night and ringing the night bell then copping abuse and what sounded like a shotgun blast. Paddy just made it to Three Ways roadhouse with the needle on zero.

The end for Frewena roadhouse wasn't far off, after one of the proprietors made headlines by shooting a customer (accidentally, he said) people were loath to stop. Like Barry Caves there is nothing whatever left of the roadhouse, only the old driveway that can be used as a rest area. Not very far along the road we came to Three Ways, just a small roadhouse on the intersection with the Stuart Highway. Like the Barkly it was just single-lane bitumen laid during the Second World War, and overtaking meant driving on the gravel shoulder and chancing the flying stones.

Even today I hear it quoted that the Americans built these roads during the war. Nothing could be further from the truth as it was a totally Australian project, and on a miles-per week basis, new world records were set.

At this point one of our better-read passengers pointed out that it was exactly 100 years since John McDouall Stuart passed this way on his successful crossing of Australia. Stuart wasn't the first across the continent, Burke and Wills had already beaten him, but of course never made it back to tell anybody.

In a short time, we came to the Tennant Creek telegraph station with the iron poles going off in three directions, north, south and east, and this overland telegraph line was now 90 years old. Tennant Creek was not a tourist town, it catered for the local miners, who must have had simple needs by the standard of the shops. It was obvious that the only essential businesses were the pubs.

We pressed on in the dark (as usual) to find a camp spot near a place called the Devil's Marbles. This was a name we knew due to publicity during the recent Redex trials and it concerned Jack Davey, Australia's best-known radio personality and trials driver. At a control point an ABC reporter doing a live cross asked Davey what he thought of the Devil's Marbles and he replied, "Didn't see them, he must have had his trousers on." This went straight to air, and being the 1950s created a country wide uproar. At this point we finally caught up with Doug and his group, and although it was originally intended we travel together we felt it was too late for that. Travellers would know that we want to feel good about the group to which we belong, and one way of doing this is to denigrate those who are not in it. While we tend to see our group as individuals we view other groups as undifferentiated mobs.

Driving down to Alice Springs we came into very heavy rain and arrived in time to see the Todd River come down in flood. This was quite exciting until Brad explained that there were only two camping sites in Alice Springs, Heavitree and Greenleaves, where we were booked in and they were both on the other side of the river. Although there was a pedestrian bridge this was no help to us.

Inquiries turned up the Church of England hall (which unfortunately burnt down a couple of years later). Showers of rain were still about, and we were thankful for the shelter. At first some of our party were in revolt on reading the "No alcohol to be consumed on premises" notice, and someone asked, "Surely they don't expect us to exist on food and water". However, a range of different teapots ultimately solved the problem.

We found with Territorians they measured distance by the clock, not the speedometer, and quoted distance in hours rather than miles, but when we asked how many hours to Ayers Rock they laughed and said the dirt road would be impassable for days. We had very little understanding of these conditions and managed to talk Brad into attempting this drive. The Bedford slipped and slithered all over the road, then catherine-wheeled and bogged facing back toward Alice Springs, we took this as a sign, and became covered in red mud from the spinning wheels as we pushed it out of the bog. And so, it was back to the hall and the teapots.

Finally, back in Alice Springs a conference was called, where we agreed that to wait for the Ayers Rock road to dry out was not an option. That said, the only way out was north up the Stuart Highway, back the way we came. "Darwin," somebody said, "We could go to Darwin". Brad looked doubtful, "How far to Darwin?" he asked. We answered, "Only about 1000 miles".

Brad must have realised the amount of night driving involved, but still he didn't interfere as we all planned ahead.

I have one talent, if it can be called that, I am a night person, (or was) and I took over the job of making sure that Brad stayed awake during the long hours of night driving. If his head nodded forward I lit two cigarettes, put one to his lips and he would come good for maybe twenty minutes, when I would repeat the process. (My heavens how things have changed.)

Katherine proved to be not much better than Tennant Creek for shopping. The main street today goes straight north on a bridge over the river, but this was far into the future. Then it turned left and followed along the riverside and on the corner stood March Motors. Eric March had the principal store in Katherine, it may have been the only one. You could buy anything from used cars, canned food, milk shakes (made unfortunately on powdered milk) and even week-old newspapers.

Eric was drumming up business for a proposed new venture. Apparently, the Katherine River cut through a sandstone plateau east of the town and he believed there could be tourist potential in this gorge. The following year he proposed purchasing boats and running tours on the river.

The locals made sure to correct our pronunciation, they insisted on Kath-rhine, so naturally we obliged. Today southerners (all non-Territorians are southerners) have pretty well usurped this pronunciation, but old timers still say Kath-rhine.

One night when Brad couldn't drive any further we stopped, and everybody rolled out and went to sleep in a row alongside the road. In the morning a sign alongside us proclaimed "Green Ant Creek". Fortunately, the green ants never found us, but like Brad, "we never had a clue" what green ants were anyway.

The road deteriorated and as well as railway level crossings there were regular low level one- way bridges over creeks. One of these, Coomalie Creek, was in the news a couple of years later, when a young Redline driver, Kevin King crashed head-on into a road train. Kev spent 12 months in Darwin hospital, but later returned to coach driving.

On February 19th, 1942, Darwin became Australia's Pearl Harbor, as 242 Japanese aircraft dropped more bombs on Darwin than were dropped on Pearl only two months earlier, and using the same task force under the command of Admiral Nagumo. Even the Japanese commander was later quoted as saying "It was like using a sledgehammer to crack an egg". The bombing raids continued until November 1943, numbering 64 raids in total.

17 years had passed since the end of the war, and Darwin had largely been rebuilt but the scars and wreckage were still everywhere to be seen. Driving into Darwin today on the left-hand side of the Highway is the thriving industrial suburb of Winnellie, but in 1962 it was a huge rubbish dump with piles of wrecked aircraft and all manner of demolished building materials. Darwin came into existence for one reason only, the British Cable Company made an offer to extend their cable from Singapore with an extension across Queensland to the east coast.

The people of Adelaide didn't have to wait a hundred years for Rupert Murdoch to show them the power and money available to those that control the distribution of news and information, they made the then spectacular offer to throw up 2000 miles of telegraph line north to Darwin in the time limit of two years. This had enormous significance as news now arrived in hours instead of months, and the O.T. line stayed in operation for nearly 100 years.

We sought out the sites of Darwin and on the foreshore of Fanny Bay, opposite the famous old jail inspected the monument to Ross and Keith Smith who in December 1919 landed a Vickers Vimy bomber at that point, after taking 28 days flying from England. That flight was the first of thousands that made Darwin the northern gateway to Australia. Brad made us feel like genuine pioneers as he explained that this was the first Redline coach to reach Darwin as he parked in Smith Street.

Who ever heard of the passengers running a coach tour, because this was what was happening - we had to work out distances, times, places etc. then lay it all out for Brad to drive to. We planned to cut across to the east coast and proceed down the Highway through Rockhampton, where Brad was back in familiar territory and could show us many things of interest. Camping places were hard to find and sometimes we just pulled in and set up tents among sugar cane fields. Coming closer to Brisbane the problem of where to camp came up, and Brad solved this by simply driving into a public park at Petrie. We erected our tents and took over the public facilities. A train line ran around the side of the park and we provided entertainment for the morning commuters as we prepared breakfast.

By the end of the trip people were discussing what impressed them the most. For me it was easy as I was absolutely impressed with the capabilities and professionalism of these long-distance drivers. Brad was obviously only typical as he fixed flat tires, repaired breakdowns, negotiated dreadful roads and I never saw him once make a driving error or lose his temper.

To an extraordinary extent we seemed to be convinced we were adventurers, in fact someone came up with the quote "We are adventurers, you are a traveller, THEY are tourists", but I dare say others saw us differently. Perhaps it was our mental defence against returning to the mundane problems of everyday existence.

Why is it that travel is so addictive? And why is somewhere else so enticing that we have to be there? Ayers Rock became our somewhere else, and the group elected Doreen planning coordinator for our next outback foray. The plan was that for next year, 1963, we would charter both Brad and a Redline coach and organise our own outback safari and in the interval we would keep everybody informed of the planning.

Meantime back at the motor business things were still difficult, with insurance assessors cutting smash repair prices to the bone and taking months to pay our invoices. Initially Toyota had only one model, the Tiara, but had now added the Crown, Corona and Corolla. (Corona is Latin for crown and Corolla is Latin for little crown) - they seemed to have an obsession about Royal head gear. The four-wheel drive LandCruiser was dead in the water, with its high fuel consumption and petrol at about 10 cents a litre (equivalent) why would city people ever buy a four-wheel drive? People were starting to appreciate the value in Japanese cars although sales remained sluggish. Perhaps someday Toyota would become a major brand, but could we afford to wait that long?

1963 There were three momentous events in 1963. President Kennedy was assassinated, Prime Minister Menzies was re-elected, we organised a Central Australian safari trip.

It was no problem filling the coach, apart from our original group other friends happily took up any left-over seats. We had crossed Queensland twice in 1962, so this time it was decided to go through western New South Wales and return via Adelaide and the Great Ocean Road.

It felt the trip really started on the rough dirt road north of Port Augusta towards Woomera. Set up in 1947, Woomera was the world's longest on-land rocket range and with a staff of some thousands, it was hard to believe they relied on such a poor road. Later we found the truth was they didn't, almost everything was carried by rail or aircraft.

Entrance to Woomera required a permit, then it was back to the Stuart Highway, and following the rail line to Kingoonya. On open country this road was relatively straight but on forested sections it wound like a snake between the trees and it didn't seem possible the big coach could fit on such a narrow twisting track. This was typical of outback roads in those days - if they were graded at all it was only with small lightweight machines mostly incapable of taking out large trees. A few years later bulldozers were used to straighten and realign many of these outback roads, although the increased speed possible then created the problem of dreadful corrugations. Kingoonya was the oddest place - the main street was a cricket ground, at the north end was a row of railway fettler's cottages, and down the southern end, a pub, a store, and a couple of houses. The road crossed the railway line for the last time and headed north past Mt Eba and the Twins stations to Mirakata, a satellite village of Woomera with large dish antennas used for tracking rockets.

Towards Goober Pedy the trees cut out altogether and the road tracked up over a series of long stony rises. The town was a small cluster of buildings on the highest ground surrounded by a moonscape, no pub but a store cum cafe run by "Ma Brewster" who was a tough looking old dear, with a hand rolled cigarette hanging out the corner of her mouth. Brad took us to meet Fay Naylor who had come through from Melbourne three years earlier and stayed on to work for Mrs. Brewster, then she went on to work with Don Field a prominent opal buyer.

Fay believed in a tourist potential for Goober Pedy and along with a partner, Ettie Hall intended to dig out an underground dugout in the hope of a tourist future for the "town".

We were generally told that Goober Pedy was Aboriginal for "White fella hole in the ground", and years later when I learned some Pitjanjatjira, I found that "piti" meant hole, not hole in the ground, just simply hole. Another much quoted translation for Goober Pedy was "boy's water hole", but this would be "nyitayira kapi piti". Goober proved more difficult although I was talking to an old timer one day who insisted that Aboriginals referred to white fellows as Goober, or perhaps pronounced as goober, or gubbah, or cobber. He pointed out that in the top end aborigines called white fellows Balandar because Indonesian fisherman told them that white people were call Hollander.

On the way north to Alice Springs Brad asked if I could hear a noise in the gearbox (being rear engined this of course was down the rear end). He looked most unhappy when I said that it sounded a bit like a concrete mixer. I was getting the impression that Redline were saving money by employing ingenious drivers that somehow carried out maintenance while on the road. Fortunately, the box held together till Alice Springs where Brad pulled it apart and then we went scrounging around trucking junk yards, where fortunately Bedfords were fairly common. We found the necessary parts and after reassembly Brad asked if I could drive the coach while he wrapped himself around the chassis and listened to the gear box.

After a run where I changed up and down a number of times I pulled up wondering if Brad was still alive. He dropped out from under the coach and I told him he looked like Al Jolson, he just laughed and said, "She sounds real beaut, she'll make it mate, ay".

This time the Todd River was dry as a bone and we made camp at Greenleaves camping park on the east side. Reg Verron the proprietor had been stationed there during the war and falling in love with the place returned and opened for business. Like most caravan/camping parks of the period the amenities were totally primitive, and you were expected to chop the wood, light the fire, and hope for a hot shower, then don't forget to add wood for the next person.

There had been a building spree in Alice Springs in the previous year, on one corner was a new ANZ bank, and opposite a new Stuart Arms hotel. Some twenty years later I was having a drink with a wheeler dealer friend called Bill Ford and knowing Bill was always planning something new I asked what was happening. He said that he had just bought the Stuart Arms Hotel and was going to demolish it and build something remarkable to be called the Ford Plaza. This is probably still the most outstanding building in Alice Springs but no longer shows the Ford name and I think Bill might have done his dough. One of the must-see places was Mrs. Jenkin's pink house, (The Ritz). She and her late husband had been opal mining most of their lives and she claimed to own the finest opal collection in the world. Mrs. J was an absolute eccentric and people had to be warned how to behave in her presence. She was famous for slamming the door in the face of the Duke of Gloucester because he was late for an appointment.

Another character was Rex Batterbee who had the elegant little "Tmara - Mara" art gallery over east side facing the Todd River. He was reputed to have taught Albert Namatjira to paint and acted as agent for the increasing number of Aboriginal painters. He had prints for sale of a painting that he had done and presented to the Queen on her visit to Central Australia, which I thought showed remarkable forward planning.

We then set off west of Alice Springs on a dirt track to see places Doreen had researched, the first being Simpson's Gap. This was a cattle station owned by ex-Territory trooper Bob Darkin who had no problem with people using the track across his property to a scenic gap in the ranges. In the 1950s the Australian film star Chips Rafferty made several western style films in Central Australia. Bob Darkin played the baddie, and Chips played the hero character in the film called *The Sundowner*.

One film called 'The Phantom Stockman" had its premiere at the station, where Bob overheard two old aboriginal men discussing the story and one said, "I followed it okay, but can't figure out why Bob Darkin was duffing his own cattle."

A couple of years later the Darkin's sold Simpson's Gap station to the Reserves Board, the forerunner to the National Parks who renovated the old homestead and paid Bob to move back in as Head Ranger, which was a pretty good deal as he couldn't run any cattle due to the dreadful drought conditions. About 1966 the Board told Bob to charge one shilling (10 cents) for entry to the homestead. I suggested to Bob that this should be beneath his dignity and he agreed saying he would bring it up at the next Board meeting. It seems the Board agreed, they made the charge two shillings, then only a year later decided it wasn't worth the trouble and scrapped it altogether.

Further west we crossed the Jay Creek at an Aboriginal settlement and on to Standley Chasm. Driving into the chasm up a stony creek bed we suggested to Brad that we could all walk and save him having to back all the way out, but he assured us there was a turning circle further in. After spending more film on the chasm and having lunch we were blocked on the creek bed driving out by a broken-down bus. There was no way around and we pushed him right out onto the flat, which proves that these vehicles were much lighter, and we were much younger in those days.

After about 10 minutes past Jay Creek on the Hermannsburg road there was supposed to be a right-hand turnoff to Ormiston Gorge, but Brad could not find it. Finally, he drove back to Jay Creek Settlement and asked some Aboriginal boys for help. They came on board and as we drove back they pointed out a couple of wheel tracks turning off into the scrub. Brad intended driving them back, but they elected to walk, so our passengers took the hat around on their behalf. Before long we came to a series of sandy river beds that gave us a few tense moments as Brad thrashed the coach through, and I said a small prayer for the gearbox. Our maps showed this as the Hugh River.

At Serpentine Gorge we came on a wide stretch of water between two vertical cliffs, a wire ran from a post on either side, and floating on the water was a pontoon supported with 12-gallon drums under each corner. About a third climbed aboard and by hand over hand pulled themselves across, then one chap brought it back. The next group climbed aboard but halfway across someone slipped backwards having a domino effect on the others. With the change in balance the whole thing up ended and threw them headlong into the water. This caused great hilarity until we saw the cameras floating around and one girl wailing that she had lost her prescription glasses. Although we dived repeatedly for them it was to no avail.

Later back in Alice Springs at the camera shop as they lined up at the counter the technician rubbed his hands and said "Ah, more victims of Serpentine Gorge I see". We naturally assumed that he had built the pontoon.

On getting well and truly bogged in trying to drive to Ormiston Gorge we realised the track went up the sandy bed of Ormiston creek and was strictly four-wheel drive. After debogging we set up camp and endured an incredibly cold night where our water supplies froze and we piled on all the clothing we possessed. The long walk into Ormiston, shedding overcoats as we went, left little time to explore but was voted a great success.

At Glen Helen Gorge, a tourist lodge nestled at the foot of a red cliff face on the bank of the Finke River that was the original homestead of Glen Helen station. The station was owned by Bryan Bowman who became a friend to us in later years. With its magnificent location Reg Ansett had bought the old homestead from Bryan as part of a grand tourist scheme that he had for Central Australia.

While there was a very welcome bar at the lodge the service was quite hopeless as it was managed by an odd couple who spent more time arguing and abusing each other than serving customers.

We didn't know at the time that our photos of Glen Helen Gorge would prove to be quite historic, showing as they did the road to Hermannsburg going straight through the gorge along the right-hand side. This was the road that Albert Namatjira drove along on his painting expeditions into the western McDonnell ranges. Not long after, a flash flood in the Finke River washed this road away completely, leaving the debris on the driveway of Glen Helen Lodge.

We became the star attraction for the Aboriginal people at Hermannsburg Mission the following day as they crowded around the tourists and their coach. We told them we intended to drive into Palm Valley and some of them seemed to think this was very funny although some older folk appeared quite concerned. One old chap said "Eh, you can't take a bus like that into Palm Valley", but being young and knowing everything we assured him that we would. The old man shrugged but said "OK, but we better give you some Marsden matting". These proved to be long strips of steel made rigid by ribs pressed into them and lightened with punched holes. Marsden matting was widely used on airstrips across northern Australia during the Second World War and since then everywhere in outback Australia people have learnt to rely on these strips for debogging purposes.

It wasn't long before we were to give heartfelt thanks for the foresight of our Aboriginal friends. Being the skilled driver, he was Brad managed to coax the coach a long way down the bed of the river before it finally sank into the sand. This was followed by hours of work pushing and digging to get it back onto the Marsden matting, then backing a length at a time back to Hermannsburg, and we reckoned the locals must have had a few laughs that night about the city slickers.

On the way to Ayers Rock we stopped to watch cattle being loaded into trucks by a station owner, Ted Kunoth. There wasn't a blade of grass on this drought-ridden property and these were the last of the cattle to be mustered on Ebenezer Station. The Kunoths are a famous pioneering family, Ted's grandfather Harry was an Overland Telegraph linesman who married a pretty dark lass called Amelia. In her book *Alice on the Line,* author Doris Blackwell has photos of both Harry, and Amelia as a young girl. Some people may remember the film *Jedda* in which Ted's niece Rosie Kunoth played the lead role. As though Ted didn't have enough problems he pointed over the road to fire blackened ruins, and said "our homestead just burned down, seems all our troubles have come at once".

I could never have guessed in my wildest dreams on that day, that in the year 2000 Ted and I would be sitting in a back yard in Alice Springs reminiscing over our lives in the 37 years that had passed.

In 1963 there was no direct road to Ayers Rock it was just a matter of following station tracks between homesteads, and Ted explained to Brad that with the drought, drift sand was constantly covering the track to Angas Downs making it not only boggy but in places hard to follow.

However, Brad knew his way and arrived safely at Angas Downs which was a refuelling stop. Like most stations they had no electricity and petrol was hand pumped up into a glass cylinder marked off in gallons, but as we needed diesel this came in 44-gallon (200 litre) drums. Arthur and Bess Liddle, a lovely couple were the part-Aboriginal owners of this million-acre property. A large number of Aboriginal people came to watch and ensured that we departed laden with spears, boomerangs, coolamons, etc.

The track then headed south to skirt around the Basedow Range, (although Arthur called this by the Aboriginal name Wilbia). The track then headed west taking advantage of a string of salt lakes, and with a surface like concrete these gave us the smoothest ride for days. These lakes are all that remains of an ancient sea, the largest being Lake Amadeus further to the west. Vince, one of our party was making a movie of the trip and filmed a sequence of us crawling across the salt with tongues hanging out. While effective I thought it rather exaggerated our privations.

This track came into use during drought years and was impassable after rain so was replaced later with a road running further to the south through sandhill country.

The next station was Curtin Springs where the young owners Peter and Dawn Severin were running a roadhouse from a tin shed and were also selling fuel. It seemed that everybody in this country had problems as Peter explained how he had to fight government bureaucracies to operate a roadhouse on a pastoral lease, but saw this as the only means of existing during those dreadful drought years. In fact, he thought other stations would have to do the same.

The road to Ayers Rock wound back and forth through huge red sandhills that were quite bare of vegetation, it was incredibly corrugated, and the coach felt as though it was shaking to pieces, so it wasn't surprising when we finally stopped to find that the heavy steel front bumper bar had cracked vertically in the middle and was hanging in two pieces.

It was surprising how excited we were getting as we kept seeing brief glimpses of the Rock between the sandhills, perhaps because the year before we had been so frustrated and thought this would never happen.

Bill Harney had started as the original ranger at the Rock just five years earlier and become rather famous as an author of books on the outback, so it was with some disappointment that we found that Bill had passed on.

His replacement was Bob Gregory who looked like an ex-army man with a clipped moustache and a no-nonsense manner. He impressed on us that climbing the Rock could be dangerous, and if the number of tourists continued to increase some form of chain or railing may have to be installed.

And the following year this is exactly what happened, posts and chains were erected on the most difficult sections accounting for about 50 percent of the climb. This left three gaps that were linked up in 1979.

Like all first-time visitors we were captivated by the sheer size and ever-changing colours of the Rock and someone recalled the late Arthur Groom who wrote "I felt like an ant at the door of a cathedral".

Arthur Groom was the author of a book, *I Saw a Strange Land,* a classic on Central Australia. He recounts how in 1946 he set out from Alice Springs carrying a cut lunch and a spare pair of sand shoes. He walked to and climbed Mt Sender in the Western McDonnell ranges, then walked on to Hermannsburg. He told the missionaries that he was walking to Ayers Rock and realising he must be quite mad and that he would never make it they insisted that he take camels and Aboriginal guides, one of whom was Tjalkaliri, usually known as Tiger who later became a friend and used to entertain us with stories about "old man Groom".

Two of the aboriginals, Tjalkaliri andTamalji showed Groom the climb and lead him up the Rock. He described it as "a bare rock ridge not much steeper than a staircase, rising from a wide beginning to a narrowing ridge of sandstone". They told him the name of the climb wasTjinteritjinteringura which means willy wagtail place. To me this seems to sit a little oddly with today when we are assured that the aboriginal community doesn't approve of people climbing the Rock, but after all what do I know?

After climbing the Rock, Groom dispensed with the Aboriginals and their camels, sending them back to Hermannsburg. He then set out to walk to Alice Springs. Arthur Liddle at Angas Downs told me one day of how back in 1946 he had come upon a white man wandering in the sandhills and had taken him back to the homestead where his father fed and revived him and directed him on how to get to Alice Springs.

Arthur Groom though is probably far more famous as the creator of Binna-Burra Lodge on the Lamington plateau in South East Queensland.

Although it looked daunting we all determined to climb, even our oldest couple Alan and Thelma. Alan was half blind and Thelma crippled with arthritis and she said Alan would have to pull her up while she told him which way to go, which is what they did. From the top of the climb we could see what appeared to be a large wooden cross that we assumed to be the highest point quite a distance away. This looked easy but there were a number of deep valleys to be crossed and we found it necessary to run down one side to get enough momentum to gain the opposite side. If nothing else this gave us great confidence in the grip of our sand shoes.

The wooden cross turned out to be a survey trig point, held upright by masses of loose rock piled around the base. With the Olgas in the distance it was time again for photo sessions.

The following morning, we were freezing as we sat atop a sandhill on the eastern side of the Rock waiting for the sunrise. In those days if you were cold you simply lit a fire so naturally we gathered some dead wood, (with the drought it was everywhere) and lit a nice warm fire. Ayers Rock was not a national park, in fact there were no national parks in the Northern Territory, it was a reserve and as such was administered by the Reserves Board.

When driving around the Rock, Brad drove into Maggie Springs on a road to where Bill Harney had his original camp. It was not really a spring but rather a soak or waterhole formed by run off from the Rock, and as this was the only water available, Harney erected a sign to protect the area. He liked writing in verse and the sign still standing read "This is neither bath nor sink, as some who come will have to drink". I am sure that this approach was more effective than the more usual This or that is illegal' type of enforcement we expect today.

The camping was on the eastern side of the Rock and had two small amenities blocks with two cold showers. These were cleverly positioned to catch the prevailing wind so that showering too long raised the possibility of freezing to death. Even so Bob Gregory worried that we were using too much water and was trying to devise a system using a coin box and timer.

The following day we were travelling to the Olgas and although this was only about 20 miles in a straight line, apparently many sandhills made this impractical so the track lead north in a big arc travelling across very stony country that Brad referred to as "The Sedimentaries". Closer to the Olgas we were slowed to walking speed by a small forest of dead trees, then finally after negotiating a series of washed-out creek beds we came into the Olgas from the northern side. After an hour or so exploring the Valley of the Winds and having lunch it was back to camp at the Rock. We hadn't seen another person all day. Ernest Giles must have been a remarkable person, even while suffering dreadful privations he still managed to describe beauty everywhere. He spoke of the Olgas as "A cluster of round minarets, giant cupolas and monstrous domes which have stood as huge memorials from the ancient times of earth, wonderful and grotesque".

We were told that Giles named the Olgas after the Queen of Spain and I and probably hundreds of others unwittingly quoted this as fact. It was only when Richard Appleton of the Australian Encyclopaedia was researching the State archives in Stuttgart that he noted a request to Baron von Mueller, (Giles's financial backer) to "name a mountain in the Australian interior after Her Majesty Queen Olga of Wertemberg", the former Grand Duchess of Russia.

Then it was back over the corrugations to Curtin Springs to refuel there being absolutely nothing at Ayers Rock, not even warm water. Brad then swung the coach off to the south on a new course, between red sandhills near the base of Mt Connor. Then for about an hour we were back on a heavily treed sand plain with the track winding back and forth through the trees. Typical of those days it was a case of no overtaking or passing and hope to hell nothing was coming the other way.

The next station was Mulga Park owned by Dave Foggerty and there were a large group of Aboriginals camped near the homestead. One fine looking old chap wanted to have his photo taken throwing a spear as he pranced about, although this was a trifle disconcerting for the photographers as he was only wearing a T-shirt. Another man with a magnificent head dress of Major Mitchell cockatoo feathers insisted I photograph him.

After leaving Mulga Park we turned east running parallel to the South Australian border at the edge of the Musgrave range. Finally, after some heavy going through sandhill country we arrived at Colin and Pat Morton's homestead of Victory Downs. Here again we listened as Colin told us unless the drought ended soon they would have to turn to catering for tourists, although from what we had been seeing there was also a bit of a drought of tourists in this part of the world.

Only a short drive brought us back to the Stuart Highway at the South Australian border where we headed down toward Coober Pedy, where after a fuel stop and a chat with Fay Naylor it was back to opening and closing gates and battling bulldust.

At Kingoonya we arrived in the middle of the night, (nothing unusual) to find Doug Fredericks working on his coach, surrounded by a group of shivering unhappy passengers. Doug had brake failure which didn't surprise me much and was about what you would expect from driving on these sorts of roads. Brad of course felt obliged to help and we became part of the shivering mob.

At Port Augusta we drove on to a genuine bitumen highway, and although this meant the end of the dust and rough ride we were saddened by the realisation that the adventure part of the trip was behind us. We regarded outback adventure and bitumen roads as being incompatible.

Adelaide was like a big country town with everyone looking as though dressed for race day, and you obviously dressed up to go to town. The ladies wore white gloves and large highly decorated hats leaving us with the feeling we were in some kind of time warp as I remembered people dressing this way in Sydney when I was a kid.

I suppose we did to some extent revel in the fact that we were the roughest looking mob in town. After all, if you have just conquered the great outback, surely it's only reasonable to look the part.

Brad dropped us in town for an eat-out celebration meal which turned out to be anything but. We nearly starved instead as we ran from one eating house to the next just as they closed their doors. Before 7 o'clock the whole town had closed down and everyone had gone home. For all that, I liked Adelaide and hoped to return some day and enjoy its relaxing atmosphere. In fact, I would inadvertently return the following year but under anything like relaxing conditions, though more about that later.

So far we had enjoyed perfect weather apart from the cold nights, but on the Victorian South Coast it turned quite foul, although it probably added to the atmosphere of this rugged coastline. We were captivated by the Twelve Apostles and London Bridge. We jokingly suggested that Brad drive out onto London Bridge for a photograph. "Nah" he said "It might fall down." We agreed, adding though not in our lifetimes. Of course, it did happen only a few years later, fortunately no one was hurt although two people were stranded on what became an island. It's relatively easy to get people off but I often wonder how a stranded coach would have looked.

The Great Ocean Road must have been a difficult drive, particularly in such weather conditions. It was narrow and winding with blind bends, the only saving grace being in the left-hand inside lane. While sharing our opinion of the road a local in Port Campbell, where we camped overnight told us that the road was due for widening and realignment in the next year or two.

In the last few days of any holiday time seems to accelerate, and it appears that you are back home before you realise it. And so, it was that we found ourselves back in Kings Cross with goodbyes, kisses and quite a number of tears.

**1962. Redline coach bogged just south of Alice Springs on tour to Ayers Rock.
Tour cancelled. This led us to chartering a Redline coach the following year, then purchasing our own coach and Sundowner Coaches was born.**

1963. Redline Coach bogged Ormiston Creek

1964/5 OUR OWN COACH "SUNDOWNER"

We relived the trip constantly and one night I found myself telling Doreen that "No doubt Brad did a fantastic job, but you know, if we wanted, could do a far better job than Redline". Doreen rather floored me by saying "I agree, why don't we". I quickly pointed out that I was just expressing an opinion, and didn't really mean it, but she persisted and so the die was cast.

We would buy a cheap second-hand bus, do it up in the workshop and see if our idea worked. We determined to keep the motor business in the meantime, after all the tour business might be a complete failure.

It was becoming obvious that Japanese cars were beginning to show up the deficiencies of British vehicles. The Brits had long dominated our car sales by always insisting their vehicles had character which we knew better as poor quality and unreliability and I think the Italians were even worse as most people quoted Fiat as standing for "Fix it Again Tony".

Therefore, I felt that our car business should have been doing better, but in retrospect I realise that I lacked both the business training and natural ability to run a motor dealership. Cash flow was always chaotic with large amounts flowing through, 6 people on the payroll, cars on floor plan, trade-ins overpriced and not moving, insurance companies slow to pay, spare parts inventories over stocked, and general lack of systems. As though this wasn't enough I was spending time trying to line up a second-hand tourist coach.

While in Alice Springs I was admiring an Ansett Pioneer Clipper coach, American designed these vehicles were built in Australia under licence. The driver Sid Lynch showed me over it. These were superb coaches that today are sought-after collector's items. As well Alan Denning in Brisbane was building coaches for Redline and Greyhound, the problem was that none of these vehicles were obtainable second-hand. So, if we couldn't buy a second-hand coach it would have to be a second-hand bus, but even these were in short supply as operators usually drove them into the ground, and they were only replaced when totally worn out.

We found two buses for sale, they looked identical both with Cycle Components Manufacturing Company bodies, one was a Bedford and the other built on a five-ton Austin truck chassis. In retrospect I believe the Bedford probably would have been the better bet, but I chose the Austin because I could still get a 30 percent discount from BMC on parts and I knew that I would need plenty of these. This bus was ex-Foggs Motors of Newcastle, so no matter how much we referred to it as 'the coach', it was very much a town bus with the usual upright tubular steel framed seats. I closed my mind to the thought that a bus no longer good enough for the streets of South Wallsend might have a bit of a problem in Central Australia.

To save money I requested interstate licence plates as we only envisaged interstate tours. Although these were becoming common for trucks apparently no one had ever requested them for a coach, and of course when a public servant has no form all is lost. Their defences finally crumbled and they modified a truck form for the purpose.

Although section 92 of the Constitution ended customs charges on state borders, State governments brought in all manner of taxes and restrictions to prevent trucks competing with their railways. Finally, two truckies, Michael Hughes and Ron Vale with industry backing fought the States through the courts who found consistently against the truckies. In 1954 the case finished up in the Privy Council in London who found that the State governments were in contravention of section 92 of the Constitution and were stifling interstate trade. In less than 10 years since Hughes and Vale, trucks and coaches had reduced the cost and expanded interstate trade enormously.

At this time, I told an old mate, Jack Wagg, of our plans and he made me a remarkable offer. Jack had a yard and small bus business in Lindfield, and he proposed that we take it over and run it in combination with what he believed would be our growing coach business. Jack would stay on and help, and we could pay him off over an extended period. We declined Jack's kind offer and ultimately, he sold out to Ron Deane. Jack passed away in 1981.

The camping gear expert Paddy Pallin was our obvious choice for equipment and when Doreen went to Paddy with a list of our requirements she explained the reason for our needs. He was so enthusiastic about what we wanted to do that he placed an advertisement for our tours on his notice board. This had a later spin-off beyond our expectations.

The Austin was duly registered as ISJ 433 (the IS prefix being for interstate). It was 35 feet long, the maximum length considered safe on the road in those days of so little traffic. In 1968 36 feet was allowed, and in 1969 37 feet, and then when traffic became thoroughly congested it was considered quite safe to operate vehicles over 40 feet in length. Also in 1969 at the behest of Reg Ansett the width was increased from 8 feet to the American standard of 8 feet 2½ in.

I am often asked why we chose the name Sundowner. Well, apart from the popularity of the movie *The Sundowners* which was produced in 1960, we felt it sat well with people travelling the outback. Some claim the name originated with the swagman who arrived at a station homestead at sundown, too late to work but to obtain a meal and shelter for the night. Then in 1908 while peddling around Australia as a record breaking long distance cyclist, Frances Birtles met up with Murray Aunger and Harry Dutton attempting to drive the first car from Adelaide to Darwin. This caused Birtles to change to cars, and he probably opened up more routes through the Australian bush than any other person in our motoring history. And what did he call his car? Well Sundowner of course, and it is now on display in the National Museum in Canberra.

To allay any misgivings, I had about the vehicle we decided that a long road test should be carried out, and so invited friends and family on a trip to Wagga and back.

My Dad, (who never threw anything away) had a copy of a magazine called "Sea, Land, and Air" dated 1920 that contained an article about driving a five-ton Leyland truck to Melbourne. It started with a dock strike forcing a decision, rather daringly it appears, to drive overland to Melbourne. Between Liverpool and Campbelltown bridges could not be crossed and detours were made, and then near Goulburn 250 yards of road was washed away, "causing a minor holdup." Police at Albury had a weight limit on the highway bridge and a detour had to be made to Howlong to cross the Murray River. In Victoria, bridges had to be bypassed and they proceeded up creek beds. In spite of considerable swaying, bridges near Seymour held up, "proving the value of Australian hardwood." The last 50 miles into Melbourne improved so much it only took three hours, and in all the journey took nine days.

The Hume Highway was only of country road standard, and 9 years earlier in 1956 rain had brought about the collapse of large sections of roadway near Holbrook that completely stopped traffic for 13 days, and with weight limits on alternate roads stranded 235 interstate trucks.

While I don't think the road alignment had improved a great deal, the bridges and bitumen undoubtedly had so we proceeded to carry out our road test. The highway wandered through Camden, then on with the narrow "S" bend under the railway bridge at Picton, then through the main street of Bargo, but the big test was Razorback Mountain.

I didn't have a rating on the Austin, but it must have been less than 100 hp and it climbed Razorback in first gear at walking speed, then I remained in first down the other side being afraid the brakes wouldn't hold. It was a long day and we made Wagga in the dark leaving me a bit disappointed about the performance although I consoled myself with the thought that the passengers would have plenty of time to admire the scenery, but at least it could make Wagga and back.

The bus had 39 seats, but as there was no luggage bin space we removed the back two rows of seats for luggage, which meant carrying it in and out along the length of the aisle. We then removed another row and spread the seats for greater leg room if not greater comfort. This reduced the seating from 39 down to 26.

The Queensland companies, Redline and Greyhound (who did their first Central Australia trip in 1960) were the only people advertising in Sydney and they both wisely left their itineraries very vague, but we (rather bravely I thought) printed them on a day-by-day basis, gambling that weather and breakdowns would be manageable.

War-time petrol rationing only ended in 1950 and people were still reluctant to travel long distances and would consider an interstate trip a major adventure requiring great preparation and planning. Travel as we know it was in its infancy, the Boeing jet had yet to be invented and flying to London cost nearly as much as a new Holden car, and travelling in the outback was thought to be so fraught with danger that few people would consider it, a bit like the medieval - beyond here lie dragons.

Doreen and I let it be known that we would arrange slide showings and talk about outback travel at group evenings. There was little ownership of TV at the time and these evenings were quite popular, and created quite a few bookings. Perhaps we should have tried selling cars this way.

We priced a 3-week trip at 50 pounds (100 dollars) and of course there was no thought of providing anything but the transport, people were expected to make their own arrangements for catering and equipment, although we could hire them our Paddy Pallin tents and camping gear.

It was about this time that I first met Ian Campbell who came to us after reading our advertisement on Paddy Pallin's notice board. Ian was geology master at Barker College at Hornsby. He had previously taught in Melbourne and had been active in organising school adventure trips. Friends of Ian's at Knox Grammar School had organised the first ever group tour to Ayers Rock in 1950. They arranged with trucking operator Len Tuit of Alice Springs to pick up the party at Finke railway siding. Len gave no guarantee they would reach the Rock and it took three days following tracks left by the famous Territory transport operator Kurt Johansson some years before at the time of the Mark Foy expedition. This trip passed into school folklore and Ian had long wanted to do something similar when he saw our advertisement.

Ian tells of how he found his way to our workshop then asked for Bill Hand and was pointed at a pair of boots sticking out from beneath a car and on inquiring was met with "won't be long mate." He told me that he wanted to run a school adventure trip to Ayers Rock, Alice Springs, and other places I hadn't even heard of. Apparently, my answer was "Gee, I don't know about that, I'd better talk to Doreen". The upshot was that we would take Barker in August 1964, and this was the start of a 26-year association with Ian and Barker College, as we organised trips for them all over Australia and New Zealand until Ian finally retired.

Finally, May arrived and we set out with 23 passengers on our first Sundowner safari trip and made Wagga once again in the dark. The next day, less than one hour west of Wagga at a place called Galore the oil pressure dropped to zero and a hammering noise came from the motor. I dropped the sump and found number five big end bearing had almost vanished. I polished the crank journal (that part of the crank shaft in contact with the big end bearing) and among the hundred or so spare parts found a set of big end bearings. With oil pressure restored we happily proceeded on and spent the next night in Mildura. Again, less than an hour west of Mildura the number five bearing went again. Feeling a bit incompetent I decided on professional help and from a nearby store rang Diesel Services in Mildura and explained the problem. They said they would send out Gary Cooper causing our passengers to joke about waiting for a tall guy with a Stetson arriving on horseback.

But Gary Cooper turned out to be the little apprentice and while he did a good job it was really no more than I would have done and felt it was time and money wasted. It didn't last long and I became very proficient every three or four hours pulling off the sump and replacing the bearing, and Doreen became equally competent at sieving the oil, while at the same time I was calculating hours divided by the number of bearings left.

Our passengers had remained surprisingly cheerful while all this was going on although they must have had extreme doubts at this rate of ever seeing Central Australia. It was fortunate that we had explored Adelaide the previous year as now it was obvious that I had to convince everyone that spending some time in Adelaide was going to add enormously to their enjoyment of the trip.

Peters Diesel was a new Company recently opened on Grand Junction Road, so after dropping everybody off at Hackney caravan park I headed off with no oil pressure and a clunking motor to see what they could do. I left Doreen explaining to the passengers how lucky they were to have this bonus. At Peters Diesel they convinced me that a new engine was the only answer, and they just happened to be agents for the revolutionary new 6 354 Series Perkins, "the finest diesel money could buy." I agreed only stipulating that they work non-stop on the changeover.

I spent the night there as work progressed and they finished the following day. I asked the boss about a trade-in on the Austin and he said "No, I don't own a boat". I remarked that I hadn't thought of it as a boat engine and he came back "No, not as an engine, I meant as a mooring". Although the new motor was a disaster financially and wiped out any profit on the trip it was a joy to drive after the Austin.

Doreen had arranged an entry permit for Woomera, this entailed submitting a passenger list to Canberra then the Federal police at Woomera comparing names on the list. It seemed anything but a foolproof system, but after much flourishing of paperwork they lifted the boom gate and allowed us in. The place was very busy with an excellent small shopping centre, in fact the best we would see until Alice Springs.

Most of the road to Kingoonya was still a narrow winding track through the trees, but dozers and graders were at work making a whole new wide straight road. A huge upgrading of outback tracks took place during 1964 and 1965 where station tracks were widened and realigned. Leaving Kingoonya we crossed the railway line and headed north where shortly the road forked; as there was no signpost I chose the left-hand fork as it appeared to carry the most traffic.

In a short time, it brought us to North Well station which was owned by Sir Phillip MacBride, a Government Cabinet Minister. Shearing was in progress and the reason for the most used road was the number of shearers and other workers driving to and from the Kingoonya pub was greater than the main road traffic. The shearers invited us to stay and watch and share a mug of tea with them. They were knowledgeable about the country and identified the local trees pointing out sugarwoods, myall and mulga. One fellow remarked that mulga *(Acacia anuera)* was the most common tree in Australia, although most Australians would never have seen one. He was probably quite right, as travelling the outback you pass through seemingly endless forests of mulga.

The road that we used the previous year had been closed due to washouts and we detoured further to the west on the Ingemar station track, then on to Goober Pedy. This was later graded and became the main road. One of the annoying things about this road was the number of gates that had to be opened and closed. We used to stop and have tea at 5 o'clock, then drive on till 1 O o'clock to make camp.

One night I stopped for a gate, somebody got out and opened and closed it and I drove on. Then about 10 minutes later a passenger awoke to find their seat companion missing. I turned around and drove back and found him huddled and shivering by the gate post, it turned out that two had got out and I hadn't noticed, one needing an urgent tree stop while the gate opening was in progress and I had driven off and left him. It was a very cold night and he was in a miserable state when we returned.

On Ingemar station there were two gates only about half a mile apart and Sid Lynch of Pioneer Coaches told me of a game some of their drivers played when driving two up. On stopping at the first gate the co-driver would open and close the gate and then hop into the rear luggage bin which was quite large on the Clipper coaches. The driver then drove off ignoring the frantic passengers who by that time are yelling "you have left the other bloke behind". Then as they slowed for the next gate the co-driver let himself out and raced past the coach coughing and wheezing and opened the gate leaving the passengers totally bewildered and believing they had seen the greatest athletic achievement of all time.

One of the interesting things about night driving in this country was the number of creatures to be seen in the headlights; the most common were little desert jumping mice that went bouncing across the road like ping-pong balls.

Kangaroos, dingos, and bandicoots were also to be seen and unfortunately the occasional feral cat.

Along the way we renewed friendships made during the Redline trip with people such as the old Aboriginal chap at the Mulga Park Station camp. He insisted on being photographed while leaping up and down waving a spear as though auditioning for a Toyota ad. This was quite a spectacular sight with someone only wearing a T-shirt.

Everybody who has driven out west of Alice Springs in recent years will be aware of the well- signposted bitumen road, but in 1964 there was neither, but although still not signposted we found that more traffic had made the track more obvious.

Further west we came to the wide sandy bed of the Hugh River. I remembered Brad storming across this point, but I didn't have his experience and became hopelessly bogged. So, on this trip we had to abandon trying to get to Ormiston. I think perhaps someone before us had bogged and wrecked the track - well either that or I learnt a bit because on all subsequent trips crossed the Hugh without any high drama.

Coming home on a gravel road in Queensland I had a rather terrifying experience when a truck going the opposite way threw up a hail of stones. As they hit the windscreen it disintegrated into a thousand pieces and came back and hit me in the face. Pieces of glass showered the length of the aisle, although fortunately I was the only person affected. I stopped and looked in the inside mirror to see my face covered in blood and was truly thankful I had been wearing sun glasses. When the blood was washed away I found only a dozen or so tiny cuts that were really of little consequence, but what was of greater importance was having to drive home with no windscreen. I hate to think what it would have been like in rain, as it was I and also the front seat passengers had to rug up against the freezing blast.

It was due to this traumatic incident that I came to meet Jack Violet, manager of CCMC where I took the coach to fit a new windscreen. Cycle Components Manufacturing Company seemed a strange name for the people who built the coach. It was started by a famous cyclist, Stan Hillsden. He started by building his own racing cycles, then tubular chairs and bus seat frames operating originally under the name SJH Cycles. Then he tendered for and won a contract to build complete bus bodies. Stan was a lovely old bloke who got the travel bug in his retirement and did a number of trips with us.

I suggested to Jack that the Company name was hardly appropriate, and he agreed saying they were getting around to changing it to Customs Coaches Manufacturing Company (thereby keeping the same letters) and at the time of writing they are working on a contract replacing the Sydney Bus fleet and are now the biggest manufacturers of bus bodies in Australia.

Jack explained that safety glass that shattered into many small pieces was being phased out and being replaced with laminated glass, and even though it could be starred or cracked would stay in place and not disintegrate. As a result of the windscreen incident Jack became a very good and valued friend, and his daughter Sharon came with us to Central Australia several months later.

After three Central Australian trips the August tour with the passengers from our first Redline tour was something completely different as we set off for the Gulf. The mountainous road north of Roma was in a shocking state, and unbeknown to us we drove past Carnarvon Gorge as it was a year or two before it was opened to the public.

We finally reached the sea at Karumba where we compared the realities of this country with our expectations. It seems we all assumed it would be dense tropical jungle instead of the flat savannah grass plains stretching right to the coast.

Karumba was originally a stopover for pre-war Qantas flying boats on their way from Darwin to the east coast. Then during the second world war was used by the RAAF as a Catalina flying boat base and although the Catalinas had long gone the huge concrete aprons dipping down into the river were a reminder.

The RAAF buildings had been converted by Ansett into an expensive fly-in, fly-out hunting/fishing lodge with uniformed waiters serving cold drinks around a swimming pool. There was a mermaid painted on the bottom of the pool that apparently was done by Percy Trezise, one of the Ansett pilots. Percy went on to become an authority on Cape York cave paintings and the proprietor of the Laura Hotel.

In later years, huge amounts of prawns were discovered in the Gulf, and Karumba became a thriving town built around prawning, fishing and tourism. The Ansett lodge has long gone and is now a pub better known for its "Animal Bar" than its uniformed waiters. On future trips Doreen would bulk buy prawns and cook up evening prawn feasts. Unfortunately, being allergic to prawns usually meant that I would retire to the rear and open a can of baked beans.

On a recent trip I overheard some of our people talking to a passenger from another coach, and he asked what our food was like. They told him that Doreen explained days ahead what was available and where, and they purchased their own supplies and cooked their own meals. This meant (1) a cheaper coach fare, (2) interesting shopping with locals, then (3) they ate what they preferred, how much they wanted, and perhaps more importantly when they wanted to eat. They also told how some packed the luggage while others helped in other ways, in fact everyone had a job to do. The fellow looked amazed and asked did they all share in driving the coach as well.

In the early 1960s the major coach companies running camping tours were Redline and Greyhound out of Brisbane, and Pioneer and Murray Valley out of Adelaide. We all used this same system, then later other companies started up such as Australian Pacific in 1967 and Centralian and to tap the growing market they invented the "tenderfoot" tour, this meant the staff did most of the work, and meals were provided. Also, to ease the logistics they stayed more in the caravan parks that were starting to appear around the country rather than bush camp.

As most of our people became regulars and obviously liked our system we saw no reason to change, but the others all changed to 100 percent tenderfoot tours and with no need to differentiate the term tenderfoot, it dropped out of use. By not changing this left us in some people's eyes as the odd ones out.

But August/September 1964 was the Barker College tour, so could a group of teenage college boys provide for and cook their own meals? Probably not, but this was a charter trip, and Ian Campbell was experienced in organising school adventure trips. All boys were appointed to jobs - packers, buyers, quartermasters, cooks, etc. They worked well as a team and I was fortunate over the years to catch up with some of these fellows and be told how that trip had changed their lives.

Early in the trip at Port Augusta we had a sickness problem with one of the boys, Drury Heath. With no doctors on duty at the hospital we drove all over town trying to find one. I think Drury became embarrassed at all the fuss and he assured us he was feeling better, so we proceeded on to Coober Pedy. Further north at the camel/whip well that they called Mala Bore, the clutch pedal went to the floor and I had to carefully judge gear shifts without it. I didn't think the poor old gearbox could stand much of that treatment and determined to strip down the clutch overnight in the Granite Downs Station workshop.

Jim Davies, the owner of Granite Downs was a famous outback character known to everybody as "Old Ironbark". First off, I asked Jim for a refill of water, meaning of course bore water but he replied, "there's rainwater in that tank, take that". I said, "Oh no I wouldn't take your rainwater" but Jim replied, "Take it, I wouldn't touch it, bloody stuffs got no taste". A few years later he sold out to the McLachlan family and bought the pub at Aileron north of Alice Springs. Granite Downs is now part of the Aboriginal Lands, and whereas in those days it was on the cross roads of the Oodnadatta Track and the Stuart Highway, it is bypassed today with the highway aligned further to the west and the Oodna Track diverted south to Marla.

That night I stripped the clutch down with Doreen, Drury and another boy who insisted on staying up to help me. I couldn't find a thing wrong with it, so reassembled it, tried it, and the pedal went straight to the floor. I finally realised that vibration had worn the splines where the pedal sat on the cross shaft; it was a long night and I had had enough so I grabbed Ironbark's welder and welded it up solid.

Young Drury had stayed cheerful and been a great help that night and it came as a shock when he simply collapsed the following day. I radioed the Flying Doctor Base VJD Alice Springs and described the symptoms and they directed us to the airstrip at Kulgera. We got

Drury aboard the aircraft and Ian said he would have to go as well with his parent authority in case of medical treatment.

Ian told later that he was having a wonderful time admiring the view, when he realised that he was the only person awake. Drury had had a busy night, and it appears the pilot had too as the plane was flying itself. As they approached Alice Springs the pilot snapped awake much to Ian's relief and said, "I often have to operate like this". No wonder he collapsed, Drury had both appendicitis and German measles. He was a good kid and we left a ticket for him at the hospital for a flight out to Ayers Rock and back.

In 1989 we were invited to Barker College and had the pleasure of being presented with gifts "In Appreciation of the many wonderful expeditions from 1964-1989". Naturally some could not attend and sent their apologies - this one came from Drury Heath, Perth, Western Australia:

> "The 1964 trip sure goes down in my history book. North of Coober Pedy the yoke on the clutch shaft gave up, so I vividly remember Bill crash changing gears for quite a distance over the dunes to Granite Downs Station - what a driving feat. It was a very mechanical style bus we were in.
>
> Most went for a guided tour of the Station but a couple of us stayed to help fit the clutch. I seem to remember Bill muttering about not fitting under buses too well, so we did the dirty work.
>
> That night I felt crook, and the following day the Flying Doctor was called. Poor Ian Campbell!! Forced to take a ride in a plane with me to Alice Springs. No wonder, I was crook with German measles and appendicitis!! End of trip for me.
>
> What a coincidence when we met Bill and Doreen in Perth 28 years later, and what a change in the bus! My son Simon is still amazed by it, in fact he wants it when they retire."

Drury's mate on that trip was John Pike who wrote this letter when he could not attend the reunion in 1989:

> "After leaving Coober Pedy the bus finally succumbed to Bill's driving - clutch trouble. Drury, Heath and I volunteered as helpers. Bus repaired, we headed for Alice Springs, this time Drury succumbed to Doreen's cooking - appendicitis and unfortunately Drury received an early flight home. At Ayers Rock, Ron Hayman asked could I keep an eye on the group during the climb. But once started, all promises were forgotten as the race to the top began.
>
> In raging dust storms with Central Australia behind us we headed home through Queensland. I will always remember black soil and rain at Blackall, the bus had slipped sideways and was stuck, so it was all out and push! The bus started to move in the slippery mud and all of us had to try and jump back on board on the move. After a freezing night at Tenterfield the final day was quiet as all on board realized we were nearing the end of a fantastic trip.
>
> I'll take this opportunity to wish Bill and Doreen all the best for the future, and contrary to what you said at the time Ian, I did remember more than the paralysed cat at Angas Downs.
>
> I have been back to the Rock twice since, but I can proudly say I climbed long before there was a chain up the Rock.

> In closing Ian, during the trip we plotted to leave you behind, but I'm glad we didn't because without you this wonderful trip and many more to follow would not have been possible."

One of our unexpected pleasures have been dozens of thank you letters we have received over the years from ex-Barker boys from all over the world.

Back to the 1964 tour – after being assured Drury was in safe hands in Alice Springs Hospital, Ian Campbell flew to Ayers Rock to continue the tour.

On driving back from the Rock, we stopped at Ted and Val Kunoth's Mt Ebenezer Station to admire their new log cabin roadhouse made from desert oak trees. Like Peter on Curtin Springs, Ted was hoping that tourism would save them during the drought as Ebenezer was one of the worst affected stations and was absolutely desolate.

About 10 minutes east of the homestead we came on a burnt-out Redline coach. The heat must have been really intense, the aluminium engine parts of the Commer diesel lay all over the ground in blobs. There were exploded cans and things like souvenir tea spoons lying all around it. The boys climbed into the wreck and as they looked out the window gaps were photographed for a "This is the way we went to Central Australia" photo. The driver Laurie McBeth later told me that he had decided that the coach was jinxed and had had a major problem on every trip that year. (I believed that all Commers were jinxed, they were built by the Humber car company.)

Laurie told how a passenger came up from the back complaining about the heat. Laurie just agreed, then looking into the rear vision mirror saw flames billowing out the rear of the coach. He yelled "All out" and left so quickly himself that he left his wallet behind.

Within minutes the whole coach was ablaze. The remains are still there today on the old road two or three hundred metres south of the present road.

About 20 years later a lady passenger told me that a girl friend had been on a Redline trip in 1964 when their coach blew up, and had I heard about it. I stopped on the main road and we walked over and photographed the old wreck for her friend.

On an earlier trip Laurie made it to the Rock with practically no gears, and I helped him reset the gear transfer rod. While we were lying under the coach working, Laurie's passengers came back dragging loads of dead wood. Next thing Bob Gregory the Ranger arrived, he abused the people, told them to take the timber back where they found it, then screamed "Where's McBeth? I'll kill him." Laurie and I lay underneath not game to move until Bob gave up and left.

A sign appeared on the road to the Rock stating "The Ranger is a pedantic twit". Surprisingly it stayed there for years until it was lost in a road re-alignment.

One more trip to Central Australia in September was the end of what we could only consider a very successful years operation and Sundowner Coach Tours was most certainly in business.

I doubt that many people find their ideal occupation in life and until then I know I hadn't felt suited to any job that I had tried. Now I found long distance driving the easiest and most fulfilling thing that I had attempted. The year had been a great experience for us both as Doreen is at her best when organising and planning and she excelled with both.

Many things on the coach were reaching their use-by-date, particularly the seat frames and I was constantly having to borrow welders to repair them. We actually wrote one seat off when I came suddenly on a washed-out creek bed and braked too late. The poor fellow in the front seat shot into the air hitting his head on the parcel rack then came crashing back into the seat which collapsed beneath him. I thought I had killed him, but he came around and took it all in the spirit of adventure, although the seat didn't fare nearly as well.

As the year drew to a close we were forced to make a decision about the motor business. The Toyota franchise was not transferable except with their OK and they insisted that any prospective buyers required an apparently inexhaustible amount of finance, so it became impossible to sell. It seemed ironic that one of Australia's first Toyota dealers was going to be the first to exit the franchise, but I could see nothing else for it. Ultimately, we were forced to sell the business as simply a car workshop, and with an economic downturn at the time we had no choice but to accept far less than I believed it was worth.

When we had first achieved the Toyota franchise my dad invested a deal of money in the business, so at the time we changed the name of the company to E. A. HAND Pty. Ltd. Putting it into his name was a form of goodwill, and when we sold out I repaid him the money he had invested. This meant that we came out with very little to show for the 10 years of work trying to build up the business.

However, a problem now arose about where to garage and service the coach having lost the workshop. At this point a friend stepped in and made an offer of his B.P. service station for our use, we worked out a deal for these purposes and also as a pickup and discharge point for our passengers. This proved highly satisfactory and even had a spin-off with B.P. as I will relate later.

With no power steering and heavy controls, handling the coach was not that easy but we agreed that Doreen should also be licensed to drive it. The registry official seemed totally amazed and said first up "You must have a job with a bus company before you can apply for a licence". So, I said, "Oh, that's OK I'll give her a job." So of course, she passed everything and obtained her coach driver's licence. As 1964 came to a close we could look back on quite an incredible year. We had made some wonderful friendships, overcome great difficulties, and learned all manner of valuable lessons.

1965 was a year of constant repairs - things like the copper fuel lines that work-hardened and cracked and I gradually converted them to plastic. Then there were the springs - in hindsight these should have been replaced at the start, but instead had been progressively renewed during the year by the busy spring makers in places like Alice Springs and Mt. Isa.

So, our diary entry for our first trip in April 1965 seems quite remarkable as it states, "Perfect trip, on time all the way".

I have lost count of how many times I climbed the Rock, although Doreen did more as sometimes working on the coach had to be my priority. The big wooden cross or trig point was still at the top of the Rock and on the May trip a young passenger, Ray Hopkins, was put out by the fact that there was nowhere that he could leave his name at the top.

We discussed this with the Ranger, Bob Gregory and it was agreed that Ray would make a steel box with a lid flap and provide an exercise book and pencils, but as Bob didn't climb the Rock we would have to collect and replace the book at regular intervals. The exercise books filled in about three months and we replaced them and passed them on to Bob Gregory. In one book we found a whole page in Japanese and we pondered how a group of Japanese had found their way out to the Rock. Another had a double page map of Australia drawn by Evan Green and Jack Murray showing a publicity trip they were doing for the

British Motor Corporation. Evan and Jack driving a Mini Minor and an Austin 1800 drove a figure 8 course around Australia. Although it was never revealed at the time, a mate of ours was hired to lead them.

Johnnie Bamforth traded as "Alice to Anywhere" 4-wheel drive tours and he told us how the two cars had to be towed half the way behind his Landcruiser. Johnnie got no mention in the ensuing publicity but accepted a handsome cash payment instead.

We continued with the Ayers Rock books until 1968 when a new ranger, Derek Roff took over and expressed amazement at the arrangement. About this time the wooden trig came down and was replaced with a stone cairn with a plaque and a map of Australia on top. The original map rather upset Tasmanians when they found they had been left off the map.

During the early sixties, although still in black and white, TV ownership was growing apace, and a popular program was B.P. Pick-A-Box, a game show hosted by Bob Dyer, who in company with Jack Davey were top TV personalities.

Dyer wanted film footage of outback Australia to use in B.P. advertising and one of his reps. contacted us for this purpose. A pair of young film makers had just won an award for their work, and it was proposed they accompany us on an outback trip. Alan was Australian, a tall, thin intellectual type and Tony a Porn, all go-go and excitable. They came on the July 1965 trip and proceeded to shoot off miles of film.

Tony went to extraordinary lengths, like making a rope harness so he could lie out parallel to the road while hooking his heels on the doorstep. With a heavy camera on his shoulder he then filmed the front wheel bouncing up and down on the deep corrugation.

I used to wonder if Tony was really mad, or just liked to act that way. He was totally extrovert and one day in a pub he sidled up to an elderly local and asked, "Gooday, and what do you do?" The old timer looked him up and down and said, "I minds me own bloody business, so bugger of".

At Ayers Rock they filmed the whole climb business, carrying all their heavy cameras and sound equipment right to the top.

On earlier trips we had become friends with a remarkable young Aboriginal chap at Hermannsburg Lutheran Mission called Gus Williams. Gus had arranged to take our people into Palm Valley where we would have a campfire concert and spend the night.

As this was strictly 4-wheel drive, Gus arranged the vehicles which we augmented with a Land Rover hired in Alice Springs which Doreen drove. After setting up camp and lighting the fire we would drive the vehicles back to Hermannsburg and pick up a mob of Aboriginal people, including as many kids as could fit in or on. We promised Alan and Tony some unforgettable footage in Palm Valley and around the camp fire.

As we drove along the sandy bed of the Finke River on our way into Palm Valley they were able to film the first commercial gas well in the Northern Territory being flared. It was quite a dramatic column of flame on the Palm Valley No. I Well. This Well was subsequently capped and nearly twenty years passed before a pipeline was installed and it was brought on stream. Gus Williams, a talented musician in the style of Slim Dusty had enthused enough young fellows at the Mission to form a band, so we always tried to round up enough of them for a campfire concert. The kids loved dancing around the fire, they jerked and twisted and threw themselves around and the moment the music stopped they dropped to the ground. There was some disgrace in being last and that kid was pointed out and laughed at.

As well as the usual crowd we often had well known painters bring down their wares, such as Keith and Ewald Namatjira, Edwin and Otto Pareroultja, Claude Pannka, Joshua Ebataringa, Benjamin Landara and many others. Gus himself was a nephew of Albert Namatjira. Tjalkaliri, who accompanied Arthur Groom also came that evening and performed some traditional dances.

Alan and Tony were completely blown away with our campfire and filmed and recorded everything, trying Gus's patience by asking for many second takes, but reassuring everyone that they would feature on Bob Dyer's TV shows.

Another week passed with Tony doing his usual athletics to capture special effects, then they started to argue about how their material would be edited. Their relationship deteriorated quickly and after two and a half weeks they were barely on speaking terms. The upshot was that Tony took out a court order preventing Alan making any use of the material without his say so. He then took off back to England and hasn't been heard of since.

Bob Dyer's people tried to get access but to no avail, and we never did see any of the film material which today would be quite historic stuff.

However, with Alan we played the sound tapes of Palm Valley and decided that regardless of Tony we had to do something with them. Alan edited the tapes and we produced 100 vinyl 10" L.P. records. These were sold at a profit with the proceeds going into a special account we opened for Hermannsburg Mission to purchase sporting goods and musical instruments. After 3 pressing runs the record company informed us that they were ceasing production of vinyl L.P.s and that was the end of our record business. For obvious reasons, even though a profit was made, we personally had to prove a slight loss to ourselves.

Alan subsequently wrote articles about the outback and when he married sometime later, brought his wife along on a Central Australian trip.

I have always been a big picture sort of person, with a need to find and overcome exciting challenges, but I admit to a lack of patience with the detailed planning this requires. I could just as easily have lurched from one disaster to the next, except for the great good fortune of marrying Doreen. She is a born organiser, nothing flusters her, and nothing is ever too hard.

We allowed plenty of time between trips for coach servicing and rebuilding, so while this kept me busy, Doreen needed more to keep her occupied and she enrolled as a part time N.R.M.A. Pilot Guide. This required meeting up with an out-of-town driver and driving them in their car to wherever they wished to go in the City or suburbs.

One extreme request was driving a woman to Wagga, another was to pick up and deliver a Winnebago Motor Home an American had brought out from the United States. Apparently, his daughter knew Jon Konrads, a famous swimmer of this time, and this kindled a desire to see Australia. He came up with a remarkable offer, would Doreen and I take time out to drive and look after he and his wife on a tour around Australia. It was intended to be relaxed and enjoyable as time and money was no problem. If only, but of course it was impossible, there was no way we could simply cancel tours with passengers already booked, and we regretfully had to decline the offer.

1964. First coach departing from our car showroom at Gladesville on first Central Australian Tour.

1964. Ayers Rock compound - amenities, water and wood supply. No other campers.

1965 AROUND AUSTRALIA TOUR

In 1965 we decided to attempt an around Australia tour which was quite a daunting prospect and required a great deal of thought and planning. We chose September as the driest time in the Gulf country and the Kimberley where there were all dirt roads, also this would bring us into Western Australia by springtime when by all accounts the wildflowers should be in full bloom.

Today I wouldn't attempt to drive the old Austin around the block and would consider it sheer madness to even dream of driving it around Australia. Maps were poor and even contradicted each other particularly in W. A. Northwest where they were shown as a web of dotted lines. As near as we could calculate the distance would be about 13000 miles (about 21000 km) which is further than flying from Sydney to London.

What problems could we expect? The Perkins motor should be trouble-free except for belts and filters and was the least of our worries. I contacted a mate, Bruce Sutton who had a truck wrecking business called Homebush Truck Spares, and Bruce crated up second-hand clutch, gearbox, and diff parts and let me have them on loan. The only other thing I could think of was brakes - well forward progress was more important, you can always run into a tree or throw out an anchor or something.

Nancy, an ex-workmate of Doreen's accompanied us as far as Bowen in Queensland where her family had a tomato farm. After they had plied us all with rich tomato soup Nancy acted as local guide showing such places as the beautiful Horse Shoe Bay. She later married David Irvin of Ingham who in later years acted as our guide and sugarcane expert in Ingham. Then as the years passed and after their children had grown up they became regular Sundowner passengers.

The Bruce Highway from Brisbane to Cairns was narrow and in poor condition and was known as the glass highway being lined with glass from shattered windscreens as this was in the days of safety glass before laminated glass became the norm.

After the sites of Cairns and the Atherton Tablelands it was back to dirt tracks around the Gulf, so it was a relief to rejoin the bitumen at Mount Isa and down to Alice Springs.

Like a surprising number of people in Alice Springs some of our friends had never been out to the Rock so we squeezed them in for the journey out and back. After climbing the Rock their little daughter Shirley became too scared to face coming down, and I had no choice but to bring her down on my shoulders. This is something I wouldn't recommend because when I reached the base I took my shoes off and found blisters across the tops of my toes.

Although we were to see much more difficult feats, one time a coach arrived with a Catholic school group and a young priest bent over while they strapped a load of wood on his back. At the top it was assembled and became an altar and they held a Mass. Then the poor follow had to bend over, be loaded up and carry it all down again. On another occasion a Scots group in kilts rather raggedly marched up the Rock playing bagpipes. They danced on the top and declared it the Stone of Scone in the name of Scotland and said they would take it home. Some wag called out "Bring Scotland out and shove it underneath, that would be easier".

Then there was the time when Doreen and a group were caught in a rain storm on the top and had to wait for hours for the slippery rock to dry, then returned looking like a pack of drowned rats. I could go on and on, like when the helicopter crashed on top of the Rock, but the most foolhardy would have been when a crowd of drunken hoons bet one of their number that he couldn't ride a trail bike up the climb. Amazingly he got nearly a quarter of the way before laying it over, then it took the whole mob to get it back down. Of course, by the 1970s and with a huge increase in tourist numbers most of these things didn't happen anymore.

Driving back to Alice we stopped to have lunch with Val and Ted Kunoth in their new desert oak log cabin restaurant at Mt Ebenezer Station. Val had happy young Aboriginal girls as waitresses, and Ted had built new toilets. He labelled them "Weeis" and "Qeeis" which thoroughly confused the patrons. These terms for boys and girls were commonly used by everybody, both black and white in Central Australia. They don't appear to be any Aboriginal language, but rather what is called stock camp lingo. In the local Aboriginal dialect it would have been "Wati" for men and "Kungkas" for girls. Outback folk were forever coming up with ever more unique names for toilets, like Dunnie's Pub at Lyndhurst where Alan Dunn had "flip dry and drip dry." Then the fruit place in Queensland that had "mangoes" and "no mangoes".

After Alice Springs and on the way to Darwin we stopped overnight at Mataranka station, where our host was Bill Richardson. Bill was an ex-mayor of Darwin and had opened his property to the public because of a magnificent thermal spring which was situated in a grove of palms. We drove the coach right to the edge of the spring and after setting up camp in a clearing in the palms walked back to the homestead where Bill and some staff cooked dinner for us, then he entertained with stories of his early days in the Territory.

I spoke of toilets, well Ritcho supplied a toilet in a grove in the garden, and stretching between the trees were the webs of giant nephila spiders, so not suprisingly I never saw anyone brave the path to the toilet. We then walked back to our camp beside the warm pool and had a swim before turning in. Ritcho has long since passed on and Mataranka is now a major tourist resort with a large modern amenities block and trowels no longer in use.

The next night's camp was Berry Springs. What a wonderful place the Top End is. Once again, we were camped on the side of a thermal pool, at no cost at all. This beautiful place was laid out during the war as a military rest and recreation area.

After the sites of Darwin, it was back to Katherine where as good as his word Eric March had boats available to tour the gorge. I was interested to see that these aluminium punts were made by De Haviland Aircraft. Eric had his man George Wittern running our boat tour and generally looking after our needs.

The Victoria Highway stretching west from Katherine was a new road alignment and was really just a maze of detours, and very little rain would have turned it into a disaster. At the Victoria River crossing we parked on the low-level causeway that obviously would have been way under water in the wet season making the road impassable.

With open windows being the only air-conditioning and bulldust swirling in, we were hot, grimy, and with the water so inviting everyone voted for swimming. Although we had problems with open windows at least it didn't spread germs the way air-conditioning does today.

Which reminds me of a driver's joke at the time. A lady opened her window, and the lady behind her said "If you don't close that window I shall freeze to death". " Well, if I have to close it I shall suffocate" replied the first. The driver didn't know what to do and asked a nearby man. "That's easy" he said "I would open the window and freeze one, then close it and suffocate the other". Today on the Victoria River there is a high-level bridge, a roadhouse, and numerous signs warning of crocodiles.

Information that there was a store at Timber Creek proved correct, the only problem being that it was closed and padlocked. An old Aboriginal bloke, the only inhabitant in sight, told us that "the missus went off with some bloke and the boss loaded his gun, locked the store and went off after them". Timber Creek was a pretty spread out town, with only two buildings, the store and the police station being a mile or two apart.

At the Western Australian border, the day became one and a half hours longer as we adjusted our clocks back, and then it was on to Kununurra the fastest growing town in Australia. The storekeeper Howard Young had come here two years earlier from Sydney's North Shore and had an interesting story to tell.

It was one thing to build the Ord River scheme, but it required pioneer settlers. Howard was working in a bank when he saw and was impressed with government literature about the potential of the new Ord River irrigation area, and how you could ballot for rich farmland, and all with government subsidy. Howard sold up in Sydney and with his mate Bill Withers bought an old Sydney double decker bus. Then with their two families aboard set out for Kununurra. It must have been a heroic journey with the back platform of the bus nearly demolished after dropping into washouts.

Bill and Howard both missed out with the ballot, and at first didn't know how lucky this would prove to be as Howard and his wife Beryl started the store and trucked from the port at Wyndham, while Bill Withers secured the B.P. fuel franchise. Only a few years later, just as the subsidies were winding down plagues of insects drove most of the cotton farmers to the wall. Although the town somehow weathered the downturn and today with better know how the Ord River scheme has finally become successful again.

A coach in town was such a novelty that Howard asked his wife Beryl to mind the shop while he came aboard and acted as our guide showing us around the cotton fields and ginnery, the experimental farm, and the town lookout. He showed us the start of the diversion dam and explained how it would become part of a new bitumen highway to Wyndham. Howard had a couple of truck-loads of a most unusual stone behind the store, it was cream with purple stripes running right through and he called it zebra stone. (More boxes of rocks for the poor old coach.)

Today people expect, even demand satisfactory roads, but it wasn't always so and any track that didn't actually destroy the vehicle was acceptable. We crossed the Ord River on the rocky Ivanhoe crossing and proceeded up and down stony hills on the original track blazed by the Duracks from their Ivanhoe station to the coast. We were being thrown around by the rough road when suddenly the coach became airborne, and on stopping discovered that we had dropped an auxiliary fuel tank, and as it fell, pole vaulted over it.

With no camping in Kununurra we had decided to camp on the road to Wyndham, but with the light fading quickly we were forced to settle on this most forlorn spot and rope up the tank in the morning.

The port of Wyndham was on a narrow strip of land hemmed in by a mountain range facing the sea, its only purpose being meat export. Apart from the meat works there was the inevitable pub and a few tin shed Chinese shops selling the usual week-old newspapers. A couple of crocodiles were sunbaking where the blood drain ran into the sea. With no room to expand on the coastal strip a separate town had grown inland with a causeway across mud flats joining the two. Here was better shopping although nothing fresh, only cans, but with a garage manned by those multi-talented outback types that can fix anything. They set to and rehoused our fuel tank perfectly.

At our bush camp that night people were complaining about the foul taste of the water we had picked up in Wyndham, and the reason became obvious when listening to the news on Radio Kununurra. They reported that after complaints the Wyndham authorities had checked and found a decomposed crocodile in the water supply.

After much bulldust and many washed-out creek crossings to Halls Creek and beyond we finally made the crossing on the Fitzroy River. It had steep banks with the road running down to a narrow concrete causeway barely above the sandy river bed. From the debris along the banks it was obvious that it had been at least 40 feet above the causeway during the last wet. On the far side was the hospital followed by the police station and I wanted to talk to the cops about a gorge we had been recommended to see. The Sergeant studied the coach and shook his head, he thought it was too big to handle the track, but was quite amenable to us giving it a go.

It was quite OK as far as Brooking Springs station that was owned by the Skuththorpe family famous for their rodeo riding sons. The track was tight, but we finally made it into Geikie Gorge and the photographers took off doing their thing. Seemingly from out of nowhere a storm blew up bringing torrential rain and we rushed back to the coach. I wanted to drive out before the road became impassable, but we were missing four passengers. It was getting dark when the rain eased, and our lost souls returned after apparently sheltering under a rock overhang. I bit my tongue and drove out through the mud until we came to a creek crossing. I thrashed down one side and thought to make it up the other, but almost over the top the back wheels started spinning and we drifted backwards.

By this time, it was dark, and it was everybody out with torches to collect any material available to lay on top of the mud. Doreen told me later that she picked up a stick that definitely wriggled, and she threw it away and told nobody. In the meantime, the police sergeant, realising we hadn't returned, drove out to Brooking Springs, alerted the Skuththorpes and they all arrived in three Land Rovers. With the Landies linked together they finally pulled the coach out and we headed back to Fitzroy Crossing, arriving back at 11.10 pm. We wanted to shout everybody drinks (as you do in the outback) but the pub, which for some reason was half a mile out of town was closed. No problem to the cop he simply ordered it open for drinks all round. While a few lined up for Bob Skuththorpe's autograph we set up camp opposite the pub. It probably wasn't intended but the dirt road outside the pub was bog proof as it was overlaid with flattened cans. There was just a centre bar under a skillion roof and when the drinking finished, cleaning up was easy. Everything was hosed out onto the road where traffic squashed the cans into the road.

A couple of years later it would have been a bit crowded where we were camped as when Aboriginal drinking rights came into practice it became their camp while they were taking a break from the pub.

Of course, it's all changed today, a bit like Halls Creek. The old town, if you could call it that, is deserted and everybody has moved to the new main highway. Lots and lots of Government money has gone into a new town with housing, bitumen road, high level bridge over the river and a modern roadhouse. In fact, instead of being one of the most way out places around, it now just looks like anywhere else.

The publican must have liked the Sundowners as he opened two hours early with drinks for breakfast, ultimately slowing our departure. A couple of years later, driving into Geikie Gorge we found people had moved in and were running boat tours. George and Lisa McDonald had seen the possibilities, and with the OK of the local station people had set up in business. How easy this once was. George always trailed a line and almost always caught a barramundi which Lisa cooked up for the group. This happy arrangement continued for a number of years until the WA government declared the area a National Park. The McDonalds were tossed out and Park Rangers took over.

The years moved on, and one day on the Palmer River in North Queensland we came upon a couple panning for gold, who turned out to be George and Lisa. George showed no surprise at all and said, "Don't you find Australia's a small place, wherever we move in the outback we keep running into old friends".

The road improved markedly towards Derby where we stopped along the way to see the huge hollow boab they call the prison tree. With an entrance barely wide enough to fit through it accommodated everybody inside with room to spare. Nearby a bore discharged into a spillway that filled the longest cattle trough I had ever seen. Alongside the bore was a tin shed bathhouse, and it was possible to swing the spillway around into the bath and enjoy a beautiful hot bath, creating another long delay but much enjoyable fun.

But not much fun the following year when we found the bathhouse demolished and notices erected warning not to walk around the area in bare feet due to leptospirosis in the ground which apparently bore into the skin and which originate in cattle droppings.

Apart from photographing its magnificent boab trees Derby proved a disappointment with only limited canned food, so we were off slipping and slithering through heavy rain to Broome.

There were no caravan parks in Broome mostly due to the fact that it was next to impossible to drag a caravan over the existing roads and all supplies were brought by boat. However, we were told to talk to Johnnie McQueen the piano player in the Continental Hotel who apparently arranged camping. Also, the only restaurant in town was Mrs. Kim's who tottered around on tiny bound feet.

At first Mrs. Kim said that our "big car" had too many people, but we prevailed and finally she agreed to feed the mob, providing Doreen and I helped and acted as waiters. The only drink available was Beagle Bay lemonade that was produced in a bottling plant by Catholic fathers at an Aboriginal mission. Mrs. Kim had no menu but assured us that we would have "plenty food" and would enjoy it, and by the end of the meal everyone agreed and booked in for the following night. It was shades of old China to see Mrs. Kim shopping in a coolie hat and a pole across her shoulders with a basket hanging from each end.

In subsequent years she joyfully greeted us when we returned always in the "big car". In 1966 a new road was bulldozed through the pindan scrub from Port Headland to Broome, and a few years later was bitumened. This brought a huge influx of tourists and Mrs. Kim couldn't cope and imported Tong, a young Chinese cook to take over the work. Then Tong was lonely and was sent back to China to find a wife, which must be relatively easy as he was back in no time with Mrs. Tong. Mrs. Kim then told us that it was time for her to go back to China to die, and Tong would take over. Tong then built a big new restaurant that quickly became the in place in Broome. As the tourists started coming Tong told us that a successful man like himself needed an heir and Mrs. Tong promptly obliged and produced little Kevin. Still, Broome wasn't big enough for Tong and he sold out and went to Perth with the family to make their fortune, but Tong had shown the way as Old Wing built a restaurant for his son, Young Wing. Then there was Chin's, and restaurants were popping up everywhere - Mrs. Kim would never have believed it.

It was dark when Johnny McQueen led us out to his camping area on a headland on the edge of town, and when we stopped I asked where were the toilets. I walked off in the dark in the direction he pointed and the next thing I had walked out into space, and found myself in freefall. I crashed onto a sandy beach and lay totally winded, then after carefully checking for broken bones made my way around the foot of the cliff and found a way back up onto the headland. Happy to still be in one piece I issued a warning to use a torch when moving around in the dark. I reckoned that Johnny was on a pretty good thing as he was charging us 2 shillings (20 cents) each per night.

A problem for shipping to Broome was the great variation in the tides, and ships could only come and go at high tide. When the tide ran out they were left standing high and dry, and to overcome this problem a new jetty was under construction further up the coast.

With all supplies coming by boat there were often shortages, like the time the town ran out of matches as they had forgotten to load them down south. But a few years later when the new road was built, and supplies were able to be trucked in even Beagle Bay lemonade succumbed to Coca-Cola, which wasn't surprising.

One night, Doreen and I walked into town to see a new movie *West Side Story* at the Sun Pictures where we sat in the open air on deckchairs. At interval we realised we were the only white faces in the crowd, all the others graded from yellow to black, but that was Broome in the 1960s.

Although everybody could talk with authority about the coastal shipping service we found it difficult to get information about the state of the road. They referred to it as the "madman's track" but no one appeared to use it. We were told that no attempt had been made to drive a road through because of the nearly impenetrable pindan scrub behind the Eighty Mile Beach.

The first stretch across the Roebuck Plains to the La Grange Aboriginal Mission at the northern end of the Eighty Mile Beach wasn't too bad, and then passable to the Talgano tracking station. Talgano was part of the Woomera rocket range that stretched 3000 miles to the north-west coast. Some years later it was dismantled, and the buildings sold off, and I believe were used in building the Fitzroy River roadhouse.

The beach became the track and when the tide went out was miles wide, and the hard-packed sand was like concrete. With a profusion of beautiful shells along the tide line, even including big baler shells, we had trouble controlling our collectors who demanded regular stops. This had its down side some three weeks later when the critters inside some of them stunk the coach out. With the tide in it became necessary to use an alternative that was really only two-wheel tracks that wound back and forth through the coastal dunes.

Around one bend we came on a poor fellow in a bogged car who had been struggling for hours and almost given up hope of getting any help. After pulling him out we suggested he drop his tyre pressures, as we had done, and is necessary in sand driving.

After having tea in daylight, we pressed on as there was nowhere to camp in this country. At about 10 o'clock we made the De Grey river, and what an idyllic camp spot with pools of water under river red gums.

The following year we found things a great deal easier as a road had been bulldozed through to Broome, then followed some years later with bitumen and a roadhouse.

After fording the river, we came to a road sign "Mt Goldsworthy 10 M" on our left and decided to check it out. It turned out to be a mining town still under construction, but most importantly it had a small but well stocked supermarket. This was the best choice we had seen since Darwin and the Sundowners went wild collecting all sorts of fresh and frozen goodies.

Just after most had passed through the checkout a big florid faced man appeared shouting "who is in charge of this coach rabble." Doreen stepped in and held him at bay as he explained that this was a heavily subsidised company store for employees only and not open to the public. By this time all the Sundowners had escaped with their purchases, but it still remains the only time I have ever been thrown out of a supermarket.

After refuelling in Port Headland, it was off to the Hammersley Ranges by way of Marble Bar and Nullagine. I thought Nullagine was in the grip of a heat wave, but the locals assured us that this was about the hottest place in Australia and was about normal. Everyone headed for the pub with their tongues hanging out, giving me a chance to chat up the locals this being the best way I know to pick up information. I met up with Snowy a geologist with BHP who was part of a team doing a mineral survey. He drew me a map to follow after we left the Hammersley Ranges. It showed the location of a place called the Millstream, which Snowy assured me was the finest water hole in the West, then his map went on to Pannawonica, their base camp, a place of such an abundance of iron ore that he claimed in the future would become a major mine.

I thanked Snowy, dragged the protesting Sundowners from the pub and headed off to the Hammersleys. These proved to be the most beautiful ranges and we spent time exploring the deep magnificent gorges like Yampire and Dales, and the Fortescue Falls, then finished up in the surprisingly large town of Wittenoom.

This town existed for one reason only, to mine the fine quality blue asbestos, that nobody considered for a minute could ever be dangerous. This was a company town, and even though prices were subsidised here nobody was thrown out. There was a company store, a two-storey hotel, a service station, hospital and Mario's coffee lounge.

The following day we were invited to have a mine inspection which proved very interesting. The asbestos looked like bright blue cotton thread and occurred in seams up to 3 or 4 inches thick in a soft blue rock that reminded me of the Reckitts blue that mum plopped in the copper when she was washing the sheets back in Goulburn.

There were big plans for the blue asbestos mines, with the vy.A. Government Geologist predicting the production of asbestos would eclipse that of gold. Asbestos is flame proof, won't burn or melt, and can be woven into cloth, and was the perfect insulating material.

It was also used in the production of fibre, for which at that time there was unlimited demand. It was quoted to us that the asbestos mines in the Hammersleys had enough material to last one hundred years.

It was a typical mining operation, with blasting and crushing except that the air was full of the threads of asbestos that covered everything and everybody.

We along with the miners had no idea that in the 1970s the study of asbestos would be given the priority it had long deserved when health and safety research turned this material from a wonder substance to a potential source of death. This of course closed the mining operation although the commercial side became privatised and remained to cater to the increasing tourist trade.

Back in town we showered off the asbestos in the excellent caravan park run by the Tablelands Shire Council. Then using Snow's map, we found our way to the Millstream and agreed that he hadn't exaggerated - apparently fed by underground springs it was surrounded by palms and paper bark trees. The flowout created a paper bark swamp, and Snowy had shown on his map the track crossing right through it and this looked a daunting prospect. The water was flowing strongly about 6 inches deep as the track wound back and forth among the trees. We found however that all was well, that with such a mat of tree roots bogging was not possible.

This track took us on to the Pannawonica camp where there was general amazement when a coach pulled up, and I announced that Snowy had sent us. BHP certainly looked after their wilderness camps where they flew in fresh supplies on a regular basis, and as Snowy was our mate we were plied with fresh orange juice and strawberries and ice cream.

I had rather dreaded this section of the trip with its isolation and dirt tracks, it was now 11 days since we had left the bitumen at Katharine. But we had travelled through some of the most scenic country imaginable, camped on beautiful swimming holes, met wonderful characters, and for me at least had no mechanical problems apart from a couple of flat tyres.

Carnarvon proved to be a surprisingly big town (well in comparison to where we had been) and it was there one night we had a really strange experience.

Doreen and I decided to have a meal out on the town, so we dressed in fresh clean clothes and walked into a restaurant cum roadhouse only to be blocked by the manager. "Hold it mate, we have dress standards here" he said. I thought my clothes looked pretty good and said so. "Not you" he said, "The woman with you is wearing pants, we don't allow that".

We had no choice but to walk out of this tin pot eating house in outback Western Australia. If the reader has as much disbelief of this story as I had at the time, I can only swear it's absolutely true.

After passing through Carnarvon we reached Geraldton, and were finally back on the bitumen although it was only single lane with broken shoulders. We were now in flower country and that night we camped in a clearing with tents surrounded with masses of beautifully coloured wild flowers.

After only seeing on average less than half a dozen vehicles a day we were now starting to come into traffic. Still we were slowed by constant stops to identify and photograph the amazing profusion of wild flowers. The booksellers in Perth were in for a busy time with sales of wildflower identification books to eager Sundowners.

Doreen had found nowhere in Perth that would cater for campers and had settled on Coogee Beach south of Fremantle, where we were left in no doubt that our NSW pronunciation was totally wrong and should be "Coo gee". It was almost a bush camp with a large grassed area facing the sea across a sandy beach, and it would have been perfect for swimming except for most of us it was too cold after our time in the tropics.

While there was a shower and toilet block there was a problem of no hot water, however each morning a council man came around and directed me to drive to the council sports ground where he unlocked the premises for our hot showers. As everybody stayed in their sleeping gear we must have looked a weird coach party to the early morning commuters, dressed up on their way to work. The council charged the princely sum of 10 shillings ($1) per day all up, even including the trip to the hot showers.

Having spent six weeks travelling up the east coast, around the Gulf, down to Ayers Rock, around the North West, and down the west coast to Perth, I felt quite genuinely that all we had to do now was just turn left and we were back in Sydney. But however, it turned out that

Perth was a bit further than it felt, of course had it been bitumen I may have felt vindicated but that certainly wasn't to be.

All agreed that Perth was a beautiful city, particularly from Kings Park where we had dinner one night and watched as the lights came on across the city. Doreen and I were kept busy taking in as much as possible to advise people on future trips.

When doing this some years later the two of us booked on a river cruise where a smorgasbord lunch was provided with their clam chowder being recommended. On the lunch bell everyone leapt to their feet and fought their way to a queue. I can't abide standing in queues and instead we sat and admired the scenery. When finally we got to the tables the only thing left was a few bread rolls. Then a while later people started rushing for the rail and were being violently sick over the side and the skipper was phoning for ambulances to meet the boat. We considered it a most interesting trip but failed to add it to our list of recommendations.

After three days in Perth it was down the coast to Augusta and the most south westerly point of the continent, Cape Leeuwin lighthouse. I had assumed that we would be on sealed roads around the south west but from Augusta to Pemberton our map showed more of the dreaded dotted lines, that turned out to be linked up forestry tracks with many stretches through swampy country.

Negotiating along one track the coach sank down and bogged and we were fortunate that a forestry tractor came along and pulled us through. This track went by the rather grand name of Stewart Rd and several years later we came to grief on it again.

With cold misty rain falling I was driving slowly and carefully when the left hand front wheel dropped suddenly and the coach, almost in slow motion, rolled over onto its side into a swamp. I shot my arm out my window and stayed hanging in the seat, but the passengers were not so lucky and finished up in a pile of thrashing arms and legs.

I was shocked to see the woman in the front seat with blood all over her face and it was a relief to find it was caused only through her biting her lip, and by some miracle no one else was hurt. The coach had an escape side window and a few of us got out and pulled the others up, then caught them on the long jump to the ground. The weather was miserable, and everyone was in a state of shock. Someone remarked that I should take advantage and give the coach a grease, but this failed to raise a laugh.

One old chap had the forethought to bring out a bottle of rum, and such was his state of shock that he sat down on a log and drank the lot, and then collapsed. People then took it upon themselves to force him to walk up and down being afraid he would die on us. Meanwhile a car came along, and the driver introduced himself as Dave Thompson a butcher from Pemberton. He told us that a timber truck had rolled over here the previous week and the road had not been properly repaired. He said, "Don't worry I'll get help, Aunty Rose will get you out" and he then drove off.

A couple of hours passed as I sat on a log and studied the chassis of the coach and wondered about "Aunty Rose" who would want to be a miracle worker. Finally, Dave returned followed by a truck carrying a bulldozer and a group of rough looking fellows led by a little old lady they all called Aunty Rose. After surveying the situation and having the bulldozer unloaded she told them to go back and borrow a second one, she then told Dave to drive back and advise the neighbours to prepare some hot meals for a coach load of people.

Aunty Rose directed a cable to be attached to the chassis of the coach, then out to a pulley attached to a big tree and back to the dozer. Then the second bulldozer arrived, and this was attached by cable to the front of the coach. I was ignored during the entire operation as Aunty Rose was in total command and too busy for small talk. She instructed the drivers as the bulldozers inched forward and the coach rolled back on to its wheels and sat square in the middle of the track. However, it refused to start, and I then had the job of bleeding the diesel injectors. By this time all the gear had been sorted and packed and we proceeded to the farm, run by Aunty Rose and her middle-aged son Lionel.

There we were greeted by neighbours who had arrived with car loads of soup and all manner of hot food. I took Dave Thompson aside and asked for an idea of what all this should be costing us, and he explained that this was a Seventh Day Adventist community and would be most offended by an offer of money. "They live by their good deeds, and you have just given them that opportunity", he said. I felt it all rather embarrassing but had to accept what Dave told me.

Because it was dark and raining, I asked Dave if he could suggest any accommodation. "I have been thinking about that," he said, "and I think my abattoirs would be your best bet". I had extreme doubts about this until he explained that the building was brand new and yet to be used. It proved to be clean and dry, what more could we ask? Some people thought it made an interesting entry for their diary, after all not many people get to sleep in an abattoir.

The next morning, we drove around to Thompson's meat shop in Pemberton and bought up all the best cuts as a means of paying our rent. After what was most definitely an exciting climb to the top of the Gloucester lookout tree it was a relief to find we were back on a bitumen road to Albany.

Somehow our thank you to Aunty Rose still felt inadequate, so it was agreed that we would buy a box of good kitchenware and have it sent back to her, which certainly made their day in the hardware store in Albany. I was finally able to wash the coach and was amazed to find no damage at all, not even a dent or scratch.

Well, going back to our first around Australia trip, we were driving up the main street in Albany when the coach slowed to a standstill, the motor screamed at full revs and we slowly drifted backwards. This understandably was accompanied by much blowing of horns behind us, which was fairly understandable as motorists tend to panic when seeing a coach reversing into them. I applied the brakes and jumped out and chocked the wheels, then with Doreen behind the wheel asked her to try and drive forward while I checked underneath.

I thought the clutch had gone, but no, I was amazed to see the driving flange behind the gearbox spinning but the tail shaft not moving. Obviously, the tail shaft had been pressed on but never welded when the vehicle was first built, and I couldn't help thinking of all the hundreds of inaccessible and isolated places around Australia where this could have happened, but instead it chose to be in the main street of a large town. To me it was nothing less than a miracle, although it didn't impress the locals with a tourist coach double parked on their main street.

I walked down the hill to the harbour where there were ship yards and found people with a mobile welder. They towed the welder up to the coach, and after only five minutes work had us mobile again.

After Esperance and the goldfields, it was out on to the Nullarbor Plain, and with the state of the road it became obvious why most people, truckies included, put their vehicles on the train. At least it was not monotonous, there were stretches of potholes, then deep bulldust, sometimes limestone outcrops, and of course corrugations.

While in Perth it was easy to feel the isolation from the rest of Australia, the only reliable links with the rest of the country being by rail or air. In the Northern Territory they referred to all outsiders as Southerners and in the West they called them Eastern Staters, and in their newspapers identified arrival times for trains or aircraft as ES arrivals.

The small roadhouses only had enough water for their own use and it was only obtainable from a few catchment tanks that we sometimes camped beside. It was quite inconceivable that some day Australians would actually pay good money to buy water in little plastic bottles.

Today people sometimes leave the highway and drive out on the original road to see the old Telegraph station at Eucla, and this is the only part of the old road still in use. While ploughing through bulldust one day I glanced in the inside mirror and couldn't see the passengers for dust, the floor had split open the length of the aisle, and was opening and closing like a concertina, but our stoic Sundowners took it all in their stride. After all, imagine the stories to be told when we get home.

Then on a rough section the gear stick started jumping out of gear, and I had to jam my knee against it to hold it in, this along with a couple of broken spring leaves I had noted the night before made me wonder if the old girl wasn't disintegrating beneath us.

While driving the 1000 miles across the Nullabor I had thought this is something I would never want to do again, but once back on the bitumen I thought maybe it wasn't so bad after all. The friendship of other drivers and people who lived along the way helped a lot in those days.

The sealing of the Eyre Highway was a slow and drawn out project. The Western Australian Government finished their section in 1969, and having most to gain, offered to proceed on into South Australia if the S.A. or Commonwealth Government would share the cost. This never happened, and it was 1976 before the South Australian section was finished and it was then possible to drive from Adelaide to Perth on black top all the way.

It was almost to Pt Augusta before we finally reached the bitumen and by this time a crack had developed from the top of the door right across the roof. We still managed to take in Adelaide and Melbourne and to my great relief, and I imagine some surprise to our passengers, made it back to Sydney right on time.

Obviously, the poor old girl was finished as far as we were concerned, and I was quite amazed when Jack Violet of CCMC offered to buy it back from us. He seemed totally fascinated by where one of his vehicles had been and what it had done. A friend who was involved in rebuilding it told me that behind every panel they removed it was packed solid with red dust and they pondered where it had all come from.

Also, the mechanical overhaul was delayed somewhat when they found some things couldn't be stripped down as they had been welded together, as it was a matter of holding things together when no replacement parts were obtainable.

The Perkins motor however gave sterling service, only ever having two problems. The first was picking up water in a fill of diesel which had a horrible effect on the fuel pump. This caused us all sorts of delays, but as it was a Barker School trip it didn't matter a great deal. Adults have a fetish about getting home on time, but school boys don't care and would prefer that the trip went on forever. The other was when the glow plug failed. Diesel engines in those days required preheating with a glow plug and it worked by turning the ignition key to the left and counting so many seconds before turning it to the right to start the engine.

Camped in the middle of nowhere on a freezing cold morning it appeared we had no hope of starting, so I pulled the air cleaner off and pushed a lighted newspaper down the air intake while Doreen turned the ignition key. It started immediately and as a Perkins glow plug seemed unobtainable anywhere, every time we had a cold motor it required another spill of newspaper. So, I would suggest that Perkins owners keep a newspaper as an essential spare part.

I have been referring to it as "the coach", and when sufficiently irritated "the bloody truck", but of course it was still only a suburban bus, it's full history being... Built 1956 by Cycle Components Manufacturing Co. Sold to Foggs Motors South Wallsend as MO 4436. Purchased by Sundowner, 1964 became ISJ 443. Sold to CCMC 1965 then on-sold to Tempe Bus Service in Sydney, where it became MO 4864 and continued in service until 1974 when it was withdrawn after an accident.

In the year 2000 while holidaying in Alice Springs, we stayed with Tim Lander and he showed us over a new tourist attraction, The Transport Hall of Fame. Looking at these historic vehicles, I couldn't help thinking about how much we lose by junking so much stuff after it passes its use-by-date.

Old ISJ443 really deserved a pride of place in The Hall of Fame where it would have been quite unique. But the fact was that in 1965 we had neither the space nor the money (or even the desire) to keep an old bus. Most of these sorts of things are found in the Outback, where having no place to dispose of them they sit around in the back paddock until some day somebody realises their historic value.

SIZE COMPARISON
Europe & Australia

England and Wales	60,000	sq. miles
Germany	184,000	"
France	213,000	"
Northern Territory	523,000	"
U.S.A.	3,027,000	"
Australia	2,975,000	"

1966 THE NEW LEYLAND

Our new coach was our greatest achievement for 1966.

In February 1966 our pounds, shillings and pence disappeared to be replaced by the decimal currency system, and a pound became two dollars. A problem arose when 12 pennies became 10 cents (where did the two pennies go?) and people claimed to be ripped off as prices were rounded up. Everything seemed to go up with the changeover, and Ayers Rock prices became 1 dollar entrance and 50 cents camping fee.

Even Sundowners were forced to increase prices when we charged 110 dollars for our 3-week trips and a whole 240 dollars for the 65 days Around Australia.

Also, although they had another 50 years supply of high grade blue asbestos, C.S.R. wisely closed down their Wittenoom mine and processing plant.

But back to the new coach. Between trips in 1965 I had managed to fly to Brisbane to talk to Alan Denning about building a new coach. Alan is often described as the father of coach building in Australia as he had designed and built the original outback coaches for companies such as Redline and Greyhound.

I found a deal of common interest with Alan, for starters we had both worked on aircraft during the Second World War and had both gone into business using that knowledge. The big difference between us being that Alan was undoubtedly a genius.

Before speaking to Alan, I had been interested in the new Ansett coaches, built in Melbourne by Ansair and called Scenicruisers.

Fortunately, an Ansett Pioneer driver, Owen Parker had kept me up to date, and Owen's news kept getting worse. Our rough outback roads were proving too much for their bodywork and

as well, the motors were blowing up. These were **G.M.** Toroflow engines, although you hardly ever heard the term as they were more generally referred to as Horridflows. Like most Ansett drivers Owen was a staunch company man, but fortunately his mateship came first when he said, "For God's sake mate, steer clear".

I picked up the Denning Leyland Viking in Brisbane in December 1965 and it became **ISM-**

154. For extra leg room we had decided on only 32 seats and typically, when we sold it eventually to Centralian Tours in 1970, they closed up the seats making it a 36-seater.

One thing I hadn't realized was that apparently Leyland didn't believe in power steering, which seems unbelievable today with even the smallest of cars taking it for granted. After battling with the Austin, this was too much, so the first modification was an after-market power steering system.

This coach was built on a standard Leyland chassis, and because of its length required a two-piece tailshaft supported midway by a centre bearing. This caused the first dramatic failure when climbing Bulladelah Mountain first day out on an Around Australia trip. I carefully drove on with the tailshafts hammering away and threatening to break through the floor until we reached a garage. A few rough looking young blokes were just shutting the doors, it being Saturday afternoon and I had to beg them to reopen and see what they could do for us. With no Leyland parts available they sleeved a larger bearing and fitted it and then fabricated a housing around it. "Better job than any bloody Leyland" they told me. Pretty good blokes really seeing that three of them had worked for a couple of hours and then asked if 10 pounds ($20) was OK.

Must be something about Around Australia trips, as on the next one the motor quite literally blew up once again on the first day. While we set up camp on the old Pacific Highway just south of the Hawkesbury Bridge, I got a call through to Leyland and by some miracle they sent up two mechanics on a Saturday afternoon. My diagnosis must have been spot on as they arrived with a bunch of pistons and on stripping the motor found a hole in the top of number five piston.

"Looks like you got a faulty batch of pistons" opinioned one mechanic, so because they would only replace a failed part, I felt it was only fair to let me borrow the rest of the set. Then later in Cairns while getting a service at the Leyland dealer, I told them to fit the other five pistons and bill it to Sydney. They went ahead, and I never heard another word about it.

About a week passed with no problems which was pretty good for a Pammie coach on outback roads, then running down the Stuart Highway about an hour out of Alice Springs, the gearbox started to shake and rumble. We set up camp and after making a few phone calls, I discovered that our mate Doug Park had left Co-Ord Transport and set up his own business.

I told Doug about our problem and he and his offsider, German George agreed to work around the clock provided I kept the grog up to them. Not that they were alkies or anything like that, it's just normal practice in Alice Springs to supply the grog when you ask for a favour.

We found the gearbox bearings had collapsed and when I rang Leylands in Adelaide and quoted the part numbers from the bearings, they told me that by these numbers the wrong bearings had been fitted and they would jet up the correct ones. A proper genius crowd the old Leylands!

At least they arrived on time and by keeping the grog up to German George, the gearbox went back together. Over the years, we and other poor souls in strife contributed enough money for Doug Park to finally reach his dream of building the best tourist accommodation in Alice Springs. He called it The Travellers Village and we were happy to become some of his customers.

As Doug had to incorporate the best of everything, you know, swimming pool, spa, tennis courts etc., he was forced to take out a bank loan. Then being really lucky with his bank manager, was talked into borrowing at wonderful cheap interest with Swiss francs. The Aussie dollar took a dive and of course the rest is history. The new owners got Doug's dream at bargain rates and renamed the place "Red Centre Resort".

On the coach I reckoned that something as basic as wheels couldn't be a problem, but I was wrong. Being in the days before tubeless tyres, the wheels were what were called split rims, that is the tyre and tube were locked onto the wheel by an outer rim that was held in place by a lock ring, or giant circlip.

I slowed down on a particularly rough section of road one day and then watched in amazement when a tyre appeared in front of the coach, bowling along the road ahead of us. It kept rolling and disappeared over a hill.

On stopping we found a front wheel sitting on the inner rim and missing the lock ring, outer rim, and of course the tyre. Being in the bush this was no great problem, but had it happened in traffic it could have had a few nasty consequences. They started cracking from the bolt holes and these cracks spread out across the wheels. Being Leylands, they refused to accept any liability and referred me to Sankey Benson, the wheel manufacturers. The bloke at Sankey Benson quizzed me about our operation and then threw his hands in the air and said, "They fitted the wrong wheels for your type of operation, not our fault". These Poms surely knew how to wear you down and I simply cut my losses and bought a set of American Budd wheel blanks and had them drilled to English Standard, thus ending the problem for all time.

They probably didn't realise it, but the great British motoring industry was about to fall in a heap, because for years they had hidden behind the Commonwealth Preference Scheme and this was about to end. In a short time, we were to see the Fodens and Leylands disappear to be replaced by Macks and Kenworths, and even Qantas was forced into a bitter fight with the Government to buy Lockheed aircraft instead of De Havillands. (How clever was Qantas).

TASMANIA - It seems like I'm always getting ahead of myself, but I have trouble stitching it all together in any sort of sequence, so I'll get back to the first trip with the new coach.

Ian Campbell and Barker College must have been happy with their Central Australian tour regardless of having to sit up on bus seats in the Austin. Ian proposed a tour of Tasmania in January 1966 for his Barker boys. We knew nothing whatever about Tasmania, but Ian assured us that he had studied geology there and knew the place very well.

January apparently is the preferred month and I got the impression that the rest of the year is pretty much a write-off in Tasmania.

Pricing the trip was difficult, but we settled on 54 Pounds ($108) which was less than Central Australia, but on the map, Tasmania looked very small, no doubt you could drive around it in a day. This was our first trip through the Fruit Check between Albury and Wodonga on the border, and we must have looked an evil crew the way the inspectors went through the coach making sure we weren't smuggling fruit into Victoria.

In Melbourne we boarded the "Princess of Tasmania" where you had the choice of paying to sit up in a lounge chair all night or lying on the deck. Being a flat-bottomed ferry, it had a peculiar rolling motion that could make anyone seasick even in a mild swell. Over the next 30 years we were to use 4 different boats, each one being a great improvement. From the "Princess" we progressed to the "Empress of Australia", then the "Abel Tasman" and finally the quite magnificent "Spirit of Tasmania".

There was great activity at the dock with police with guns everywhere and we finally found out the reason. It wasn't because of the Barker boys at all - they were loading millions of dollars of decimal currency for Tasmanian banks for the soon-to-be changeover from pounds to dollars, so we sailed under the tightest security imaginable.

In Devonport we were fortunate to meet a local character and tour operator, Dennis Maxwell, who operated everything from school buses to four-wheel-drives. Dennis drew us maps, recommended camp sites, was a mine of information and an all-round good bloke. With Dennis and Ian's experience we were to camp in some of the most beautiful places, but unfortunately as the years passed they were either flooded by Hydro Dams, became day picnic areas in National Parks, or were simply fenced off. Dennis has remained a good mate for over 30 years and has visited us in Sydney on a couple of occasions.

There seemed to be some doubt that a large coach could be driven to Cradle Mountain and I had wondered about Ian's opinion, when he admitted that he had always used a Landrover on his travels. However, it proved no worse than many outback roads, except that many of the creek crossings could be a problem after rain.

As we got closer to Waldheim Chalet the road became extremely narrow and for the last 100 metres, just possible with trees brushing against the coach. Being the only people there we had the Waldheim Chalet complex for our own use. Rooms were allocated, and the boys used up energy chopping up firewood for the huge fireplace in the dining room, and not wanting to see the fire wasted, Doreen and I set up our swag on the dining room floor.

The Chalet was built by an Austrian, Gustav Weindorfer in 1912 and the entire building, including furniture was built out of split King William Pine. It must have been a mammoth task as he was not only builder and architect, but had to manufacture his own building materials. It was partly burnt down a few years later and rather poorly repaired and is no longer used for accommodation.

With the Barker boys we sloshed through rain and mud and were constantly attacked by leeches and although the scenery was magnificent I had doubts that an adult group would enjoy these conditions. Since then we have walked and climbed Cradle Mountain many times, but thankfully have never again endured the conditions on the first trip.

After Launceston Ian thought it a good idea to drive up Mt. Barrow - "You can see half of Tasmania and even Bass Straight" he told us. The winding road got tighter and tighter until finally we were stuck on a bend with a rock face on our left and a sheer drop on our right. I had no choice but to back all the way down the mountain, after listening to Ian tell me his Landrover had no trouble reaching the top. If I was going to commit suicide it was probably better to do it alone, so it was everybody out and I had 30 odd kids waving directions. Backing a coach anytime is not that easy and can become rather nerve racking around tight bends with sheer drops. However, I finally made it and was grateful when Doreen suggested afternoon tea.

Then one kid told me "I followed you all the way down with my camera, and I reckon the picture would have been worth a fortune if you had driven over the edge". I treated this with as much good humour as I could under the circumstances.

Ian continued to prove that he really did know Tasmania and we took in all the places of interest and enjoyed his chosen camp spots. At Lake St. Clair Ian decided the boys needed some exercise so we all trooped off to climb Mt. Rufus, up one way and down another. This was another place "Where you could see half of Tasmania". It proved much tougher than it looked and tested us all, although we did have a snow fight at the top.

Down near the camp we met a couple of girls who had caught and killed some tiger snakes. Asking the obvious question "What are you going to do with them", we were told, "We are gunna skun em". West coast Tasmanians all seem to speak this way. Not much different to Western Queensland where we were told by a local, "We are gunna rung the trees", whereby someone asked, "Is there a special time to do that?" and got the answer, "Acorse, when you got a sharp axe".

The road to Queenstown around Mt. Arrowsmith was a narrow, winding dirt track and was nearly as bad as Mt. Barrow and enabled us to feature in not one but both of Tasmania's newspapers. An edited version from *The Advocate* said –

"BUS SAVED FROM 100FT. GULLY"

"An interstate Sundowner tourist coach with 30 passengers was prevented by a culvert and saplings from rolling down a 100ft. gully after a road shoulder collapsed under it on the Lyell Highway near Derwent Bridge on Saturday. The roadway crumbled when the bus moved over to allow another bus to pass. The bus tilted at 45 degrees almost off the road. No one was injured and the passengers from the other bus helped prevent the bus from overturning. A local Mr. E. Triffett pulled the bus back with his logging truck and said, "it was amazing the bus didn't roll over". The driver then sounded his horn on every bend on the tortuous Mt. Arrowsmith section of road to Queenstown."

This is *The Mercury* version -

"Thirty tourists had a narrow escape from death or serious injury with their coach balanced above a 30ft. drop on the Lyell Highway this morning. With the coach hanging at an angle of 45 degrees the shocked passengers clambered out on the road. The coach travelling to Queenstown moved over to allow an empty semi-trailer to pass. The dirt verge gave way under the 8-ton coach and saplings under the sump and gearbox prevented it from plummeting into the valley below. The driver left his passengers and went to get help. Late this afternoon the coach was still hanging precariously over the drop."

Good stories, with a few inconsistencies - so what was the truth?

A Greenline bus (a Tassie-wide inter-township bus company) came around the bend ahead of us, through the mist, and using most of the road. I pulled left and hit the brakes. The Greenline bus never stopped, much less their passengers helping. I opened the coach door and found it was over a sheer drop and it was impossible to get out. The Denning had a large sliding driver's window, quite large enough to squeeze out, so we one at a time got everyone out except for Laurie Wigney. Laurie was a teacher who had come along to help Ian and would be the first to admit was somewhat overweight. It really developed into a bit of fun as some pushed and some pulled until Laurie popped out like a cork out of a bottle.

The coach was in no trouble where it stood but the left-hand wheels, both front and back were close to the edge in soft greasy mud and I was afraid of trying to move it. It definitely wasn't hanging over the edge, but one wrong move and it could be. We waved down a vehicle coming the other way and they agreed to give Doreen a lift back to Derwent Bridge. Doreen returned with Eugene Triffett in a logging truck which he used to pull the back of the coach away from the edge as I edged backward. *The Advocate* was spot-on about one thing though, I did sound the horn on every bend, but how did they know?

When we were in Strahan I noticed a cafe advertising meat pies, and having a bit of spare time ordered one. During the long wait I watched a girl setting a table and to jolly them along I said, "Look, I just want a pie and sauce in a paper bag". This was greeted with a stunned silence and then I was told, "Our pies are not sold in paper bags, sit at the table and use a knife and fork like everyone else".

After safely making it home we felt quite expert regarding Tasmania, although it was two years before we ran another trip in January 1968. Once again, we made it into *The Advocate* when they ran a front-page article complete with photo of the coach and passengers. To quote we were introducing "Safari type" touring to Tassie, seems like they had forgotten about our 1966 visit.

Our 1973 Tasmanian tour had some drama which did not make the headlines. We were camped at Longford, south of Launceston which was famous for its motor racing circuit laid out on local roads, although with road realignments, this has all disappeared. The Caravan Park, alongside the river was planted out with a number of trees that Poms would call Helms, Hoaks and Hashes, and it was one of these that caused us a truly dreadful night. People had chosen to erect their tents among the trees, and the camp had settled down for the night when a sudden gale blew up. The rain lashed down in sheets and next thing our tent collapsed on top of us. Fighting our way out of a wet clammy tent is like wrestling with an octopus, but we made it and ran for the protection of the coach.

In a short time, others suffered the same fate until half the mob were in the coach. Then with a noise like an explosion, a tree came crashing down across one of our tents.

Everyone ran out into the driving rain to help, but with all helping it was impossible to lift the tree. A man and his wife were in the tent and we managed to drag the man out, but his wife was pinned across the chest and couldn't move. I raced back to the coach and got hydraulic jacks and blocks and Doreen told someone to use the public phone and call an ambulance. As I was jacking in a fury a helper told me that the woman couldn't breathe and was turning blue. Finally, I lifted the tree enough, so they could slide her out. The ambulance arrived and brought her around on oxygen then took her to the hospital at Launceston. At sunup the rain stopped, and it took a while to clean up our camp and repair equipment. Our passenger had a couple of cracked ribs but after four days rest in Hospital was able to return to the tour. The Tassie Tourist Bureau were running a campaign about Tasmania the Adventure Island, and they certainly turned on as much adventure as we could handle.

Copy of a letter received by Ian Campbell at the Barker College Reunion in 1989:

Dear Ian,

The wonderful experience of meeting Doreen and Bill has remained with me all my life. As you know I travelled on Tasmania 1966 and Central Australia 1967. My memories of Central Australia are still vivid - the church service at Hermannsburg, the beautiful Olgas, Aboriginals saying "Two Bob", open campfires, sleeping out under the stars, the beautiful desert flowers, and the flight over Ayers Rock. The bus accident in Tasmania, Bill cursing the leeches at Cradle Mt., the tiger snakes at Lake St. Clair, Laurie Wigney making mashed potato, and Doreen's everlasting patience.

Thank you Doreen and thank you Bill for creating a curiosity and travel bug that has remained with me ever since. So far I have been on 18 overseas trips and numerous trips around Australia. It is now my intention to settle in Tasmania and run a small hotel and winery.

Fond regards, Phillip Smith 1989.

Phillip mentioned flying over Ayers Rock - these flights were carried out by a most remarkable pilot called Harry Purvis, who incidentally taught me to fly. The single engined Cessna had dual controls and when taking our Sundowners on flights, Harry instructed me to fly out and around the Olgas and back to the Rock. He could then turn around and give a commentary to the passengers. He never taught me to land or take off, so I am only qualified to highjack and crash an aircraft. (Although with many outback flying friends, I have had the opportunity to take the controls of many different aircraft, even a helicopter). Harry always said that flying was simple, but the most important thing was to not let the ground get in the way.

Harry's stories used to fascinate us, as he had flown with most of the famous early aviators. He had worked for Charles Kingsford Smith when they went on barnstorming trips around the country. Harry certainly flew in an age of flamboyancy and danger with no radios and primitive airfields and even cows grazing on Mascot. He had flown for almost half a century as a barnstormer, a member of a Flying Circus, and an airline pilot. During the war he was the Commanding Officer of the First Transport Squadron of the RAAF and was finally Deputy Director of RAAF transport. In 1951 with P.J. Taylor he made the first flight across the Southern Pacific to South America. Their Catalina Flying Boat (Frigate Bird 11) is on display in the Powerhouse Museum in Sydney.

On a trip to England Harry bought a Fokker Universal Aircraft for 400 pounds to run joy flights. It was then bought by a Victorian transport operator who had started a service car business between Hamilton and Melbourne, but at that time the Victorian Transport Minister, a young Barrister, Robert Gordon Menzies, concerned that this would affect loadings on the railway, banned the service. The man's name was Reg Ansett. Ansett had obtained a fruit vendor's licence and sold very expensive apples and gave the purchaser a free ride. Inevitably this ploy failed in court, so he went over the court's head and bought Harry's Fokker and paid 1000 pounds (Harry was a reluctant seller) and started Ansett Airways in 1931. A replica of this aircraft was in the Ansett Terminal at Mascot.

Food and drink and for that matter anything else was totally unavailable at the Rock until an attractive, vivacious English woman arrived. Kay Queen, with Bob Gregory's blessing bought a secondhand Mr. Whippy van that she parked at the foot of the climb. Kay dispensed tea, coffee, hot soup and food stuffs, and did a roaring trade on frosty mornings.

A little later we camped under excellent conditions behind the Redline Chalet managed by our old Redline mate Doug Fredricks. By the time Redline went belly up in 1970, Kay and Harry, now married, joined with Doug and his girlfriend Lyn to buy the Redline Complex from the liquidator. They renamed it the Inland Motel and it made the headlines in 1984 when after a drunk was ejected he drove his single trailer roadtrain through the bar, killing five patrons. About this time Doug Fredricks was killed when a ConAir Beechcraft crashed when taking off from Alice Springs on a commercial flight to the Rock.

1982. Harry's plane on old airstrip at foot of Ayers Rock.
Our niece Alina has been on a scenic flight.

OUR HOLIDAYS & FRIENDS

We considered the summer months in outback Australia too hot for tours, in fact there were practically no tourists in Central Australia at this time of the year, and it was referred to as "the off season". This meant that after completing the annual coach overhaul we had time on our hands and what better way to use it than holidaying with friends in the outback - like Peter and Dawn Severin at Curtin Springs, Arthur & Bess Liddle at Angas Downs, and our Aboriginal mate at Hermannsburg, Gus Williams.

With the excellent road system today, we prefer to drive to Alice Springs, but with the dreadful car-wrecking roads in those days it was hardly an option, so we would fly to Adelaide and then catch the Fokker Friendship flight to Alice. Fokkers flew quite low and gave a wonderful view of such places as the Flinders Ranges and without long range, had to refuel at either Leigh Creek or Oodnadatta, allowing an hour or so to walk around. On one trip we disembarked at Oodnadatta and intended to walk into town to catch up with friends, but after the airconditioning in the aircraft, the air outside felt like the equivalent of a blast furnace and forced us back.

In Alice on one trip we caught up with Robbie and Helen Collins. Robbie was a young New Zealander who had (1) fallen in love with Central Australia and (2) fallen in love with and married Helen Gregory, the daughter of Jean and Bob Gregory, the Ranger at Ayers Rock. Robbie was running four-wheel drive tours and having a new Toyota Landcruiser and a lack of customers we talked him into taking us out to Hermannsburg to see Gus Williams. After spending time at Hermannsburg, Gus suggested we drive out west to the Aboriginal Settlements at Papunya, Haasts Bluff and Areyonga.

Without putting too finer line on it, I couldn't see Papunya listing for the Tidy Town Competition and according to Gus's uncle, there were a few inter-tribal problems as well. It seems that the white fellas who put the whole show on the road didn't allow for the fact that housing four different tribal and language groups in one settlement wasn't a brilliant idea.

Uncle pointed out that his mob, the Arunta were proper gentlemen compared to the Pitjanjara, who didn't have a lot of time for the Warlbri, and at the bottom of the pecking order and most recent arrivals were the Pintabi. This last group were brought in from the Western Australian desert during the great drought, and some years later in good seasons couldn't wait to leave and return to their own country.

We drove south from Papunya to Haasts Bluff Settlement just as a huge storm started to blow up. While the scenery at Haasts was magnificent, our welcome wasn't, and it appeared that the white fella Superintendent had been too long in the bush and had developed a deep dislike of all other white fellas. A Catholic missionary Nun once told me that all white staff belong to the three "M"s - The Missionaries, The Mercenaries and The Misfits.

As even Gus couldn't achieve a welcome mat and with the storm brewing we headed east to Areyonga. Before long the rain caught us, and it teemed down. With Gus becoming worried that the Finke River would come down and strand us on the wrong side, I began to drive faster. Robbie had invited me to drive, but after I belted through a couple of washaways a bit quickly, he suggested that I might treat my Toyota that way, but it was not the way that he drove. So rather than hand over in disgrace, I dropped back to a more leisurely pace, although I knew that Gus was still worried about the Finke. When finally we arrived on the south bank of the Finke, the river was bone dry and Robbie could afford an I told you so expression. We spent the night at Hermannsburg and in the morning drove down to check on the river and Gus could afford his I told you so expression, as the Finke was a raging torrent, a hundred metres wide.

Quite a large part of our bookings were Church Groups who were always interested in attending the Flynn Memorial Church in Alice Springs. One of the ministers, Rev. Jim Downing was running teaching classes in Pitjanjatjira, the most widely spoken Aboriginal language across the outback. We could see some benefit in this and enrolled in some classes - well as much as our time would allow.

Gus was a bit upset when I told him saying, "Why don't you learn a real language like Arunta instead of that yabber?" and insisted on teaching us some of his language.

Working on the assumption that phonetic spelling is the only logical method, I can't understand why the experts keep changing spelling. The people of Hermannsburg are Western Arunta, although the spelling was officially changed to Aranda, which is simply the German spelling used by the Lutheran missionaries (and still pronounced Arunta). Now the official spelling has become Arrente, which seems a little odd as it's still pronounced Arunta.

The people say Pitjanjara, but it is spelt Pitjanjatjira. Then the Warlbri now have their name spelt Warlpiri and the Pintabi spelt Pintupi.

So regardless of the condemnation that will probably come crashing down around my head, I intend to stick to what sounds right and write phonetically.

In the early days of settlement, the Afghan camel teams going to Alice Springs from the south followed the course of the Finke river, first to Hermannsburg (which in those days was bigger than Alice Springs) and then turned east and followed the valleys to Alice and the following year Gus suggested that Doreen and I plus Gus's wife and kids might like to drive down the Finke following their route. We loaded up into a Landrover and the going was easy as far as the Palm Valley turnoff, but after leaving the Palm Valley track to follow the course of the Finke it became obvious that the Landie was not up to the job in the soft sand, it was both under powered and under-tyred.

Gus however is a pretty determined bloke and some time later he came up with a borrowed beach buggy for us to try again. The buggy amazed me, fully loaded it bounced over the sand where the Landie had bogged down. We stopped and netted fish in the beautiful big waterhole, dreadfully misnamed "Boggy Hole", then saw the old Illamurta Police Station, built to protect the early camel trains from "wild blackfellows". Then on to Running Waters where a rock bar forces the river running under the sand to the surface. When it was time to cross the river, Gus stopped and walked ahead to check. He started to sink and fought his way out, saying we would have to drive on and find a rocky place to cross as the place we had tried was quicksand. He explained that standing in quicksand you must never wait to sink above your knees, but lie on your back and draw your leg up, and rollover to the bank. Quicksand is caused by water beneath the sand, but is still more supportive than water when you lie down.

We did a number of trips with Gus in this way and of course during the years we continued with our Sundowner campfires and it helped when Gus bought an old four-wheel drive bus and began to take tourists into Palm Valley. As well as ourselves he was supported by Kevin Bryant, better known as K.B. and Eric Blizzard, both Centralian Tours owner/drivers and both pioneers of early outback coach travel.

One night when preparing our campfire down in Palm Valley, Gus asked if I would drive back in our hired Landrover and pick up some of the boys, and driving back too fast in the dark I missed the track and bogged. Cursing my stupidity, I hacked into the sand with a spade, quickly cleared it and backed out. When on arriving back at Hermannsburg I went to check the time I found I was wearing a watch strap and back, but no watch movement and realized it had jumped out and was back in the bog. There was no sign of the "boys" (not unusual) and I was wandering around in the dark when I was suddenly taken from behind in a half nelson and I could just see a knife against my throat. Then I listened to a litany of complaints about we whitefellas. I reckoned it was mostly the grog talking and I realized who the young fellow was (I'd better call him Joe rather than his real name). I kept agreeing with him as much as possible, but if I nodded my head the knife pricked my throat. We seemed to be going nowhere fast and I took a punt and suggested that we sit down and discuss things over a couple of cigarettes. I was relieved when he agreed, and we sat and talked as he grew increasingly maudlin. Finally, I simply got up and walked away.

When I got back down the Valley and told Gus what happened he wanted to beat "Joe" up, but I talked him out of it, firstly I didn't think it was Gus's style and anyway I didn't think it would do much good. By a strange twist of fate, some 20 years later "Joe" suffered the same attack as I did, except that his assailant didn't stop, and he died. I have often wondered, didn't he say the right words, or didn't he have a pack of cigarettes, or what? There was a frightening amount of violence in Aboriginal communities in those days which caused us to lose some good friends. Even Gus's lovely daughter, Ingrid, was killed during a drunken brawl.

In the Valley it was impossible to use tent pegs in the sand and we just used to roll out our bed rolls without tents, and when I was rolling ours up one day I forgot to check and was stung by a scorpion. I was extremely careful what I did and where I went in the future.

One night everyone was enjoying singing and dancing around the fire when a Ranger vehicle pulled up and a rather uptight Ranger stepped out and announced that our campfire was illegal. We replied that this was our patch and we had been doing it for years. But he had a trump card, unbeknown to us, the entire area had just been declared a National Park. After we had soft soaped him, the Ranger calmed down and agreed to join us around the campfire, later saying that he couldn't remember a more enjoyable evening. We gave him our next date and the upshot was that he said he would collect the wood for the next campfire. They don't make Rangers like that anymore. Of course, it couldn't last and after a year or so our Ranger mate was moved on and a new Ranger appointed.

Accommodation was built up the Valley and the new man moved in with his wife and with the isolation, both vowed to give up smoking. Shortly after the Finke came down in flood and completely cut them off from the outside world, necessitating an air drop of food. The inevitable happened when the drop smashed into a cliff face and the food component was a total write off, but a couple of cartons of cigarettes came through unharmed. Their situation was getting quite desperate by the time a vehicle could get through and found them living on a diet of fresh air and cigarettes.

Gus Williams scored a few firsts, such as Aboriginal Coach Driver in 1968, Honorary Ranger, and in 1981 received the award of the Order of Australia for "his services to the community". Then in 2001 both Gus and his son Warren received Country Music Awards.

I remarked to Gus one day that with his physique he should have been a footballer, and he said that as a young fellow he had played for a white team in Alice Springs, but couldn't stand it when they won as they all got drunk. He was left the odd man out, not because he was black, but rather the only non-drinker. He was appalled by the problem of drunkenness, and lobbied tirelessly among his people to have it banned on settlements.

Gus was introduced to the Pope when he visited Alice Springs, and I asked him what he thought of him. "Well of course the Holy Father is not one of our mob (Gus is Lutheran) but he seemed a thoroughly nice bloke" Gus answered. In 1982 the Hermannsburg Mission that was founded by German Lutheran missionaries in 1877 was handed back to the Aboriginal community with inalienable freehold title.

CURTIN SPRINGS In the early 1960s, as nothing whatever could be bought at the Rock, Peter and Dawn Severin's Curtin Springs Roadhouse became an important stop if only for cold drinks.

The first lessee was Abe Andrews who made an epic journey from Pt. Lincoln in South Australia, transporting his family and goods in a wagon pulled by donkeys. (The wagon is on display in the grounds of the Old Timers Folk Museum in Alice Springs.) Andrews took up 1600 square miles of land west of Angas Downs and 60 miles east of Ayers Rock on a natural spring.

When Abe died in the 1950s his sons Merv and Ossie took over and ran the Station until they sold out in 1958 to Peter and Dawn. Merv and his Aboriginal wife then moved into Alice Springs where their pretty daughter Oriel made a name as a Country and Western singer and went on to relative fame in Adelaide.

With the drought forcing Stations to de-stock, Ozzie bought a truck and did well for a time carting cattle. But of course, his business crashed when de-stocking finished. We met and became friends when he then took up driving the Alice to the Rock Tour for Pioneer Coaches. Ozzie told us that his first experience with passengers was in 1950 when he carried some of the Knox Grammar party in a 1938 Ford Truck for the organizer Len Tuit. He said it took 3 days from Finke rail siding to the Rock. (This of course was the trip that inspired Ian Campbell.)

Ozzie's mate Ron Dingwall was his co-driver and Ron went on to become a coach driver on Tuit's Ayers Rock Tours. This ended rather abruptly when the Department discovered he was only 16 when the minimum age for a licence was 21.

Oz could talk for hours with tales of the early days and when possible, I would lure him over to our camp fire to entertain our passengers.

Len Beadell wrote about staying with the "Happy Family" where the son would ride a motorbike through the house, scaring the chocks off the furniture, and how the daughter would entertain them playing the guitar.

Ozzie told how he was the young fellow on the motorbike, and how Merv's daughter Oriel inherited the guitar after her aunt was killed when thrown from a horse.

They used to drove their cattle more or less in a straight line into Alice Springs across Angas Downs and Oz advised us never to pick up water at a certain bore. He told how he was thrown when his horse bolted and the only chance to survive was to walk back to Angas Downs. With very hot weather, when he came to this bore, he drank as much as he could before walking on. "It gave me the runs so bad that I walked into Angas with my pants over my shoulder" he said. Later I told Arthur Liddle, "Quite true," he said, "magnesium sulphate, you know, Epsom Salts".

In 1960 Ozzie planned a holiday with a friend in Perth and checked with Lennie Beadell about following his tracks across Western Australia - "Taking a short cut" he said. He broke down near the granite outcrop called Giles Tank in the Great Victoria Desert, and was saved by a mob of Aboriginals walking to Warburton.

When we were planning our first Gunbarrel crossing we turned to Ozzie for advice, and he pinpointed on a map where he had broken down. Sure, enough we found his old brown DeSoto car, and no doubt it is still there today, although it's impossible to know as this section of road is now Aboriginal land and so off limits to tourists.

What is the origin of the name Curtin Springs? Well, I asked Ozzie, and of course got a long answer. "We just called it Andrews Country, but in the 1940s the Lands Department asked for a formal name. Dad had picked up a booklet all about Russia and Joe Stalin and reckoned he was simply wonderful, so he submitted the name Stalin Springs. This sort of upset the bloke behind the counter, and he said don't you reckon our Prime Minister would be better, so Dad said OK and it became Curtin Springs". Well that was Ozzie's story anyway.

As there was no motor fuel available at the Rock, Peter Severin decided to install pumps (he had been selling it out of drums). We stopped one day to watch them digging the holes for the underground tanks, and they unearthed a marsupial mole, a beautiful small golden-haired creature, and the only one I have ever seen. As they live permanently underground the poor little critters have lost the use of their eyes.

ANGAS DOWNS When Len Tuit of Alice Springs began driving tourists to Ayers Rock, Angas Downs was the half way stop, as Bill Harney recorded in his book *Ayers Rock and Beyond.*

It is sometimes misspelt Angus by people associating the name with cattle, but in actual fact was originally a sheep station, that ultimately failed because of the dingoes before it became a cattle property.

Bill Liddle took up the land in 1927 and named it after George Fife Angas, a director of the South Australian Company who brought out many immigrants including Bill Liddle's grandfather.

Angas stands as a statue in North Terrace, Adelaide and Angaston in the Barossa is called after him.

At first it was just a fuel stop for us, but in time we became firm friends of Arthur and Bess Liddle. Arthur was one of three sons of Bill Liddle and his wife, a part-Aboriginal woman. Harold built Tea Tree Roadhouse, Milton had a wood and taxi business in Alice, and Arthur took up the Station. Bess was one of the Breadon girls, part-Aboriginal and descended from Alan Breadon who had managed Henbury Station.

Arthur and Bess came to treat us like family and camping alongside the homestead was a highlight of the tour for our passengers.

Quite a mob of tribal Aboriginals lived on the station and it was the first opportunity for most of our passengers to mix with tribal people. The people were Pitjanjira and very primitive by our standards when compared to the Arunta people of Hermannsburg who had worked with missionaries for nearly 100 years. Also, we were able to buy real artifacts produced by the desert craftsmen before loads of tourists caused them to hack out anything, then decorate with poker work done with the white fella's steel wire.

Boomerangs were always popular but it's a misconception that they are purely Australian as we have seen boomerangs in the Cairo Museum from ancient tombs and they were used in India and in the South West USA. In Tasmania they were unknown, and the Top End and on the Queensland coast - no boomerangs. Just like the Didgeridoo was purely from the Top End and unheard of in Central Australia, or anywhere below the tropic for that matter.

Of course, returning boomerangs are really toys and it had to be explained to people that real hunting boomerangs travel in a straight line and the spinning blades do the damage when they hit.

A problem for a lot of tourists was the Aboriginal attitude to the daily shower, or really any shower, but these people live in dry desert country where it would be criminal to waste water that could mean the death of another party coming through.

Our present day obsession with cleanliness is only recent anyway, and our great grandparents were never bombarded with advertising suggesting they may be on the nose, and with their deep aversion to washing, some of our ancestors must have stunk like pole cats.

It reminds me of back in the 1940s when Uncle Bob kindly supplied board and lodging to my mother and her smart alecky son. I must have really tried his patience as among other things, he insisted it was ridiculous anyone should need to bathe more than once a week. But of course, Uncle Bob was born back in the 1800s in what we call the Victorian era when the British public were stunned to learn the Queen was barmy enough to think she needed a bath once a week.

So, I wouldn't be too hard on tribal people about not washing as I reckon their ancestors probably recoiled and held their noses when they met the first white fellows.

Today cattlemen complain about the tourists washing in and fouling their troughs, but to desert people defiling a water source was a matter of life or death.

Tribal people had no means of boiling their water, and one of the most useful things they took from the white fellas was the empty powdered milk tin. They made them into billycans with a fencing wire handle, and called them "wayatjara", waya their pronounciation for "wire", and tjara means that "that which has" (that which has wire).

Also, I have seen in settlements all over outback Australia, kid's toys made from milk tins with the lids back on and a hole punched through the bottom and the lid, fencing wire pushed through like an axle, and then drawn back into a long handle. The little kids push these around chasing each other and making motorcar noises.

Arthur always referred to people like himself as coloured, and the tribal people as black or blackfellows, and he meant nothing derogatory by this in any way. I like to think that all people are simply people, although it's pretty obvious that deep down we are all tribal and owe allegiance to our own tribe. But to feel better about it, we keep changing labels, and Arthur would now be an indigenous Australian. I feel that we have a habit of reviewing past actions and ideas through the lens of the latest mores, which are really only society's latest prejudices.

A famous American singer once said, "I was first called a Negro country singer, then later, a Coloured Country Singer, then I became a Black American Country Singer, now I am an Afro American Country Singer, so what's next?" The reason, of course, is that some names are seen to be disparaging and come to be avoided.

There were 30 or 40 tribal people living on Angas Downs and the young girls seemed to enjoy doing housework, making bread etc. and were always clean and well dressed. The men helped Arthur with station chores, which appeared pretty spasmodic, and I don't think they were expected to do a great deal.

The Aboriginal people were a bit like an extension of the family and were paid in kind rather than money, which wasn't much good to them anyway in those days. There seemed to be only one firm rule, no grog allowed. We had to warn our passengers on overnight stops, that this applied to them as well.

Arthur and Bess had three school-aged children, Laurie, Lorraine and Johnnie, then there was Laurie's school mate Tim Lander. Tim was white with blonde hair and blue eyes, but he spent all his holiday time at the Station and became known as Arthur's white-haired boy.

Tim's parents had managed a station and like most young people brought up in the bush, both Tim and Laurie were extraordinarily capable young fellows.

Passing through regularly we became friends of the family, then Arthur suggested we take our holidays there. He really became a best mate and when he passed away a couple of years after we retired, I flew up to Alice for his funeral.

An old chap called Alex Barney who also lived on the station was also a coloured man, but not Aboriginal. Alex was South Sea Islander, born on the Queensland coast. He ran away as a boy and became a member of a shearing team working out of Barcaldine. He answered an ad to shear Billy Liddle's sheep in the 1930s where he fell in love with Central Australia and stayed on.

On our holidays Alex adopted Doreen and me and one of our jobs was helping him give out the station rations each week. These consisted of flour, tea, sugar, treacle, meat and sometimes clothes, blankets, tarps, etc. according to the people's needs. When we relayed the information to our Sundowners, they deluged us with boxes of clothes that made Angas Downs look like St. Vincent de Pauls.

As well as station rations of course, the people found and ate bush tucker, and while watching them cooking a snake one day, someone remarked "Pity they weren't in the garden of Eden, as they would have passed up the apple and eaten the serpent".

Most people assume that tobacco was introduced by the whites, but Aboriginals were quite possibly the first people to use it. There are several native species of Nicotinea, the most desired being Ingulpa, and with the people not being nomadic anymore, this had to be supplied in rations. It was called nicky nicky and made for the stations by W.D. & H.O. Wills.

Until 1962 the North Australian Workers Union actually banned Aboriginals from taking out membership. In 1965 they applied to have them brought into the award. This was called industrial justice and the court was told that both the employers and their Aboriginal stockmen should be "Thrown into the water and learn to swim". Predictably the Aboriginals sank. The Union said that, after all, any Aboriginal "disemployment" or social dislocation resulting could be covered by the welfare system. And to think today we have an Aboriginal problem and people wonder why.

To be fair, there are two sides to most stories and contrary to the feeling that arose later in the uninformed public, the fact that so many Aboriginals were being employed as stockmen was an asset to Aboriginal life and assisted in their assimilation. The families were together, children were going to State schools. But most importantly the men were learning and employed in useful stock trades and many earning a living. Those we saw were all well fed, I believe better than today in town reserves where meat in particular is so expensive. They had no contact with grog, and appeared much happier than they look today.

Many things I have read paint a misleading picture of the conditions of Aboriginal labour in this period, about how the Stations exploited these people, in fact when helping out with the rations that catered for whole families, I sometimes wondered who was exploiting who and many old Aboriginal blokes still talk about their love of horses and cattle and how working with cattle supported them on their own country.

Living on welfare won't ever replace the status and lifestyle many of these people enjoyed.

Although few things are completely black and white (no pun intended), we mostly knew of conditions on family-owned properties, but on some of the big company-owned stations, things were probably different. Ted Egan and others tell of harsh treatment of Aboriginals and even white staff by managers forced to show profits for their big city and sometimes overseas based companies.

Meanwhile, holidaying at Angas Downs, Alex was treating Doreen and me as though we were his grandchildren and it was hard to believe he was turning ninety, without a wrinkle he looked

20 years younger, and although he no longer drove he always wanted to show us new country.

When we admitted to not having climbed Mt. Connor, it was into Arthur's old Landrover and off we went. After leaving the road, Alex insisted we were on a track, although I couldn't see any, and I just had the Landie plunging through the scrub, but I had to give him full marks when he brought us out right at Paddy de Conlay's old homestead as the southern foot of Mt. Connor.

Paddy was a mate of R.M. Williams in the days before Williams became wealthy producing stockmens' boots and such. He must have been a good mate because Williams financed him into the station back in 1943. When Paddy died the Government decided that it probably never could have been a viable property, and divided it, giving the southern half to Dave Foggarty on Mulga Park and the top end including the Mount to Peter Severin at Curtin Springs.

Mt. Connor is a huge mesa with near vertical sides except at the south end, where the catchment has created a rocky gully and forms what they call Aneri Soak. After a fairly stiff climb we came out on top where it was more like a flat plain covered in trees than a normal mountain. We followed the sun to the western side and were finally rewarded with a view of Ayers Rock and the Olgas way to the west.

One day there was a bit of a strike by the people, they were tired of the processed nicky nicky and wanted some real tobacco, so Arthur hitched up the trailer and invited us on a trip up into Kings Canyon country. He told us his father once lived in a cave near Kings Canyon. I asked was this to get out of the weather. Arthur replied "No, it was so he didn't wake up with a spear in his back".

Arthur drove north on a bush track to the old original homestead in the Liddle Hills (called after his father). At the old homestead, built in the 1930s and now a ruin, he showed us the remains of a T-model Ford, his father's car and the first to brave this country. Further north we came to Wallara Ranch and stopped to have a drink with Jack Cotterill.

Jack was a great personality. He was a motor mechanic who had migrated from England with his wife and two young sons. He was determined to open up Kings Canyon to tourism, but as it was too far out, he leased a block on Angas Downs from Arthur and built a half way staging point he called Wallara Ranch.

This was all very well, but there was no road to the Canyon, so using a four-wheel drive, Jack and his son Jim dragged a piece of railway line up and down to create some sort of road. It was still four-wheel drive in many places, but finally we came out at the Canyon. Up a side gorge east of the canyon we found tobacco growing in abundance. We picked and packed the big leaves into hessian bags and stacked them in the trailer. Then we returned to an overjoyed mob back at the station.

To give the ingulpa a bit of a boost, they sometimes added pituri, which is a common bush in this country, but I don't think you would want to overdo it. It is listed in books as Dubosia hopwoodii, "A powerful narcotic".

During the early 1960s the country was blowing away in dust storms and years later we saw red banks of outback dust in glaciers in New Zealand. The stations had all de-stocked and sandhills were moving across the country. First a stillness would descend on the country, and everything would be quiet, even the birds would disappear. Then from the west a reddish- brown curtain would appear right across the horizon, getting progressively higher in the sky and slowly move toward us. Everyone rushed to take precautions, windows closed down, anything that could become a flying missile put away. Then as the sun began to disappear a red glow would come into the air, and the wind would hit with a dreadful fury. Cars left outside could be left with a dull sandblasted paint on one side, while still shiny and new on the other. Dust storms were the chief topic of conversation and when talking to an old timer one day he said, "yeah mate, opened a can of beans the other day, and would you believe it, full of red dust".

Journalists from down south had a field day writing stories about how the country had been ruined through over-stocking. They said it would never recover, as they photographed any animal skeleton they could find sticking out of the drift sand. I thought that Arthur was going slightly mad when he took to saying, "you won't know this country when it rains".

We had seen the Todd River come down in 1962 and the water disappeared into the sand and we had seen the Finke come down and it had no effect. Anyone could see that this was a desert pure and simple and always would be. Then in 1967 it started to rain and in 1968 it seemed to never stop, and Central Australia became an inland sea. The railway line was swept away, and vehicles were bogged everywhere. It was a crash course for us on de-bogging. I learnt more about de-bogging and what equipment was necessary in six months, than most people would learn in a lifetime.

The water retreated, and it was impossible to put a finger between the wildflowers, the whole country was a carpet of colour. Botanists came out and identified new plants that had never been seen before and I reckoned that even Arthur couldn't have foretold this. He agreed saying "It was nearly this good in 1934". A long time to wait for miracles and I don't expect to see it ever again. Sure, there have been dry years since, but nothing compared to what we saw, and even the really good years have never produced a fraction of the carpets of flowers.

Just as the people rejoiced after the rains, so did the pests. First, we had a mouse plague, and where we had had sand getting into everything now it was mice. They swarmed into the homestead, into the coach, and into food boxes - mice add absolutely nothing to the joys of camping.

One night having dinner at the table, Bess ripped off a shoe and hurled it across the room knocking out a mouse running up the wall. And if we thought this was bad, things got infinitely worse when as the mice started to disappear they were followed by a rat plague.

One day there was a great commotion as Elsie, one of the housegirls, was giving birth and this was followed by deep gloom as Elsie gave birth to twins. Traditionally, it is difficult enough to bring up one baby in the desert and to be saddled with two, near impossible. I couldn't see any problem, but Arthur said that the old men believed that it was a curse, and seeing that this was a pretty big deal, they wanted to kill, not just one, but both of them. Arthur radioed the Flying Doctor (Angas had an easy call sign to remember 8 Sierra, Echo, X-ray, or SEX) who flew out immediately. The doctor proposed that he take both the twins and Elsie into Alice Springs and asked if they had been named. Arthur thought quickly and said, "We'll call them Charles and Todd". The doctor filled out birth certificates and as a J.P. (from the motor dealer days) I witnessed them. I don't think that Arthur understood much about being a J.P. because he remarked "Gee, they'll think you have a big beat, ay." No trouble putting the twins on the plane, but Elsie was scared out of her wits at the thought of flying, and we had to pretty well wrestle her on board. Charles died some years later, I don't know how, but Todd grew into a strapping big man and would be middle aged now.

It was deadly quiet of a night as at that time they had no generator and relied on batteries and lanterns. One night we were waiting for Arthur to return from town in the old Falcon when Tim said, "I hear him coming", I could hear nothing. Then Bess said, "No that's not a Falcon, Holden I reckon." I could still hear nothing. Then much later a Holden drove past and disappeared into the night on the Ayers Rock road. These people had phenomenal hearing.

Today a bitumen road runs out to Kings Canyon and it is possible to drive on around the range, past Areyonga Aboriginal settlement and on to either Glen Helen or Hermannsburg and so into Alice Springs. But in those days no road went past the Canyon, in fact it was fourwheel drive just to get there.

So, we used to think there must be something about the power of God when Pastor Keleski drove his Holden Ute from Areyonga, around the end of the range to Angas Downs on a regular basis. He not only drove but carried building materials as he was building a church on the station. We of course were roped in and became God's little helpers. Keleski already had a black Pastor in the camp, Pastor Peter Bulla, and intended that Pastor Peter have his own church. Attendance was lax to say the least, but Keleski wasn't daunted, he obtained a movie projector and on Saturday nights showed cartoons, Micky Mouse and such. People flooded in to watch, then camped nearby and were easily rounded up for church the following morning.

When the award wages came in and the rations system was ended, Government trucks took everyone in the camp out to a new settlement called Docker River near the West Australian border and the interaction between our people and the Aboriginal community ended, then the white ants had a field day eating Keleski's church.

One holiday we were picked up at Alice airport by Arthur and Tim, and Arthur proposed that I drive and use the old original road to Angas Downs. This started as a droving track used by the Andrews family at Curtin Springs, and partly used by Jack Cotteril when he pushed his road through to Wallara and Kings Canyon, it was far more direct than the present road that uses two sides of a triangle.

1965. Angas Downs.

1967. Road to Kings Canyon.

1972. Hermannsburg. Gus Williams and Tjalkaliri (Tiger).

1967. I bogged Arthur Liddle's Landrover trying to cross the Palmer River on the way to Angas Downs.
Tim Lander on spade.

1968. Angas Downs. Arthur Liddle, Mum, Florence (Doreen's mother) and Alex Barney.

1974. Angas Downs. Bruce 'Tracker' Tilmouth.

Ossie Andrews drove and assisted Len Tuit with the very first tours to the Rock and the droving track left the Stuart Highway just south of the Finke River crossing and went in nearly a straight line to Angas Downs. The road, or more properly track, was almost non-existent and after driving through the river red gums of the dry sandy Palmer River we drove on for 3 or 4 miles to reach the old Mt. Quinn homestead. Ozzie had told me of his stopovers there when it was a going concern and owned by Alf Butler and Bob Buck. There is a photo of Alf Butler (a little man with a big moustache) standing in front of the homestead in Bill Hamey's book *Ayers Rock and Beyond.* Bob Buck became famous as the bushman that found Harold Lasseter's remains in the Petermann Ranges. (Refer Ion Idriess's book *Lasseter's Last Ride).* The old homestead now was just a dilapidated mass of slabs and stone with very little left.

Further on we came to a creek washaway and I put my foot down to race through, but instead sank into the sand and badly bogged. Arthur just shrugged, but Tim, only a school boy at the time, gave me a pitying look, and I felt a proper dill as we dug the Landrover out. Finally, we reached the station boundary and Arthur told us the reason for this trip. Under the BTEC Scheme to wipe out infected cattle, all property had to be fenced and the fences would go up the next week, closing off the old track for all time, and meaning that we were the last people to use this, the original tourist road to the Rock. We came out at the station airstrip. The strip was first class due to the fact that Prince Phillip had been visiting Central Australia. Phillip announced that he would like to fly himself out to the Rock. As Angas had the halfway strip, in fact the only strip, a team descended on the place and did a first-class job, bringing it up to a standard fit for royalty, just in case.

One day folding metal beds were set up alongside the homestead, the Aunties, that is Bess's sisters were coming for a stay. Every day Bess swept the sand under the beds which I thought was overdoing it a bit, until she said, "It's to see where snakes have been."

Doreen joined the ladies in the back of the ute one day and they went off to collect berries. Tomatoes and Deadly Nightshade are both Solanums, and a couple of hundred years ago people, knowing this, weren't rushing in and stocking up on tomatoes. Many different Solanums grow in the outback, and it pays to know which is which, some edible, some poisonous and some produce the chemical for the contraceptive pill. What Bess called berries were in truth, little, strongly flavoured tomatoes and one of the few bush tucker items that I find in any way edible.

Doreen colours up very well after being in the sun, so all the ladies looked like "coloured" people as they drove off on their collecting, and naturally Bess took the gun "Might see roo, ay?" Not a great deal of time passed before they came roaring back, with everyone looking in a state of shock.

As Doreen told me later, they were all out picking the berries, when two Toyotas appeared over the hill. They were full of Red Ochre Men who ordered the women off the road and out of the way. Red Ochre Men are elders in charge of initiation and round up boys to make them into men. They can generate a wave of fear as they move around the country, which certainly worked on our ladies. Doreen said that they were a fine-looking group of old men, and she said to Bess "We don't have to move, we're on your property". But Bess wasn't waiting to parley and they all leapt aboard, dragging Doreen with them, so we didn't have much of a feed of berries.

During school holidays Arthur and Bess played host to the children of their relatives in Alice Springs. They were a bright lot of kids and our Sundowners would talk to them around the camp fire. Like all adults they would ask "What are you going to be when you grow up?" The answer was usually "I'm going to join the Industry". "What's that?" "You know, the Aboriginal Industry, that's where the money is." And some of them did, so if anyone reading this was among those Sundowners, I'll bring you up to date at the time of writing.

Of Arthur's three kids, Lorraine studied hard and became a barrister, and her daughter, young Catherine is an ABC newsreader in Adelaide. John did join the "Industry" and became a force in local Aboriginal politics, but ultimately gave it away to become The Education Ranger at the Alice Springs Desert Park. Laurie was and is a top bloke who always held down a steady job, although wasn't driven like many of the others.

Laurie's mate Tim Lander was the only white kid in the mob, and Tim now owns his own contracting company in Alice Springs. Among the relatives, Ian owns Kings Creek Station (more about that later). Jeffery was the road boss for MacMahons in charge of building the bitumen road out to Ayers Rock. Bob became a council alderman, then started his own consulting business. Ronnie worked as an Aboriginal advisor in Canberra during the Whitlam years, then in the tourist industry where we continued to be mates.

Bruce was the real character among the kids, he took on the nickname of Tracker and rose up through the "Industry". He was fingered by Bob Hawke and Senator Collins to be Senator for the Northern Territory, but Tracker was too independent and didn't cosy up to the right factions, then killed his chances of becoming Senator Tilmouth when in a burst of anger announced, "I'm just treated as their pet nigger", which of course proved to be a very bad career move. I could go on about more of those young people, but I think it is remarkable what many of them achieved.

We were holidaying at Bess and Arthur's town house in Alice Springs when I noticed an Aboriginal woman sitting in the backyard. Bess said, "That's my old Mum, she can't speak English, and she won't come into Arthur's house as under Aboriginal law, mothers in law and sons in law must never meet face to face". (Pretty smart people). So, we had Grandma who couldn't speak English, daughter who couldn't read or write, but who later became a famous painter, grand-daughter who became a barrister, and great grand-daughter who is an ABC newsreader.

I include this to bring early Sundowners up to date and for city people who rarely hear of successes in the outback.

I read in *The Weekend Australian* in 2003 "The N.T.'s Deputy Administrator is the much-respected Pat Miller, an Alice Springs Arrente woman".

We knew Pattie as the pretty young niece of Arthur Liddle who married a young fellow we called Miller the Driller as he worked for Water Resources.

GREENLEAVES CARAVAN PARK on the first Redline trip we were booked to stay at Greenleaves Caravan Park over eastside, Alice Springs, but with the Todd River in flood we never got to see the place. So, working on the assumption that Redline made very good decisions, we booked in there right from the start of our tours. Although the amenities would get a minus one star today, they were pretty average for those days.

To call it a caravan park is a misnomer, as few people drove their cars up the south road from Adelaide, much less tried to tow a caravan. The normal procedure was to put your car on the train. Then, coming through outback Queensland was no better and a used car dealer we knew as Honest Neil made a business of buying cars that had been driven to Alice Springs and the owners wanted to sell, either believing the car wouldn't make it home, or they couldn't face the return trip. Poor old Neil finished up getting shot, creating speculation on whether the assailant was an irate car owner or an irate husband.

Greenleaves was divided into camping bays by a scatter of weeping ironwood trees and each with a fireplace-cum-barbecue. Camping coaches were really the biggest part of the business and we all had our regular bays. As well, Reg had caravans that had been brought up by train and rented out to semi-permanents, many of whom were real characters and enjoyed telling their stories to the "tourists".

Reg Verran, the proprietor was an ex-concert pianist and entertained the customers on at least one evening a week, then there was Kangaroo Joe Jackson, who was a retired outback shooter. Joe had a lifetime obsession with film making, and if asked would show some of his hours of film shot back in the 1930s and 40s. We spent many evenings in the caravan of Paddy and Kath Ethell, one reason being they kept a very nice drop of sherry.

Paddy was a journalist, and he produced a top line colour magazine about Central Australia called *The Inland Review*. We used to bounce ideas off each other, as we were both interested in stories and places of interest to tourists. He wrote many articles, a lot under assumed names, and for readers of *The Inland Review* it would appear that it was written by a team of expert writers. Many years later when Ayers Rock became Uluru, tour operators were advised by the powers that be, that coach drivers that relayed stories written by Bill Harney, Charles Mountford, and Peter B. English, could be severely dealt with in some unspecified manner as these people in some way had written things that under the new order were no longer acceptable.

Bill Harney spoke half a dozen Aboriginal languages, lived most of his life among Aboriginal people, and wrote a number of books on the subject. He was chosen as first ranger at Ayers Rock because of this background. He started at the Rock in 1957 and finished in 1962. Bill was married to an Aboriginal woman who passed away, then his son Billie drowned in Alice Springs Water Hole when trying to help another person.

Charlie Mountford was a fully accredited anthropologist who wrote a number of books about Central Australian aboriginal people. Then of course, there was no such person as Peter B. English, it was simply one of Paddy's favourite titles, and in his defence I can only say that he researched his subjects thoroughly and was more accurate than many of today's writers.

We live in politically correct times and I agree that the changes are made with worthy motives. I'm just another old timer, but I believe that distorting history is one thing, rewriting is quite another.

As well, Greenleaves had an Italian Restaurant run by Mumma Maria and husband Gino. Not that Italians were very much appreciated in those days - they were still called wogs. They drank vino instead of good Aussie beer, and spoke in dreadful broken English. So, it wasn't easy sometimes to get our passengers to try the delights of Italian cuisine. To describe Mumma Maria I couldn't go past something Tim Lander told me. Walking along Todd St., Tim saw a parking cop booking Mumma's car. She caught him and when he refused to back down, she nearly floored him with her handbag. It finished up with the cop trying to get away up the street and Mumma chasing him screaming in Italian.

One day when we had Gus Williams with us we had to see Maria at home for some reason. We no sooner entered than she set us down and opened a bottle of vino. Very hospitable people the Italians, but Gus didn't know which way to look and said, "I'm sorry Mrs. Deano but I don't drink". To which Maria replied, "Donta be silly, all you blackfellas drink". We smoothed things over, but I don't think that Maria was convinced.

In another caravan we had a Dutch couple and Henk was a professional painter. They had migrated to Australia and Henk couldn't make a living as a painter in the city, and finished up coming to Central Australia. This was a good move because tourists will buy a painting when holidaying in an area that they wouldn't consider buying when at home, it's called a holiday souvenir. He painted in oils in a rather colourful and flamboyant style, but tourists loved his work, so much so that between us and some of the Murray Valley Coach drivers like Neville Hobbs and Ivan Walkley, Henk had no trouble selling his production.

There was no stopping Henk Guth when he got going. He took over an old house in town and rebuilt it as a modern art gallery that attracted all the tourist buses. He then set up a painting assembly line and mass-produced paintings that sold at an amazing rate. In the 1980s a local we knew wanted to buy Henk out and a figure of one million dollars was quoted, but I think his bank manager failed to co-operate, no more Swiss francs or something.

So many people from that era have passed away including Henk Guth and Ivan Walkley, so it came as some surprise when reading the July/September 2003 issue of *Australian Geographic* to see a photograph of Neville Hobbs. He was listed as one of twelve "Transport Legends of the Outback" during a ceremony at Arkaroola in the Flinders Ranges.

It described Neville as a bush/tourism trailblazer who drove coaches through the outback in the 1940s, which was something I never knew, although I was always a bit in awe of him.

He drove for Murray Valley Coaches, at that time a very big company based in Adelaide, and taken over by Greyhound in 1974.

During our first year of camping at Greenleaves we watched as a M.V.C. coach drove in to set up camp, with as was their custom, the camping gear in a rack on the roof.

The driver, a big powerfully built man then climbed onto the roof and unloaded the luggage, then helped set up the tents, He then constructed a barbecue and cooked everyone's meal, chain smoking all the time.

I was just a new chum and not in the same league as this bloke, but decided to walk over and introduce myself and so met Neville Hobbs, who became a great friend over the years. Like many drivers of that era he was hard smoking (3 packs a day), hard drinking, and tough as they come, but beneath it all, kind and free with advice. He never knocked the new chum driver, saying "Remember we all had to drive and learn on our first tour".

BRUCE & JACKIE FARRANDS - RABBIT FLAT

Again and again as I have been writing this missive, it has occurred to me "What if?", and the thought that our entire lives are ruled by chance. Chance encounters, chance decisions serve to create "What ifs?".

There is a Roadhouse in the middle of the Tanami Desert, half way between Alice Springs and Halls Creek called Rabbit Flat that may never have existed if Doreen hadn't talked me into that first Redline trip.

On our June 1966 Central Australian trip, we had a French girl Jacqueline Bererdengo as a passenger. Jackie had lived in and around Paris most of her life and in 1964 decided to see the rest of the world. Her first choice was Australia "as it is the easiest country to get to without much money, they nearly pay you to come here". She spoke very little English, and even then, with the French accent her English still sounded like French. She was staying with friends in Melbourne when she booked on the Central Australian tour.

French was a compulsory subject at school and as I always failed miserably I found that my French barely existed. It was obvious that our teacher never ever assumed that his students might actually want or need to speak the language. However, difficulties aside, Jackie loved the trip, so much that she booked on the 9-week Around Australia Tour.

Jackie reported to Doreen one day, "Bill is starting to understand me". This was an exaggeration and came about as I had started nodding my head and smiling as an answer.

One day in October Jackie asked me, "Ist the twelfth Doreen's birthday no? I buy leetle gift, foreign keys". I was nonplussed, and even more so when she gave Doreen four hankies.

During a visit to Curtin Springs Jackie told us she had fallen in love with Central Australia and how could she get a job there. This was overheard by Peter Severin, who came up with an idea. Joe Mahood at Mongrel Downs was married to Marie who was the French teacher at Alice High School before she married, I bet she would appreciate having a young French girl as general help. Peter radioed Joe who said it was a great idea and it was agreed that Jackie would continue with us around Western Australia, then leave in Melbourne, pack her gear, fly to Alice Springs and Joe and Marie would drive in and take her back to Mongrel Downs.

It didn't work as easily as planned and when we returned to Alice Springs, Jackie was marooned there as the country around Mongrel Downs had been deluged with 16 inches of rain and nothing could move for over two months. The Mahoods finally got into town to take Jackie back and the station must have been all she could have wished for as she even fell in love. The next time we saw her, it was with her new husband, Bruce Farrands. Bruce was a laconic, snowy haired young fellow with a wicked sense of humour.

Although Bruce's main asset appeared to be an old green truck, they had a plan. They were going to build a hotel/motel out in the middle of the Tanami Desert where water was available, near the old Tanami gold fields. Then, and even to this day, they used the Aboriginal pronunciation of "Tchanamee" which of course has to be correct, although I suppose the common "Tana-my" will win out in the long run.

Bruce told us that the old "Madman's Track" that the gold fossickers used coming down from Halls Creek was being graded and Ansett Pioneer were preparing to run a tour from Alice Springs up to Halls Creek, across the top and back to Alice Springs using Clipper coaches, and were relying on Bruce for a half way overnight and fuel stop. Of course, it was taken for granted that Sundowners would become customers, what could we say?

He pointed out that the Birdsville Track would become too tame for adventurers, and anyway it was only 300 miles long, the Tanami was over 700 miles, no comparison really. Against all odds, they did as they said and built Rabbit Flat Roadhouse.

The rain in 1967 that flooded Mongrel Downs was the start of the breaking of the drought, but their first year in business in 1968 coincided with the floods right across the Centre. They were flooded in for months, and rather than tourists the first party to make it in was a geo survey group that could not have operated without their help. Their one saving grace was being appointed an official weather station, which means recording all instruments every four hours and radioing the results 24 hours a day. While this is terribly demanding work, it pays rather well.

With Land Rights, the entire Tanami country was made Aboriginal land and the fact that Bruce and Jackie had a tiny spot right in the middle seemed to drive the Aboriginal organizations into a fury. They tried everything both legal and illegal to get rid of them. One night, Bruce spent the whole evening hiding after radioing for help while those outside hurled rocks and abuse. "They had guns and so did I" Bruce said, "but I knew better than to fire the first shot, it was the longest night I've ever spent, and was I glad to see the police". Finally, Bruce and Jackie won a court case that gave them their land claim, but it took years to achieve it.

Even so he must have gotten on well enough with the locals as they gave him a totem name, and always called him Jungula. One night with a big mob camped opposite, fighting started up and one fellow ran across the road for Bruce's help. He explained that the

Jungula skin group were copping a hiding from another group and it was Bruce's duty to come and help. Bruce had to explain that although fighting was a great pastime it wasn't really his thing, and after all he was really only an honorary Jungula. But he and Jacky did the right thing the following morning and patched up their brotherly victims.

The notion that the Government or anybody else should help them never entered their heads, and although I have had many people tell me that Bruce was mad, I could only pray that our country had a couple of million like him and Australia would lead the world. At least Bruce learnt to be a great philosopher, I remarked one day when talking of problems that nature could be cruel. "No, nature just displays blind, pitiless indifference" was his answer.

In 1976 Jackie was pregnant and we jokingly suggested that it looked like twins. As it was she gave birth prematurely and Bruce all alone had to do the honors. He delivered the baby and hit himself with a stiff drink, then Jackie went into labour a second time. Bruce said it was like a nightmare, where the same thing keeps happening over and over.

The twins Danny and Glen did early schooling through School of the Air/Alice Springs. It was possible to go to the bar, and a small disembodied voice would ask what you wanted, then after he climbed upon a box we would see one of the boys.

Jackie was a mathematical whiz and taught the boys maths memory systems, and apart from always giving the correct change, they loved getting our passengers into dart games. Of course, they were unbeatable, but the clever thing was they never wrote down the score. No matter how many played, they kept every score in their heads. This fascinated our people and they would give them maths problems to solve, which was "child's" play for them.

The boys went on to become Army officers, with at least one serving in East Timor. At the time of writing Bruce and Jackie are still at Rabbit Flat and have no intention of leaving.

1976. Bruce and Jackie with twins.

1966. Around Australia Tour.
Leyland beside tall termite mound, Top End.

1967/9 OFFER OF PARTNERSHIP EXPANDING ROUTES TO BIRDSVILLE & OODNADATTA

There seems to be a regular stream of letters to the newspapers lambasting all Australians as a mob of racist red neck hicks. But what does the majority of this mob do when asked?

In the Referendum to extend full rights to the Aboriginal people in 1967 over 90% of us voted in favour, although I don't expect this extraordinary result will placate the letter writers who have a need to lecture us. The Referendum was brought about by a petition to Prime Minister Robert Menzies who was enthusiastic about the idea, and went ahead to organise it, but had left office by the due date, and it was passed under the Prime Ministership of Harold Holt.

Then in December 1967 a quite unbelievable event took place when the Australian Prime Minister simply vanished. Harold Holt waded into the surf in Port Phillip Bay for a swim and was never seen again.

The Leyland Motor Company produced a monthly journal rather fancy and in full colour, printed in England and distributed around the world, illustrating the capabilities of their vehicles. We were approached to feature as they informed us their research had shown our Around Australia Tour was the longest coach tour in the world.

I had doubts about this and thought that the overland London to Bombay would be longer, but they assured us that at 13,000 miles, ours was longer. They printed photos we gave them of passengers carrying rocks to fill washed-out creeks, and other typical outback scenes. The main problem was they showed "Two tours, the Around Australia lasting 22 days and the Central Australian Tour lasting 8 days". It appears the Pommie editor couldn't believe a tour of 65 days and modified it all accordingly. But he must have thought we were pretty smart doing 13,000 miles in 22 days. The rest of the article was rather good, and the front cover of the Christmas December 1967 issue featured the Australians in shorts enjoying a summer evening around a campfire, with of course their prized Leyland in the background.

How many times have we witnessed events that have later been written up in newspapers or magazines only to be amazed by the inaccurate reporting? So, it came as no surprise that the Leyland magazine article had so many mistakes.

1969. Doreen with Birdsville youngsters

In the outback of Central Australia, crossing a creek presents a problem and it is a case of all hands to the pump to provide a way across.

Where to go for that annual holiday is becoming a problem for people of all nationalities, as jet air travel brings the four corners of the earth within easy reach, but the citizens of Sydney have the chance to take a really unusual holiday. Bill and Doreen Hands run "Sundowner Coach Tours" and offer the enterprising tourist a choice of two tours which give a chance to explore Australia and really absorb local colour. The tours are operated with an Albion Viking coach and in order to preserve the personal service Bill will not increase the fleet though there is sufficient traffic potential. The body on the coach was built to Bill's specification by Dennings and is 33ft long. It features 330ft^3 of luggage space, fuel capacity for 1000 miles, drinking water capacity of 50gal, jet air conditioning, deep anti-glare panoramic windows, two refrigerators and seating for 32 in luxurious reclining seats. The coach also has two way radio for emergency use and also for tuning in and calling up the isolated homesteads sometimes visited and even the Flying Doctor.

The two trips are Around Australia, lasting 22 days and the Central Australia Tour, lasting eight days. Who could resist such temptings as "overnight camp in beautiful Palm Valley, watch the changing colours of Ayer's Rock, camp fire meetings with Aboriginals, swimming at Lake Moondarra on Mount Isa" etc.

The trips are planned so that they can be operated throughout the year, even during the wet season, but of course the route often follows unmade roads. The tour around Australia goes from Sydney up the east coast of Queensland through Brisbane, Rockhampton, Townsville, Green Island to Cairns and Mossman then strikes west to Normanton, south to Mary Kathleen and Cloncurry before again heading west to Mount Isa and into the Northern Territory via Camooweal to Tennant Creek. The tour then heads south to the famous Ayer's Rock via The Devil's Marbles, Barrow Creek, Alice Springs, the MacDonnell Ranges and Palm Valley before returning to Tennant Creek and then continuing north to Darwin via Katherine and the vast Sturt Plain. From Darwin the coach returns to Katherine before continuing along the northern seaboard crossing into Western Australia and passing through Ord River, Wyndham, Halls Creek, Fitzroy Crossing, to Broome on the western coast. The tour then heads right round the coast via the Eighty Mile Beach to Port Headland, strikes inland to Marble Bar and Wittenoom Gorge in the shadow of Mount King, Mount Vigors and the Mulga Downs. After the gorge the coach heads back to the coast and continues through Onslow, Carnarvon, Geraldton, Perth and then along the southern coast via Albany, Esperance, Norseman between Lake Dundas and Cowan, Eucla, into South Australia to Port Augusta, Port Pirie, Adelaide and Mount Gambier. Crossing into Victoria the tour passes through Melbourne and back to Sydney in New South Wales via Wagga Wagga and Goulbourn. In total, a round trip of nearly 10,000 miles.

The Central Australian tour covers 5,500 miles and goes from Sydney via Goulbourn, Wagga Wagga and Hay to Mildura, junction of the Great Murray and Darling rivers, then on up the Murray Valley to Renmark, Berrie, Port Pirie and Port Augusta to Woomera, where the rocket range is situated. The tour continues to Kingoonya and then north to

Gleaming and new, the 'Sundowner' shortly after leaving the Denning works and before numerous trips in and around Australia.

Searching for local colour

the Coober Pedy opal mines and along the edge of the Great Victoria Desert to Victory Downs and Ayer's Rock, and then along Palm Valley to Alice Springs and on up to Tennant Creek. The coach then heads east to Camooweal, Mount Isa and Mary Kathleen, the uranium town before continuing to Cloncurry and then striking down through central Queensland to McKinley, Kynuna, Winton, Barcaldine, Blackall, Augathella, Charleville, Morven, Mitchell, Roma, Condamine, the Moonie oilfields, Goondiwindi, back into New South Wales to Moree, Narrabri, Gunnedah, Tamworth, the Glenbawn Dam site and back to Sydney via Newcastle.

Obviously some nights have to be spent at places where there are no hotels or camps. On these occasions the meals are cooked in the open and the passengers sleep under canvas on air beds.

The Viking coach is the VK41 machine, powered by the Leyland O.400 engine developing 2400 rev/min and giving a torque maximum of 330 lb/ft at 1600 rev/min. Transmission is by six speed overdrive gearbox.

The coach is driven mainly by Bill with Doreen acting as Hostess, but she also holds a licence and takes over the wheel at times. Such is the personal service of the Sundowner that anyone wishing to take a Safari holiday is invited to call at the Hand's home and discuss it and see slides of previous tours.

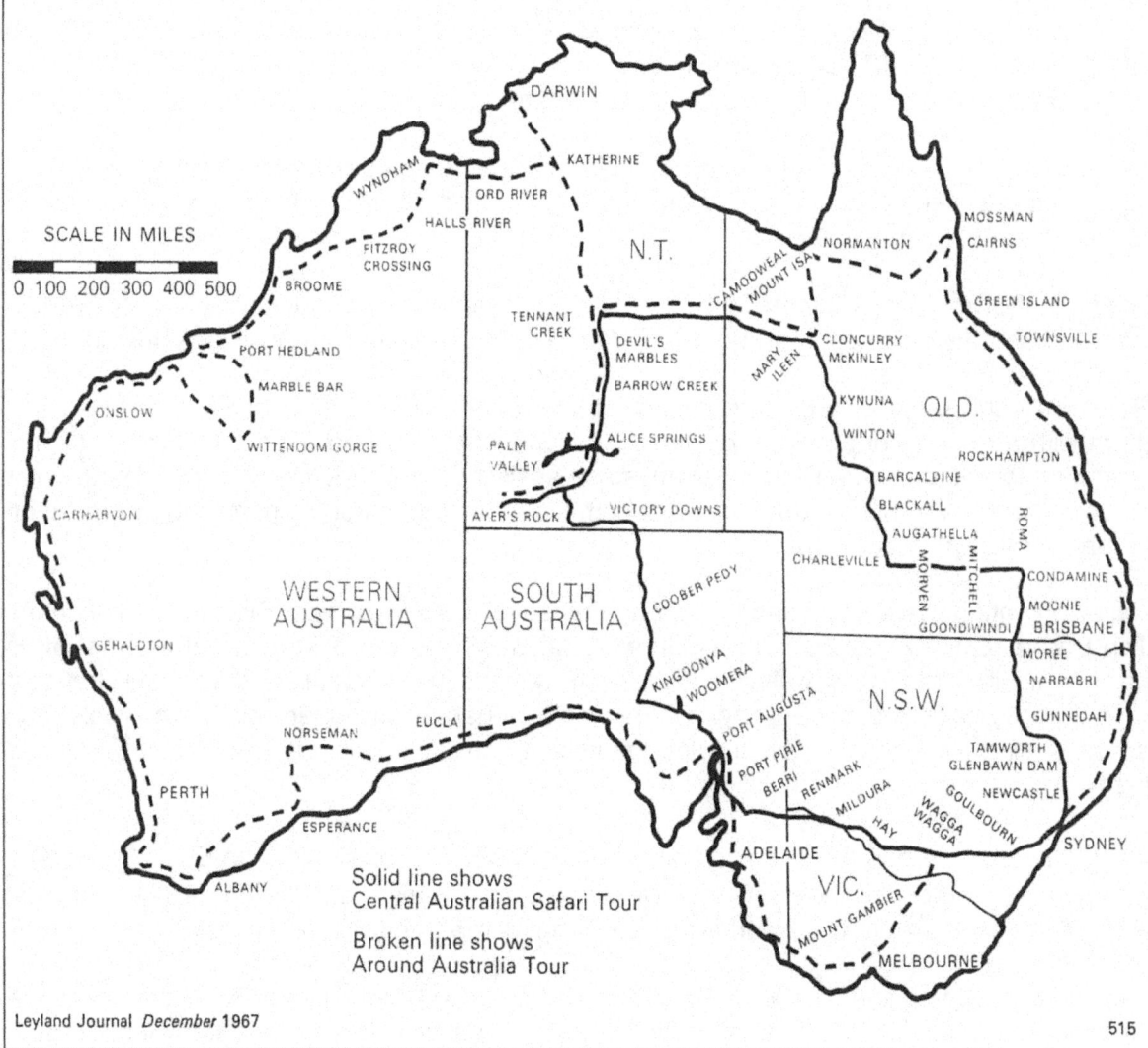

Solid line shows Central Australian Safari Tour

Broken line shows Around Australia Tour

In 1967 Rex Laws Redline Coaches was the biggest coachline in Australia, but in three years time it would be gone. There are many reasons why, but at least a contributing factor was the startup of Australian Pacific Coaches (later changed to Australian Pacific Tours, or A.P.T. in February 1967 in Melbourne by Geoff McGeary and Mayer Page. A.P.T. came to dominate coach touring and became the biggest operator in Australia.

When Redline collapsed we were made an offer by our old driver mate Brad Franklin to form a new company. Brad proposed a partnership, with our "proven ability and record" (nice one Brad) and his experience, he reckoned we would be unbeatable. We would raise the money between us to purchase the pick of Redline Coaches at the liquidation sale and Brad knew the best of the now out-of-work drivers.

He painted an appealing scenario and I suppose I get easily carried away, but Doreen asked is that really what we wanted, and it would probably mean sitting behind a desk fielding problems from broken down stranded drivers in the middle of nowhere.

Brad took it rather hard when, after quite a few planning sessions we pulled out of the idea, and it was something we never came to regret. He really believed that we could become a sort of three-person Reg Ansett, and you never know, he might have been proved right.

Brad then went on to work for Bill Boulton in Toowoomba who had resurrected the name Cobb & Co. Coaches. This company folded not long after Bill died in 1979. Cobb & Co. is an iconic name that was taken up and continued by Melbourne operator Bruce Nixon in 1982.

A number of ex-Redline drivers decided to start up their own companies. After all, they were highly experienced, and probably reckoned if Bill Hand could do it anyone could, but of course, none of them had Doreen.

Fred Carah, Derry Willis, Laurie McBeth and Ray Collins all tried their luck with only Freddie Carah lasting the distance. His Sunstate Coaches in Queensland is still successful today.

Redline's demise not only cleared the way for Australian Pacific's expansion, but supplied them with a number of experienced drivers. Because of their knowledge, Ern Pavilach and Valentine Mack became Driver Supervisors, assisting new drivers and writing up their commentaries. Val Mack went on to become one of the most respected authorities on outback tours and a good mate.

Val also wrote news articles and I read one that said, "Caught up with Bill and Doreen in the Top End recently where they, as usual, were taking three weeks to do what the rest of us have to do in less than a week". I think he may have been pointing up the fact that tour operators try to impress by fitting as many place names on itineraries as possible and embarrassing their drivers who are left insufficient time for their passengers to appreciate them.

1968 In 1968 we had a new head Ranger at Ayers Rock, Derek Roff, an Englishman who had been a member of the Kenya Police Force and a Park Ranger in the Tsavo National Park. The job was advertised worldwide, so Derek came with top credentials.

He was amazed to find that we supplied and maintained the Visitors Book on top of the Rock and immediately took over the responsibility. Derek was very different to Bob Gregory and knew how to project authority simply with his personality. He told me that he had been boxing champion in the Kenya Police, but gave up when beaten to the canvas by the Ugandan champion, a bloke called Idi Amin. He was also a top line photographer and produced the authoritive book *Ayers Rock & the Olgas*.

Derek wanted Aboriginal involvement and appointed an Aboriginal Ranger. Toby Naninga was "An Ayers Rock man", a very handsome bearded man with large luminous eyes. Toby took his job to be mainly standing at the foot of the climb in uniform, posing for photographs. Along with a uniform, Toby was given a caravan for accommodation. He told me all about this and the fact that he couldn't sleep in the caravan, although his dog took to it straight way and apparently considered it an up-market kennel, while Toby slept in a swag in the lee of it. He said it was like trying to sleep in a big tin box, and I can appreciate that, even I can feel claustrophobic in a small caravan and seem to hit my head on things all the time.

After a particularly gruelling session of standing for tourist photos, Toby told Derek this Ranger bit was a bit too hard and not worth the money. After all, the other old fellows like old Nipper got paid for just sitting around doing nothing all day. To them sit down money is a respectable source of income, whereas to us it's dole bludging.

Toby passed away a couple of years later and as he had always told me how he was a proper Ayers Rock man I asked Derek Roff if there would be a burial at the Rock, and Derek replied "No, they are taking him back to his proper country in South Australia".

One of the big disincentives for these people was the Aboriginal communal rule that all money and goods had to be shared out among relatives and those that work must keep those who don't. This works really well when dividing up, say a kangaroo, but doesn't leave much in a pay packet.

It reminds me of Wonga Way at Mt. Ebenezer Station who went into the camel ride business. In fact, he started the camel business by catching some wild camels and after taming them gave rides to the tourists. As this was a stopover on the road to the Rock, he sold a ride to pretty well everyone who came through. His staff consisted of a mob of kids who appeared to work for the fun of it, as their only payment seemed to be an occasional kick up the backside.

Ray Collins, one of the Redline drivers arranged with his boss to give Wonga Way a holiday in Sydney by taking him back on a camping trip. Redline got some good publicity as the *Daily Telegraph* did a story on Wonga Way's reaction to the City and Kings Cross, accompanied with photos. He could then regale his customers with stories about the Pink Pussycat and Manly ferries and tell them "Dis old Blackfella bin everywhere".

He told us that he was being pressured to share his income "But whitefellas don't do that and he was working like a whitefella", and he bought an old car. At this point Pastor Keleski let it be known that he would host a big Christmas get together at Areyonga. Wonga Way decided to attend, and seeing it was a party, reckoned that he would do the right thing and donate a boot load of grog. Apparently, it was a great party with fighting and other amusements and not at all what Keleski had in mind.

Quite suddenly old Wonga Way fell desperately ill and was rushed to Alice Springs hospital, where the doctors couldn't diagnose anything wrong with him. Arthur Liddle went in and sat with him for nearly a week before he passed away.

Arthur said that after many requests, Wonga Way still refused to share and finally he had been "sung" (It depends on who you speak to, and even whether you're told, if "pointed" or "sung"). It just goes to show the power of the mind - the doctors could do nothing, and Arthur felt bad about it as the old man had been a mate of his father.

1969 The Boeing Jumbo Jet or 747 flew an inaugural flight across the Atlantic in 1969, bringing in the era of affordable overseas travel, and while Neil Armstrong walked upon the moon Sundowners changed their itinerary on Centre tours to come home through Birdsville.

The highway across Queensland had simply become too crowded by the end of the 1960s. South from Mt. Isa to Boulia, Bedourie, Birdsville, Eulo to Bourke was certainly off the beaten track. While in Boulia, some of the group walked east along the road looking for the Min Min Lights, but the only lights they found were at the Golf Club.

Driving south from Boulia, we came to the Diamantina Shire Boundary fence and a most intimidating sign that explained that we were entering isolated country and to be sure we were carrying sufficient fuel and water.

I felt that the advice was a little late by this time, but it went on to say we should inform local stations of our progress, so we drove into the first station we saw. It was managed by a young couple, Sid and Rose who made a great fuss of the passengers and insisted on putting on the kettle and was the start of a regular happy morning tea stopover for a number of years. It only ended when Sid and Rose, in local parlance "split the sheets" and left.

Some years later when we were using the Nathan River Road between Borroloola and Roper Bar on a regular basis we ran into Sid and his new partner Heather (Sid must have had a thing about flower names). With his usual hospitality he insisted we camp alongside a spring fed stream on their property. This also continued for a number of years until Sid and Heather "split the sheets". I kept expecting to meet up with Sid somewhere with a partner called Marigold, but it has never happened.

Birdsville became a hit, they were simply the friendliest people, all part-Aboriginal, apart from Len the publican, Jim the cop, Bill the local Station owner, and of course the school teacher and the A.I.M. nurses. These people were house-proud, work-proud, and in no way seemed to see themselves as any different to any other Australians, which placed them apart from most "coloured" people across the country. After all this was the 1960s.

The kids adopted us and helped erect tents, blow up lilos and in general helped by getting in everyone's way. After tea half the population came and joined our campfire, where stories were told, and laughter heard well into the night.

The campground was rock hard clay that played havoc with tent pegs, but as we found on later trips, turned into a sort of glue when wet. There was a fence of sorts and gate that we were told had been erected to stop Murray's goats from eating the tents. The goats, there seemed to be hundreds of them, were of course the local dairy. The school teacher, sitting by our fire mentioned one night that he could use indoor games to keep the kids amused. We were deluged with games donated for Birdsville. Then later the Shire built a tennis court, only to find a shortage of racquets and balls, and the Sundowners again came to the rescue.

Jim Gurn the local cop didn't have much to do, which was OK as he looked pretty tired and ready for retirement, but before he went he had one brush with fame. There was a shoot-em-up bank robbery in Adelaide, which must have been the most exciting thing to happen there. Then a suspect car was identified passing through Marree and heading up the Birdsville track. Jim loaded his shotgun, made a thermos of coffee and a pile of sandwiches and parked across the track. The robbers must have been seriously incompetent as Jim led them back in handcuffs. So, Jim Gurn went out in a blaze of glory and newspaper headlines, and Birdsville got a new cop called Gordon Thomas.

If a TV show had been made about Birdsville, central casting would have chosen Gordon to play the cop. Tall, fair, with a wife and two kids, and everybody's friend. I was repairing a tyre one day and having trouble breaking it from the rim, so Gordon came down and fixed it by driving his police Toyota back and forth across it, and then helped me repair the tyre.

We were all sitting around the campfire one night when it became obvious that the kids were plotting something. Little Kenny Booth asked Doreen (they all knew that Doreen was a soft touch) "Is it right that next time you come through will be cracker night, and if so could you bring some crackers?" (Of course, Empire night, or cracker night is no more, which I think is a great shame as all Australians enjoyed the fun around a fire). So Gordon Thomas said he would organize the bonfire and one of our passengers was a close friend of a fireworks producer and could get a serious discount.

We finished up with a tea chest full of assorted fireworks and a case of thunder crackers that had been declared illegal in NSW and so were given free. Of course, with enough fire power to blow the back out of the coach we were forced to implement a smoking ban on this trip. Could this have been the first coach smoking ban in Australia?

Gordon had amassed wood for a huge bonfire and Doreen proposed that each of our passengers look after a plastic bucket of fireworks and ration them out. A little kid throwing a sparkler into a bucket of flowerpots caused a bit of drama. (Does anyone remember flowerpots?) We couldn't stop kids lighting skyrockets and throwing them at each other, and screaming "Jet propelled spears". There was a huge crowd as the word had gone around the Stations and simply everyone had come into town.

We were probably lucky in having only one small accident, when David Brook, the schoolboy son of Bill Brook, the local Station owner, threw a double bunger that blew a hole in Joannie Murray's jeans, but the AIM sisters quickly patched her up, and declared her all OK.

The following night we were listening to the ABC State News on the radio when they featured a full description of our cracker night and credited the item to the ABC Birdsville Correspondent, which created a mystery as no one seemed to know who this could be. But all up it was an historic occasion as cracker nights were banned in Queensland from that year forward. (The ban in NSW came in the previous year).

It must have been nearly twenty years later when walking up the street in Lyndhurst, South Australia, a pretty brown-skinned girl called out "Bill", and rushed up and threw her arms around me, it was Joannie Murray. She and her partner had taken over the local general store. This was typical of Birdsville kids, they all did well.

During the time we drove the Birdsville Track it was changed from a track into a well graded gravel road. So, it was a mystery on one trip to drive out of Marree and come to a sign in the middle of the road saying, "SA Police, Road Closed". I try to be law-abiding, so drove back to the Police Station to at least find the reason. There was a young constable on duty and our conversation went something like this. "What's the reason for the sign across the Track?" reply "Look I'm sorry but I don't really know, but I think it's something to do with rain up north".

Just then the sergeant came in, he pointed at the young cop and said "You, back to work", turned to me saying "And what do you want?". I repeated my question, and he became most upset. "I don't have to explain to anybody when I close the Track, now get out of here" he yelled. As I headed for the door he said, "Hey stop, look I hope you don't think I was being rude?". I assured him that it hadn't entered my head and kept going out the door quicksmart, then radioed Gordon Thomas in Birdsville for advice and told him the story. Gordon laughed his head off, and I won't quote him about SA cops. He explained that with local rain the track was under water near the border, but as we both knew there were wet weather detours around all the bad stretches. The passengers cheered when I drove around the sign and I fully expected the howl of police sirens that never eventuated. Up north the Track was certainly under water, but the wet weather detours worked perfectly.

On one trip we battled through heavy rain and on arrival at Birdsville were told by Gordon Thomas that we were stuck as all roads out were closed. With the campground turning to a sheet of brown muck, Bill Brook invited us to use the original Shire Hall. The kids helped everyone with their gear and Doreen topped up the urn to make tea and coffee, when young David Brook asked, "What's that thing?" pointing at the urn, then after studying the spec. plate said, "Don't plug it in, it will blow up the town". He explained that apart from the pub that had its own power supply, the town power was generated by the water pressure at the town bore. This was only enough for a limited number of lights and apparently didn't run to things like our urn.

David organized film nights for the town and had obtained the film *The Sundowners*, so a sheet was rigged in the main street and everyone sat on stools or chairs down the middle of the street. Apart from the sheet flapping in the wind, a major problem was that David got the reels mixed up and it was rather difficult to make much sense of it.

Finally, Gordon relented and let us have a go to get out, provided we kept in wireless contact. We slipped and slithered until finally couldn't lift out of a creek bed. I rolled the coach back and forth while everyone threw sticks and stones under the wheels as we tried to get traction. It was only when we were out that Doreen told how she had misjudged and her hand had been dragged under a wheel and had a finger nail ripped out, but she said nothing until we were back on high ground. She certainly took the prize of "Stoic" of the day and henceforth that creek became "Doreen's Fingernail Creek".

HOW A BUS TRIP BECAME A TRAIN RIDE At the Barker College Reunion in 1989 we received a copy of a letter from a boy on the 1969 Central Australian tour -

> "Dear Ian,
>
> I was glad to receive your letter and it brought back a flood of memories that caused me again to look at my album depicting some of the most exciting moments of the trip to Central Australia in 1969. What you didn't know about my climb up the Olgas was that I really thought that I would never get down again. I had visions of being the first tourist helicoptered off the top after spending days hugging those cliffs. Anyway all went well and further pictures showed us slugging through red mud near Oodnadatta. I remember how the Hand's got the bus up into a flat car and somehow our bus trip became a train ride. I notice one picture of the interior of the bus, talk about a band of callow youths. Another photo shows a group of guitar players around a camp fire, singing for the tenth time "Blowing in the Wind". There's a guy in the picture called Peter Garrett. Did he ever learn to sing and play that guitar. Regards, George Darling, Mining Engineer, Sudbury, Ont. Canada".

George's letter certainly brought back memories, and I don't know why, but Barker trips were always filled with drama, I can partly blame Ian Campbell for throwing me challenges. "We should try to get to Kings Canyon". Ian was unperturbed when I pointed out that it was four-wheel drive, knowing that a few bogs are essential to any true outback adventure trip, and anyway the boys would work like slaves to get us through.

George spoke of "slugging through red mud near Oodnadatta". It all started one morning on the way home after leaving Central Australia. We awoke to a pea soup fog that left everything dripping wet, and then after packing up, we were driving toward Oodna when a Toyota covered in mud waved us down, and the driver excitedly told us to turn back as the road ahead was flooded and we had no chance of getting through.

After he had gone I explained to everyone what was said, and as we hadn't seen a cloud in the sky for days there couldn't be much in it, and anyway people underrate the way tourist coaches can handle muddy roads. With only about 15km to go we ran into a completely flooded countryside and I couldn't hold a straight line, the tail would come around and we would crab along sideways, then I would fight to straighten up only to lose it the other way and crab again on the opposite lock. But the coach lived up to my claims and in teeming rain we finally pulled up at the Oodna Police Station.

The cops were amazed and told us that all roads were closed, and we probably wouldn't get out inside a week, but that the train line was still in operation. We got the OK to camp with the coach under cover in the huge old railway workshop building. (This was dismantled along with the train line a few years later, when the new train line was built much further to the west.)

With everyone settled in under cover I went back to the Station to ask about railing the coach out. This brought on a prolonged silence followed by a definite "NO", so Doreen and I went across to Pecanek's General Store to get some supplies. Pee was a Free Czech Fighter Pilot during World War II, and had his own Cessna aircraft. Jaroslav Pecanek and his wife Jindra had built an outback empire, they owned just about everything in Oodna apart from the Pub. As well as a fleet of road trains, they owned machinery for road making for the Department of Transport and oil rig roads in the Simpson Desert for Geo Surveys.

We told Pee that we had tried to have the coach railed out, but apparently this couldn't be done. "How much bribe did you offer?" he asked. "I would start at $20, otherwise you will be here forever" he added. (This was a fair bit of money in those days). We went back to the Station and asked the same question to the fellow in charge, at the same time sliding $20 across the counter. "No problem" he said, "tomorrow we will get you onto a flat top wagon and down to Marree".

Many years later, and after the train line had been ripped up, we battled into Oodna in similar circumstances and after checking with the Police, proceeded to Pecanek's store. I told Pee that the Police said all roads out were closed. "Vot vood the bloody police know, they haven't asked me yet" he replied, then added "we will fly in the aeroplane and find out". "Oh can I come too?" Doreen asked. "You are used to flying, Mrs. Hand?" Pee asked, and Doreen assured him that she was. "I ask because I have a fear of heights and never fly above 12 feet" Pee said, although this must have been his little joke. Just the same we never flew above 20 feet, mostly I assume to study the road condition.

The main road south of Marree was definitely out, covered in water for miles, but Pee turned back, and we followed the other road west through Copper Hills to the Stuart Highway. On some bad stretches Pee would turn the aircraft in a circle on one wingtip and point out the detours. "Now print these wet weather detours in your memory and don't forget them or you will be in big trouble, remember and you will be OK" he said.

To make a long and rather harrowing journey short, we made it through to Copper Hills Station and on to the Stuart Highway. This road passes through some of the most spectacular breakaway country in Australia and we included it on many later itineraries.

Pee was a truly great Australian and I was sad to learn that he finally lost his licence after suffering a heart attack. Not being able to fly nearly broke his heart so he sold up and he and Jindra retired down south in Adelaide.

Well, back to the Barker trip, we reported to Ian that we had arranged a rail journey to add a little variety to the trip.

With storms around we were totally safe in the huge old railway workshops and after tea on hearing a train coming I, and a couple of boys walked down to the station. It was a cattle train and no use to us, but we stayed to watch men getting in and prodding cattle up onto their feet as they had fallen down and could be trampled.

They dragged a cow off that appeared to have a broken leg and was giving birth. A couple of fellows dragged the calf out, and then the boss man arrived and asked what did they think they were doing. They said they were saving the calf, to which he replied, don't be stupid, we can't save them, drag them around the back and cut their throats. (I suppose this becomes a regular meat supply for railway barbecues.) I had to hold one of our boys up as he turned a shade of green and murmured "Gee Mr. Hand, this is sure different to Wynyard Station".

People in a truck were sharing our big shed and they came across and joined us for breakfast. The chap introduced himself, it was Tom Kruse, with his wife. Tom of course was the mailman in the old Shell film *Back of Beyond.*

Finally, our train arrived from Alice Springs, it was part passenger and part freight, with a number of empty flat top wagons, and pulled by two locos. It was broken up in the siding, and one loco backed up a flat top onto a spur siding. I was backing the coach up a ramp to drive on when a major panic erupted. The rail line had subsided and the loco slowly rolled over on its side in the mud. I have seen some hopeless situations, but this must rank as the ultimate, but one of the fettlers told us that they were capable of handling the problem. He said they were forever repairing washed out line and derailed trains, and the necessary equipment was on hand for the job.

We were not allowed onto the train and spent the night in our sleeping bags, lying on the damp ground around the railway station. The repair crews worked under flood lights all night and by morning the loco was sitting upright on a newly constructed piece of line.

After backing the coach on and seeing it chocked and tied down, I lined up with our crowd waiting to board the passenger cars, only to be told they were fully booked, even though they had been paid for. We were then herded into the guard's van (ripped-off again!). The guard's van was like a big steel box and was really a luggage compartment. There was a smaller box at the rear which was living quarters for the guard. We had had a quick breakfast, but believing meals were provided, or at least obtainable, hadn't brought much more than biscuits to eat. The coach was at one end of the train with everything and we were at the other with nothing. But as we explained, we were only going through to Marree, a three or four-hour journey (little did we know).

Not long into the journey, with everyone standing in groups talking (there being no seats) we heard a distinct bang in the distance. This was followed by another, then another, each getting louder. Then suddenly we were all thrown off our feet, some to the floor and some into the front bulkhead. Fortunately, no one was seriously injured, and we realized that the train had stopped, and the banging was caused by the slack being taken up by the couplings between the carriages. This became a regular occurrence and on the first bang we all sat on the floor and braced ourselves as we counted down. The countryside was flooded all around and the train moved slowly and stopped regularly while the crew got out and inspected the line ahead. This was going to be a long journey.

School boys don't react at all well to missing mealtimes and the guard, who was a young Aboriginal chap found some paper cups and made coffee for everyone. He then produced some biscuits. But a cup of coffee and a biscuit is starvation lunch for a schoolboy. At a stop along the way, our guard moved out and was replaced by a white fellow who locked himself in his box and never spoke to us, much less made coffee. Tea time came and went, supper time came and went and some of the kids looked like they were going to die, as this was the most deprived of food and drink most of them had ever been.

It was almost midnight when we pulled into Marree Station. This was the end of the line because with a change of gauge, everything had to be unloaded and reloaded on to another train through to Adelaide. Brilliant planning on somebody's part. The Station Master came out to meet the train and regaled us with stories of the floods. "The Premier has been flying over the north checking on stranded people, he'd be too lousy to drop them a cut lunch" he told us. I cut in and said, "Well speaking of food, we haven't had anything since breakfast". "Huh" he said and turned on his heel and walked off. Talk about the Premier.

We led the party across the road to the big old two storey hotel. It was in darkness like the rest of the town, but we hammered on the door. A rather irate woman answered and by the time we told our tale she was saying "Oh, those poor boys". She roused some staff and we were soon enjoying beans on toast and hot soup. They then arranged for us to set up camp in the local Shire Hall.

Marree was really just one big marshalling yard for the changeover of trains and Doreen and I were up at first light and down the yard to retrieve the coach. But there was no one else there. I might have been keen, but no one else was. Anyway, we got into the coach and got out some breakfast food and took it back for the boys. The workers arrived at morning tea time and then stopped to have morning tea.

The train was finally broken up and the coach was backed up to a platform. Nobody made any attempt to undo the ropes and chocks, so I got up and did it myself. I'm not in the habit of being a thief, but felt extremely hard done by the railway, so I collected the ropes and threw them into the side bin. The road from Marree down to Hawker, although only gravel was well maintained and apart from being a bit slidey in a couple of places was no problem.

The boys were supposed to keep diaries of their trip and of course Oodnadatta took up a great deal of diary space, and a map they were using advised that the name was Aboriginal for "The place where the mulga grows". This sounded like a load of old bollocks to me and thinking about it, remembered that "udna" was Pitjanjara for excrement (very expressive word I always thought), yellow in the local language is "vukata", so udnavukata could logically enough become Oodnadatta. This was later confirmed by an anthropologist who did work in the area, and I couldn't think of a more fitting name for the place in wet weather. I can envisage a mob of Aboriginals on walkabout floundering along in yellow mud muttering "Bloody udnavukata". One kid's diary entry regarding the train trip read "We can't recommend this form of travel".

One story leads to another, and this one had a spin off on our next Tasmanian tour. We were negotiating the Mt. Arrowsmith Road, where we had had cause to feature in the two local fish wraps on the Barker trip. A VW Beetle was stuck behind us and understandably I was driving very carefully, so I waved him past. He lost his tail on the greasy mud and went over the edge on the next bend. We stopped, and there was the VW way down in the gorge. Our people scrambled down and brought the driver back up, being the only occupant. While he appeared OK, he was quite incoherent. Then how to retrieve the VW? We tied the railways ropes together and they just made the right length. With the rope and the unstoppable power of the coach, we pulled the car back to the road, and found apart from some frontal damage it was driveable. I wonder if the driver realized how fortunate he was. Someone saw him go over, how many people would carry the length of railways rope? And how many vehicles would have the power to pull him back? No wonder our Barker trips were always sold out, with their diaries crammed with adventurous anecdotes when the kids returned, they automatically on- sold the next trip. In fact, it became so popular that Ian could pick and choose those he wished to take.

Boulia to Birdsville Track.
Sign at Diamantina Shire Boundary.

THE VICTORIAN NATURALISTS SOCIETY WATER & TED EGAN

Well that was the name of the crowd that had chartered us for the next trip - September 1969. Betty Maloney and Alec Blombery, well known botanists and regular Sundowners were organisers of the group, among whom we had four female doctors. It was planned that we would drive about 10,000 miles taking in highlights mainly across Western Australia, and although I didn't realize it at the time, we would be greeted by all sorts of influential people all along the way, this group really had a bit of clout.

Some of the highlights were exploring caves beneath the Nullabor, spending time with Mrs. Crocker, the noted wildlife artist at Balladonia Station, and driving into the Pinnacles Desert. Another memory is of stopping at the Python Pool south of Roebourne for photographs and then seeing what I took to be staid Victorian ladies throw off their clothes and leap into the pool in their under garments.

One hundred and thirty-two years before the first fleet made landfall at Botany Bay, Frances Pelseart was wrecked in the ship *Batavia* on the West Australian coast. Then twenty-seven years later it was the turn of the *Vergulde Draeck* or *Gilt Dragon*. Eight chests of gold and silver and two chests of assorted coin were brought ashore and buried. The captain sent a boat with seven men to Batavia in Java for help while sixty-four men and four women were left behind. Although help was finally sent they could find nothing of the place or the people, and probably more important, the gold.

How do I know all this? Well we met the expert. Harry Turner who just about made it his life's work to unravel the mystery. Harry had written a book on the subject and we all lined up for our autographed copies when our Victorians arranged to meet him. The idea was that Harry would lead in his Land Rover and we would follow into the area of coast opposite where the *Gilt Dragon* was wrecked.

The track was narrow and wound through columns of limestone, then Harry's Land Rover started climbing into sandhills. I made it over one sandhill, but lost speed and bogged on the next one. How Harry thought a tourist coach could handle this I will never know, and I had thought there would only be one sandhill, but we found ourselves in what people would call The Pinnacles Desert and much later Nambung National Park.

I hope and trust that Colin Simpson won't object to me quoting him. In 1971 Simpson wrote an excellent book called *The New Australia* published by Angus & Robertson. Quote -

> "No provision has been made for tourists to go to this quite extraordinary place, nor according to the W.A. Tourist Development Authority is it likely to be opened up for some considerable time. The Authority takes the view that it is being protected by its isolation."

Simpson was taken in by a Ranger from Yanchep National Park as a great favour to be shown the wonders of the Pinnancles Desert, and states -

> "When we arrived, the place was not at all desertedly awaiting the day when Rangers would be protectively present. In fact, there was a whole busload of people, camping types, who were gathering wood for a fire (until Yanchep's Ranger Ken Gibbes pounced on them). Their bus was sand bogged, but an attendant Land Rover was helping pull it out. One can hardly blame the tour

operator, he knew of this remarkable off-track scene, and how to get to it, and was showing it to his appreciative customers."

Spot on Colin, but it was certainly a coincidence the way we met, and naturally the girls would boil a billy and make a cuppa for the workers, and I didn't much like that Ranger fellow from Yanchep. He didn't even offer to help.

While trying to get out we slewed against a pinnacle and raked right along our stainless side panels. Another job when we get home, and although we shovelled plenty of sand, we didn't find the chests of gold.

We had better luck with many of the other places that had been arranged, like Dryandra State Forest, where the Rangers were catching and tagging the beautiful little creatures called numbats.

In Albany, after the rather unpleasant scene of seeing whales cut up at the Whaling Station, we proceeded to the Police Station where it was arranged that Inspector Spike Daniels would be our guide. The Victorians certainly knew the right people, who ever heard of the Police Inspector of the South Coast Land Division acting as a tour guide of the wildflower areas. Spike even brought a Sergeant along to help and proceeded to take us to all the top places to appreciate the masses of wild flowers. Along the way we heard that forty whales had beached themselves on Cheyenne Beach, and Spike immediately suggested that we drive out to see them. The beach approach was a little used track between sandhills and I was starting to have memories of the Pinnacles Desert. When we arrived at the beach we saw about twenty feet of soft sand ahead and then with the tide out about fifty feet of hand packed sand. Way down the beach on our left we could see a mass of black blobs in the distance stranded by the receding tide. It was a similar set up to the Eighty Mile beach, I gunned the coach across the soft sand and then from the tide line it was like driving on concrete.

I drove down among the stranded whales and that was my first mistake. The second was parking at right angles and facing out to sea while everyone got off. I tried to reverse but nothing happened. I jumped out to look and found the front wheels sinking into the sand. Well we had plenty of debogging equipment. I threw down boards and using our big specially made jacks, lifted the front wheels and got boards under them, then jumped backing and reversed and nothing happened, our back wheels had sunk.

The tide had changed and was coming back in and at this rate we were going to lose the coach. Doreen got out the twenty or so plastic buckets that we used on bush camps and told the people to form a chain and build a horseshoe wall of sand around the front of the coach. Spike Daniels meantime went off over the sandhills to look for help. By the time I had jacked up and boarded the rear wheels, the boards under the front had sunk and the front wheels had bogged again. Apart from all this, a most unpleasant thing started to happen. Whales need the flotation of water to support them and when stranded without that support, their insides start to collapse. All sorts of oily whale guts were lapping towards us on the incoming tide.

Then we were saved, Spike returned with some tough looking locals and an old four-wheel drive truck. They laughed at our predicament and said we would be out in a jiffy. They put a short towrope onto the coach, powered the truck and promptly sank into the sand.

This multiplied our problems by one hundred percent, now we couldn't move anyway with a bogged truck behind us.

Doreen's sand wall meanwhile was incredibly effective, it was becoming higher and wider all the time and like Holland we were safe behind it, for the time being at least.

Without being too boring, could I just mention some more problems, at this point it was getting dark and starting to rain.

We grabbed shovels and commenced digging out the four-wheel drive and Spike handed one to his Sergeant and told him to get stuck in. This was the only satisfying thing so far, to see a big fat Police Sergeant shoveling sand. Finally, we debogged the truck and as nicely as possible asked them to go home. Then working behind the sand wall and below water level, we jacked up the coach and finally drove it backwards onto the place where the truck had been bogged. Well, here we were stuck again, but safely above the tide level. By the time we debogged again there was only about six feet of firm sand left between the soft stuff and the sea. I drove like fury in the dark and rain with the sea and the soft sand tugging at us left and right up the beach. To get across onto the track I just pulled the wheel over and stamped on the accelerator, and the coach bucked and lurched and we were back on track.

The Caravan Park had a row of old tram cars fitted out as cabins, and although the rain had stopped, Doreen booked everyone into the trams rather than putting up tents. Both the coach and the people stunk of dead whales and we all needed a little bit of luxury.

Spike Daniels went on to some sort of fame when he was appointed Police Commissioner in Perth. The W.A. politicians were upset at alleged Police corruption in Perth. Fancy people suggesting such a thing. Like all politicians, they ducked and weaved and appointed Spike to sort out their problem. Perhaps they thought he was a hayseed from the bush, but Spike was a real straight shooter and set up inquiries that looked like upsetting some very influential people. The upshot was that he was relieved of his command and retired. It was alleged that he had suffered a nervous breakdown due to overwork. I don't know if it made much news in the Eastern States papers, although *The Bulletin* magazine ran a major digging dirt article about it. So, Spike returned back to Albany and his first love, talking about W.A. wildflowers.

The Victorians heaped high praise on us at the end of the trip and I didn't feel it was totally undeserved after scraping down the side of the coach in the Pinnacles and nearly losing it in the sea at Albany. Well, anyway we had made it our motto to give people more than they expect, and at all times do it cheerfully.

WATER One of our problems in those days was water, or rather lack of it. With constant bush camps and a large group of people, and city people at that, getting enough water required a bit of local knowledge.

For instance, in Coober Pedy water was both rationed and expensive, so to be independent, it paid to pick it up beforehand. Many station bores were barely drinkable, and some could cause tummy upsets which is not very good for coach travel.

On Ingomar Station south of Coober Pedy there were a cluster of bores with good drinking water feeding into large metal tanks, making this an ideal pick up point.

The sensible way to get water from these was to use a siphon hose, but on one trip we were in a hurry, so I climbed up onto the rim of a tank and plunged the plastic jerry cans into the water to fill them quickly. Then it was a matter of lifting the full jerry can over the rim and lowering it down to a couple of catchers, which was a pretty good balancing act.

When doing this I swung the jerry can down to the catchers and for some reason they had turned away, and being totally off balance I had to drop the jerry can. I tried to regain my balance, but my feet went from under me and I looped the loop and crashed down to the ground. I was knocked unconscious and woke up with a sea of faces staring down at me.

I found I couldn't breathe and it was as though a belt was tight around my chest and I felt dead certain I was going to die.

Our resident experts checked me over and pronounced no broken bones apart from maybe a rib or two. A lilo was blown up and I was carried into the coach and laid down the aisle, and Doreen took over the driving.

We were bumping along when the motor noise doubled and then tripled, and everything became dark as though we were under a shadow. Doreen yelled back "We're not driving on an airstrip, are we? and at the same time slammed on the brakes. My lilo slid down the aisle and I hit feet first into the front panel and looked up to see the back end of an aeroplane filling the windscreen. Regardless of the pain, I sat upright to see the plane hit his wheels on the road ahead, then lift into the air. He circled us then waggled his wings and flew off to the north. Of course, he was only playing leap frog and during the following years we were to fly with many outback characters and have seen them do similar things.

I remained in sick patient mode all the way to Alice Springs, although by this time I could stand and drag myself around. An old Aboriginal mate had remarked to me that "The hospital is now run by a mob of black fellas". This was brought home to me when Doreen drove me around to the old Alice Springs Hospital and I realised the only doctors that I saw were Indian. The Indian doctor explained that they couldn't carry out X-rays for the simple reason they had run out of X-ray technicians, so he asked me to walk the length of the room and back and I staggered up and back as requested. After some thought he decided that I had cracked a few ribs, so I asked should I have my chest bandaged, and he replied, "Good heavens no, you couldn't breathe properly."

He said the only treatment was to take it easy and lie down for a couple of weeks. I'm sure this was excellent advice and should have been followed, but duty called. I went back behind the wheel and by the time we arrived home felt comparatively normal.

TED EGAN Travelling on the Barkly Highway toward Mt. Isa we camped on a regular basis in a mulga forest and of an evening often listened to Radio Mt. Isa. One night they played a song that went on verse after verse about characters of the Northern Territory. It was a bloke called Ted Egan, and the song was called "The Bloody Good Drinkers of the Northern Territory". Then in a year or so everybody seemed to be playing Ted Egan songs. We got to know Ted rather well, in fact we had him down home in Sydney one day, and we seem to meet in the oddest places all round Australia.

We tend to marvel over coincidences, but the truth is that the more people you get to know, the more they happen.

Doreen wanted to see a show called *Bran nu Day* at the Riverside Theatre, Parramatta, so we drove over one night and parked in a side street. Parked in front of us was a Landcruiser with N.T. plates and as we walked past I saw that the headlights had been left on. (It was just on dusk).

In the foyer although it was getting dark they hadn't bothered turning on the lights, and being early we sat down on chairs in an alcove. A couple were sitting across from us and in the gloom I could just make out that under his jacket the fellow was wearing a Barrow Creek Pub "T" shirt. So, I called out "You from the Territory mate", when he answered "Yeah" I said "I reckon you have left your lights on." He stood up and the light caught his face and I saw it was Ted. He and his partner Nerys were on their way to the Tamworth Festival and had dropped in to see the show on the way.

I mainly mention Ted Egan at this point because if we are going to talk on about things in the Territory, it is almost inevitable that some reference to Ted or one of his songs will crop up.

Ted had a most wonderful song writing ability. Sitting in our living room at North Ryde one day he told us he was going to the Birdsville Races and as he had never been there would we give him some background. He asked who had won the most times and I said, "Lyle Morton". Ted hummed "Lyle Morton's a cert to win the bracelet". T hen who's the best tryer, and I said, "Bill Brook" and he continued, "Bill Brook's mare will be trying hard". T hen who's the publican and I said, "Taffy Nicholls", and he went on "We'll all meet in Taffy's Bar". Seemingly out of thin air he put a tune to it all and Ted had a beautiful song.

In his book *Penelope Bungles to Broome,* Tim Bowden writes "Ros and I accompanied Ted to the Birdsville Races and recorded (in the bar) tracks for an LP with Ted on his Fosterfone and with me adding a scratch ukulele accompaniment. Needless to say, some professional musicians augmented this fairly basic effort later, but to our surprise *The Bush Races* put out by R.C.A did rather well." The locals told us that Ted was a great hit singing in the bar.

Late 2003 Ted Egan was appointed Administrator of the Northern Territory (the equivalent of State Governor). Not bad for a Republican, and I bet Ted opened a bottle and threw away the cork.

1984. Ted Egan, his partner Nerys, with Bill and Doreen, Alice Springs.

1970 NEW DENNING COACH V6 53GM
GUNBARREL
TANAMI & DAVE SIMPSON

With Alan Denning building us a new coach we were able to use American technology, Detroit diesel motor, Allison transmission, Rockwell axles etc.

It's not that I dislike the Brits, fine people of course, excellent cricketers, and wonderful cooks, it's just that automotive design had moved on and left them trailing behind.

Another feature that had become available was the "no spin" diff that locks up and drives both back wheels in difficult traction conditions. The "no spin" diff mob asked for a photo of the coach and I later gave them one of it plastered in mud (the passengers couldn't even see out the windows) that they featured in their advertising for a number of years.

Later with this coach we fitted a third axle or what is called a lazy axle and made up a form of tank tread that fitted over the drive wheels and back over the lazy wheels. We could then have a half track vehicle for use in mud or sand.

Of course, this idea is not new, and I got the idea from a snow vehicle built by Sir Edmund Hillary in a museum in New Zealand. Tank treads of course go back much further than that, and not many people realise that the tank was an Australian invention.

As a young fellow working in outback Western Australia, Lancelot De Mole was constantly getting bogged, and he came up with the idea of laying a road ahead and rolling over it, something that came to be called a tank tread.

At the outbreak of the First World War De Mole took a model of his tank to England and showed it to the British War Office.

In 1916 the British Army introduced De Mole's tank, but gave credit to British inventors and his claims for a reward were refused. When he persisted, he was paid all expenses and granted an honorary army rank. The Canberra War Memorial has a model of his tank.

"Tank" seems an odd term for these vehicles, and came about due to the need for security. The surprise factor in their initial use was critical and their intended purpose kept secret. Keeping up a supply of clean water to the armies in the trenches was a well-known problem, so at all times, right from their manufacture they were referred to as mobile water tanks. This subterfuge fitted in nicely with their appearance.

The Leyland we on-sold to Centralian Tours in Melbourne, then years later they sold it to Tiwa Tours in Alice Springs. Tiwa was nothing to do with tours, it was an Aboriginal run bus service between outlying settlements and Alice Springs. They only had two coaches, ours and the other bought from Derry Willis. Derry had been an early Redline driver who went out and bought his own coach. Derry became a mate, but for a number of reasons he sold up and went into a different business.

He later married a pretty girl from the Philippines and invited us to join them on a holiday in the Philippines and spend time with his in-laws.

One day in Alice Springs I was chatting with Terry, the young Aboriginal driver of our old coach when we were both assailed by a dreadful stench. Terry opened the side bin and there was haunch of kangaroo covered in maggots. He laughed and said, "Looks like one of the boys forgot his lunch".

Tiwa Tours finally folded, a Government grant ran out or something and the coach was bought by Greville Cawood. Greville owned a chalet at Ayers Rock and for a number of years used it to run tourists around the Rock and out to the Olgas.

The new Denning coach might have stretched our finances, but after the Leyand it was simply brilliant. It had more power, better ride and handling, amazing reliability, and cut down travel time on an average day by at least one hour. Most people thought we were mad to specify an automatic gear box, but this proved to be so superior and reliable that I would never consider a mechanical box again. For one thing it did away with the clutch which was an ongoing weakness with the Leyland. It has taken a long time but today the majority of Public Transport vehicles are automatic.

GUN BARREL The 1960s was a time of a number of small tour operators trying to outdo each other in offering adventure tours into ever more inaccessible places. They prided themselves in telling others "I've been here, or I've been there", and there was quite a lot of competitive spirit in the business. Some, Bill King was one, built bus bodies on ex-army Bedford four-wheel drives, but we coach people considered that they were only selling an image as they rarely ventured off the beaten track. They were slow and top heavy, and we saw two that had rolled over.

We had people like Bill Kenniwell, Kevin Bryant, Eric Blizzard and Colin Jacks all trying to be first in taking people into more interesting and isolated places. Colin Jacks started in 1960 with a bus body built on an International truck chassis, and operated out of Broken Hill under the name West Darling Tours. He was something of a star and liked to impress the rest of us with his exploits. He was well known for getting back days late, either due to breakdown, bogging or simply getting lost.

I was highly impressed when Colin told me that he taken a party across Western Australia from Ayers Rock using Len Beadell's so called Gunbarrel Highway. Also, we found later that Eric Blizzard had also been through the other way, coming from the west. Sadly, we lost a valued friend when Colin passed away in 1975 at the age of 49.

Some of the hazards that Colin listed were sections of the track washed away, largely because Beadell made it straight instead of following contours, there were lengthy detours and detours on detours, then it was not sign posted, and you had to carry enough fuel for one thousand miles as there was no guarantee of obtaining fuel at Warburton Mission. Also, rather predictably Colin at one stage got lost.

Once the Birdsville Track was a challenge, but this was going to be the ultimate, so we scheduled it as a tour in 1970.

Curtin Springs had the most powerful radio transmitter with the call sign BRR or Double Romeo and it was left switched on twenty-four hours a day and Dawn Severin was known far and wide as the "Voice of the North". Dawn probably saved lives in the early days by relaying messages from stranded people who didn't have enough power to get through to the Flying Doctor Base VJD Alice Springs. We arranged with Dawn a twice-daily "sked" (as it was called) as a form of insurance.

There was no problem until the Hull River near the cave where Lasseter died. It was wide and sandy, and it was obvious that vehicles had been bogged and cut up the track. A big asset in these circumstances is that a heavy tourist coach takes a lot of stopping and I gunned it through at speed without any problem.

On arriving at the recently built Aboriginal Settlement of Docker River we found an old mate was Superintendent. David Hewitt was an adventurous type of bloke who after a few years at Docker went on to run La Grange Mission south of Broome. In later years he became obsessed about exploring the Canning Stock Route and became the top authority cum guide on the area. At one time we considered tackling the Canning with David's help, but it required first a survey trip and we never did find the time. David's wife Margaret manned the radio at Docker which gave us another back up "sked".

Then it was onto Giles. On approaching Giles there were signs advising "Keep Out Commonwealth Property". This was a rocket tracking station, and like Woomera and Talgarno on the N.W. coast could only be entered with permission from Canberra. It was here that advice from that wily old fox Colin Jacks became valuable. "Nobody in desert country will refuse you water" he said, "when they stop you simply ask to be able to fill your water tanks, they can't refuse."

Once on the base the staff came out to talk to the people and of course found they had places and things in common. These fellows were lonely, they worked 6 months on at a time. It wasn't long before we were invited into the Canteen, and then would we like showers. There was only one thing, no photos as we weren't supposed to be there.

They explained that the old section of the Gunbarrel road due to the intense drought of the early sixties had virtually disappeared under drift sand from the Gibson Desert. It was advised that we go due south to the Tompkinson Range, passing Mt. Daisy Bates on our left, then due west across the edge of the Great Victoria Desert to Warburton. This agreed with what Ozzie Andrews had told us and was the way he went.

On reaching the Tompkinson Range the track came to a "T" and we took the RH fork to the west. On subsequent trips we have taken the LH track to the area called Wingellina (say with a hard G). This was a source of chrysoprase, a cryptocristaline green rock.

On old time woomeras the spear sharpening blades set into the handle was as often or not a piece of polished chrysoprase, and sometimes wandering Aboriginal groups would trade it with us, so it was of great interest when we found the source. It appears that the chrysoprase is formed due to underlying nickel deposits, so someday we might hear more about it, although it is well within Aboriginal lands now.

Much further west at the water catchment sheets of granite called Giles Tank we found Ozzie Andrews abandoned DeSoto car, and as it looked intact I was tempted to run jumper leads to see if it would start, but decided not to waste time as Ozzie had assured us that the motor was shot.

Warburton Mission was run by an obscure religious order and was a pitiful looking dump, however we were able to refuel and ease the worry of running short.

On this trip we simply took the easy route and drove through to the old mining town of Laverton, although on later trips apparently suffering from some form of masochism we used the much longer route up to Mt. Beadell to Carnegie and coming out at the old mining town of Wiluna. In later years at Wiluna we were able to buy cases of the finest navel oranges that were produced by an Aboriginal co-operative. It was obvious that with water the red desert soils could just about feed the world. Another Aboriginal venture was an Emu farm that was set up to produce all manner of emu products, oils, leather, meat and carved eggs. There seemed to be quite a turnover of white advisers that reminded me of our old friend the Catholic nun who insisted that white staff belonged to the three "M"s, the Missionaries, the Mercenaries, and the Misfits.

Sometimes we were welcome, and the operation explained in detail, then the tourists were relieved of a good deal of money as they bought the products on sale. Then under different staff we could be treated almost with disdain as if whitefella tourists had no right looking into their blackfellas business.

With the demise of the Woomera Rocket Range the tracking stations were closed down, and as Giles had also supplied weather reports to the Met. service, this would leave a big hole in their coverage, so the Meteorology Department stepped in and took the station over. This meant that the high security that was supposed to be maintained was no longer necessary and the Met. people opened the base to travellers passing through. So instead of having to dream up some pretext to gain entrance, we found that we were welcomed, and tours of the base were arranged.

These six-week western desert trips became very popular and we started doing them on a regular basis, some turning south on the West Coast (Gunbarrel South Trips) and others going up through Wiluna, Broome and the Kimberleys (Gunbarrel North Trips).

To try and repay Arthur and Bess Liddle at Angas Downs for their wonderful hospitality we invited them to join us on our 1973 Gunbarrel North trip. We had scheduled this tour to return to Alice Springs via the Tanami Track for the first time. Unfortunately, Bess declined, and Arthur wouldn't come without her. Then he made a suggestion, "I'll bet young Timmie Lander would love to go. You know the only river in the Tanami Desert is called after his grandfather". Tim jumped at the chance. To make a happy trip Doreen always tried to match people with similar likes to sit together, so she planned to sit Tim with John Waugh, a young grazier from the Gundagai district. John travelled with us regularly and as a pleasant and extremely practical bloke was a great asset on trips.

It is very interesting to see a trip from a passengers' point of view and Jan Trompp has kindly allowed me to reproduce some of her diary of the 1973 Gunbarrel North trip. Jan and her husband Bill were a romance on one of the first outback trips, became regular Sundowners and we count them still amongst our best friends.

Jan writes in great detail, so I've taken the liberty of editing out much everyday detail and added some comment in brackets. Jan and Bill of course were familiar with the trip as far as the Rock, so we will start her diary on leaving the Rock. She refers to our beautiful coach as "Suzie" and even the "Buggy", but we remain friends.

TO DOCKER RIVER   Sunday 3rd June, 1973

It was fairly cold as we went to the "Ininti" Aboriginal store which had promised to open early on this Sunday, for our passengers to buy provisions for our next five days journey through virtually uninhabited desert, except for a couple of Aborigine Reserves which are "off limits". The set of rules, a mile long, even stated that we were not to deviate any more than two chains off the road.

Again we found ourselves on the road past the Olgas to the sign pointing off the right - Docker River 124 in the middle of Aboriginal Reserve. To our left, far distant, was the Mann Ranges. The soft, red, sandy road wound through spinifex, desert oak and rather dead looking poplars, grevillea and occasional desert kurrajong or acacia, then the country changed dramatically for a while to stark, dead trees. In no time the pinkish-purple, most beautiful Petermann Ranges came into view as we wound through the low bluish coloured spinning mallee.

Near the Hull river we stopped at Lasseter's Cave where Bob Buck found his body. It was certainly nothing like I would have imagined. I'd had a mental picture of an arid desert, a cruel country, but nothing save the Flinders Ranges could even compare with the beauty of this unforgettable area of mountains, rivers and gum trees with myriads of birds. As Harry Brumby would tell us later, the Petermanns was "plenty good country".

We drove parallel to the Hull River for some time and the bird life was plentiful. A spectacular spot, and signposted beautifully was Kikinkura or Ruined Ramparts, named by Giles in 1874. This was a remarkable cut in the Petermanns.

Soon we crossed Docker River and entered the Native community where some sat at the doors of their homes or gunyas by little fires. Around the administration buildings the natives came to greet us and wave. David Hewitt came to meet us with his unchanging smile and sought his number one man Harry Brumby. (We knew Harry from the old days as he was an ex-Angas Downs man. B.H.)

Harry was one of the leaders of his people and David asked if he wished to show us around the area, which Harry proudly did, but we had a problem understanding him. We saw the hospital and mobile school rooms. Old Harry's dog would faithfully follow, then curl in a ball and sleep at his feet and one of us would usually fall over him. I brought Harry's attention to his sleepy dog on a couple of occasions, then on returning to the coach someone discovered their bread had been dragged from the front seat and Harry immediately started yelling frantically and throwing rocks at his poor hound who slunk away blinking his eyes. I stopped Harry, "No Harry, him too sleepy dog". At this old Harry grabbed his gut and spun in a half circle in fits of laughter. David then asked Harry (not told him) if he'd care to show us the water holes some distance away called Wruuru. A really bumpy trip followed with half the kids from the camp in the coach and Harry Brumby as well.

At night, after tea, during which we had to keep the Native's dogs at bay, we wandered over to view and buy the artifacts for sale, then David showed slides in the hall of parts of the area as well as a trip he'd done down part of the Canning Stock Route and the building of the Ininti store at Ayers Rock were we'd all bought our food a couple of days ago. It was fairly cold and we rugged ourselves up against the wind. Of course, we didn't know at the time, but the dogs were getting at some of the gear in our tents, scattering it all over the country.

TO GILES WEATHER STATION   Monday 4th June, 1973

The Docker River store, partly made by the natives of natural stone, opened after breakfast and while we wandered around, the men were invited over for strictly "man's talk" by Harry Brumby. The boys returned after some time sheepishly and carrying well covered, sacred Tjurunga stones on which we girls must never look. Soon after we were saying farewell to David and Margaret, Harry and the others and in a few minutes were out on our windy, red dusty road.

On crossing Rebecca Creek, on which Bill said they'd camped on a previous trip, they'd nearly perished in the heat and today, here we were nearly perishing of cold as a film of cloud covered the whole sky. From Rebecca Creek we took to the part of the Gunbarrel Highway which Len Beadell pushed through and thankfully made "straight".

After a quick morning tea we passed Beadell's survey marker on the roadside with Gill Pinnacle, Kutjuntri, behind it in the distance. Our straight, well graded red road sped through ever changing country, but good country with plenty of vegetation and really the reverse of what I'd expected of this area. We crossed Giles Creek which was just sand, and sped along marveling that nothing had been done to the road since 1960, yet it was still rather good and we were cutting 62 mph.

Around lunch time we were nearing Giles Weather Station and saw Natives waving from nearby. It was still overcast and since we'd already taken on water supplies at Docker River, the only excuse to go in to this very "restricted area" was to find out the weather forecast. David Hewitt had given us a letter of introduction of the finest quality in case we should meet any objections, but it turned out that all the "Warning". "No Entry" signs for the last couple of miles were only there to be photographed and we were made more than welcome by the handful of lonely chaps manning the weather station. The whole place was swarming with Zebra Finches, then Aborigines with their dogs and artifacts.

Mike, the head man, showed us a beaut. green lawn on which we could have lunch and No. 23 cabin was made available for a shower which we promptly put to use, and No. 24, the toilet. The boys then opened the bar where beer or spirits could be purchased, and coffee was extended to all from the cook in the adjoining room. There was nothing these fellows couldn't supply - right down to a pile of postage stamps.

Nearby was a pool-room and all rooms were inspirational with pictures of nude girls gracing the walls. Mike showed us over the many rooms containing the weather recording equipment and explained their duties in fine details. Ian was photographed sending off the afternoon weather recording balloon, which would reach a height of 60,000ft. It seared straight up, carrying beneath it, a reflector which could be followed by the radar dish. Then to top off all the excitement, the grader which Len Beadell had driven to make the Gunbarrel Highway was driven from its hanger and put through its paces for all our eager photographers. (I was intrigued by ants rushing around on the ground as though preparing for the great flood and asked Mike for his forecast about the possibility of more rain. He assured me the rain was finished. In future I'll back the ants. B.H.)

At 2 pm we waved the men of Giles a hearty farewell and I'll think about them every time we get a completely wrong weather forecast back home. In red, sandy country we had afternoon tea amongst a garden of wild flowers which had everyone excited, not just our botanists.

The road had been excellent, but suddenly deep sand covered the road and we all piled out while Bill drove the "buggy" through but only got 100 yds. before going down. We radioed Docker River as instructed to do till we reached civilization, then the boys worked hard with planks and spades, then applied the "half track" and another 100 yds. was gained. In the end, everyone shared in carrying all the ports from the side bins. Looking back at all the people staggering along with ports in the sand was a real sight, but too late to take movies of the exodus.

Doreen called a halt at the most likely spot on a detour road close beside the main road, and here we gathered wood, made a great fire, and waited for the sound of an engine in the dark. After some time the "buggy" ploughed through the rough stuff, took to the side track and rejoined us at the fire, closely followed by the triumphant de-bogging team of men, cheered on by the girls.

We had some fun around the fire after tea recalling the rigid rule that we weren't to deviate further than a chain off the road - and here we sat by the fire at least two chains off with our tents even further. The night wasn't cold and the stars came out.

GILES TANK & WARBURTON Tuesday 5th June, 1973

A pretty sunrise lasting only a minute greeted us but the weather was similar to the day before, cloudy with a nip in the air. Before starting out, Doreen tried, amongst radio static, to get contact with Docker River. Doreen told Margaret we were OK and soon were out of the sandy zone and passing Mt. Fanny on the right, Mt. Daisy Bates on the left. At 8.15 we turned off in the direction of Laverton and Warburton Reserve. A signpost loomed up "Blackstone" but all there was we could see was an old tin hut from an abandoned copper mine. "Warburton 134" and Docker River 133". The ground was red, covered with fine black pebbles from the nearby Blackstone Ranges.

The road became more horrifying at every bend, and there were thousands. It was plain to see that many had been bogged after wet weather where creeks cut across the poor excuse for a road. With Doreen studying the meridians on the map, we eventually, after a little back-tracking, located the unused track into Fort Mueller where Giles had made camp and described in his journals. A little side road had been blocked by limbs of trees dragged across, these we removed and drove many chains to a great rocky, forbidding looking place - piles of marble like boulders surrounding creeks and gullies and certainly a perfect place for ambush as Giles had nervously recorded.

We too felt nervous in case we should be found in here and our permit confiscated. It was a most interesting place, though inhospitable and some of the more prominent boulders were covered with Native paintings and rather well kept, excepting one spot where vandals had written names, as usual. Most of us exploring, were spread out near and far when we held our breath at the sound of an approaching vehicle. None other than the Ranger, a Native from Warburton appeared with another two natives, and immediately confronted our helpless driver. They had noticed where we had back-tracked, then removed the barricade on the little road and defiantly used this road. Bill hastily covered "We thought they were covering the road so that nobody would get trapped in a bog or something up the road." A little more parleying and Bill mentioned a few other Native friends in Central Australia and told him the good time old Harry Brumby had shown us and it did the trick, for Harry was the Ranger's uncle, and he had helped build the tiny road through the Gorge along which Harry had taken us on the way to the waterholes. (I asked him how he knew we were there, and he looked at me as though I was mad, and said "Do you think it's hard to track that thing", pointing to the coach. B.H.) He told us we must go, so we reluctantly obeyed after morning tea and retraced our tracks, covering the entrance to the side road with branches and trying to wipe out the wheel marks so that even "Boney" couldn't track us.

It began raining and flocks of Budgies flew from our path which led to Winburn Rocks (also known as Giles Tank. B.H.) a pile of giant red boulders holding a water soak which Giles and later Sir John Forrest used for water supply and both left their mark. It was a grand place which overlooked miles of flat country and here we had lunch and seat-change.

As soon as we'd left the mountains, the road improved greatly and we could make up time. Old wurlies or gunyas appeared often just off the roadside. A car full of Aborigines waved as they passed, then soon we were crossing the airfield and were within sight of the buildings of Warburton. Hundreds of old wrecked cars littered the surrounding paddocks. The Mission was no longer a church Mission and had been taken over by the Federal Government, so we met with none of the nastiness we were preparing for, instead, we were even allowed to talk to the natives and were shown into their artifacts store for souvenirs to stow on the luggage rack. On the inside walls were extensive plans for the new buildings and work had already begun. Before the afternoon had passed, we were gassing up and doing some shopping at the most untidy and badly cared for store I've ever been into. Sacks of flour had spilt over in the corner and rats and mice droppings were everywhere. Everything in the shop was covered in dust.

Many of the homes built recently for the natives were made from the local red stone and looked exceptionally good. Since the plane had not arrived to receive the mail, and now wouldn't do so for a couple of weeks, we were given charge of the mail to carry on to Laverton.

GREAT VICTORIA DESERT   Wednesday 6th June, 1973

After a night of almost continual rain, it was ghastly, yet funny to pop our heads out of the tent. There was no point in our getting out early as our gear seemed to be still dry, but later we joined the other unfortunates, gathered round a bonzer fire Alec Blombery had luckily got started. Many tents were down or floating, most people's gear wet, but everyone made the most of it with a grin on their face and grabbed breakfast on the run - perhaps a cup of soup taken under the tarpaulin which repeatedly threw buckets full of water down if touched in the wrong place.

Bill ran around with buckets all morning filling the jerrycans to end water rations. Although it continued to rain, the Sundowners grouped round the roaring fire and somehow managed to get the gear dried, laughing and chatting and helping each other. Ma (Doreen's mother) remarked later, "I didn't hear a cross word from anybody".

Things were just beginning to dry when another belt of rain would send us rushing for cover. Our road was a rushing river and a great target for the movie camera, racing and foaming round the bend.

We were astounded to hear the engine of a vehicle (perhaps of a speedboat) coming from the direction we were heading and the driver of the semi, loaded with building equipment for Warburton, announced that he'd not had any real bad spots and was carrying about the same weight as we, so at least, things looked hopeful. It was announced that we'd get moving after lunch! All the awful, wet gear was stowed away and we hit out, all chatting madly. The road, for the most part seemed fairly hard underneath and we ploughed through great lakes on the road, sending water way up past our windows like a hydro-foil.

The thrill of our trip was a stretch of water about one hundred yards long and fairly deep. Here we stopped, let the photographers out, then Bill sped the buggy through the muddy water, geysering up over each side. Many of our folk were sprayed with muddy water! This sort of thing happened repeatedly and we were made to walk often, but this we all enjoyed. Ducks were swimming on our road and would flush as we approached.

The Nursing Sister at Warburton had given us directions to some permanent water holes, the first of which we found without any trouble. Gahnda Waterhole was most remarkable, deep, surrounded by caves in depressions. Here we had afternoon tea as the sun tried to shine, then we took off again to search for yet another Hole described by the Sister. Pink everlasting daisies were already welcoming the feeble sun. We chatted with the driver of a Landrover, who said the Police at Laverton had already closed the road to Leonora.

Again, the sky had been building up its blackest clouds as we made our way cautiously along the road - or was it a river. It was at Muggan Waterhole near the 27th Parallel we pulled in to camp, to dry wet gear and so some washing since water was no longer a problem. The clouds moved inland during the night, it only showered once.

GREAT VICTORIA DESERT & COSMO NEWBERY Thursday 7th June, 1973

The mud was literally shovelled out of the coach and water from the Muggan Waterhole generously thrown over the filthy windows. The waterholes were strange, surrounded by caves, the roofs of which had been blackened by continual fires lit within by natives using these remarkable desert waterholes.

Our window cleaning was in vain as we were hardly along the road when muddy lakes of great distance had to be forded.

Morning tea was at Terhan Waterhole which was just off the road and about five feet deep. We inspected this in the sun with a cold chilling wind. After a half mile walk up the road we came to the Blowhole, down which Tim Lander and Bill Hand climbed to find protruding from the mud walls, some leg bones of either a Native or a kangaroo.

The bus had to become a hydro-foil at times where the roads were flooded but none presented any difficulties. Ten more floods and we reached Beegull Waterholes where we had lunch with flocks of Lovebirds dive-bombing us. The many caves around the group of waterholes were art galleries, frescoed by ancient Aborigine. From the top of the hill one could see LakeThrossel.

We met two Aboriginal men and gave them a lift some twenty miles into the mission of Cosmo Newberry, our first civilization for some days. It was a funny place with a store, court, gas station and a couple of homes with fowls running about. All this was run by an undenominational mission where the Aborigines worked with cattle and sheep. As well, some of the old-aged live here. The man in the store was most helpful, (he'd not received wages for 25 years) and recommended we make camp in a safe spot off the bad road, about twelve miles out, but at the same time, promised some difficult spots for the morrow.

We all dug trenches around tents just in case and made perfect radio contact to Docker River for the last time. A few who remained around the fire at night, made a presentation to poor John Waugh - a toilet roll to replace his own which had been soaked two days ago and abandoned this morning.

TO LAVERTON & LEONORA   Friday 8th June, 1973

The darned rain picked on us at dawn - just enough to wet the tents and tarpaulin and harass the breakfast makers. Only a few miles from camp, a great lake loomed up, half covering the road. We drove straight through, puddling mud all over us. We almost ran into a roo and the country was very lush and green. A stationary car on the road provided speculation and mystery. It had probably been there before the big rains, and there were no tyre tracks and certainly no occupants, although a couple of spent fires lay nearby, so we presume the owners to be Natives.

We passed the "Laverton 8" turnoff and met a truck driver, who on being questioned, wasn't sure if the Laverton-Leonora road had been reopened. Soon we hit the bitumen near the turnoff to Windarra where Poseidon Nickel Mine is situated, at this turnoff was an old smelter and deserted homestead.

In minutes we were in Laverton, which had had rain for two weeks and on checking at the Police Station, found the road for the next thirty miles was open, but the rest was "clay country" in which many vehicles were already hopelessly bogged. The police radioed Leonara while we awaited their advice - a very bad stretch 26 miles this side of Leonora. We hung around, bought provisions and went over to the Coach House Cafe where we bought all the hot pies. They had to restock with frozen pies which the lady admitted had just got through on a big semi-trailer. We conveyed the message to Bill Hand who searched out the semi's driver, then reported to the Police who gave their permission to go. We unloaded the Warburton mail and it began raining again as we approached the signs plastered right across the road "Road Closed". The Laverton area had already had twenty inches of rain in the last two months and four inches in the last week and all W.A. and N.T. were experiencing history-making rains.

We were back on the dirt road again and heading into the clay (horror) areas. At 11.15am we had a wee-stop-of-a-tree-stop then carried on to the inevitable bog. It looked bad, so my Bill always in shorts, waded through and said the bottom had been recently paved with bricks. A vacant grader standing nearby had possibly just finished this work - and just in time, so things seemed right. Off we went, everybody bracing themselves against the impact... fizzer - we breezed through and the whole coach was roaring with laughter - its passengers too! Betty even reclaimed her recent nomination of my Bill for the Queen's New Year Honour List. One laugh followed another - there was a sign pointing to Laverton "GATEWAY TO ALICE SPRINGS".

The last twenty miles heading into Leonora was exceptionally bad with great muddy, boggy, slippery and flooded sections, but we proceeded with care keeping on the crests. One great lake we ploughed through, the water came up the steering column at Bill. Then, there it was, a gigantic bog filled with sticks, so we cut a pace and raced into it. The Buggy slid, lurched with more power and literally bulldozed through triumphantly. The sun was at least aiding in drying things a little.

The next obstacle was in the form of a lake of deep water covering the surrounding paddocks in which ducks were swimming. This sheet of water was OK underneath and we seemed to be "out of the woods" with only seven miles to go, when we came across a bogged car with a grader ready to rectify matters, but with caution we went round the outside, showering him with mud. The rest of the road wasn't too difficult, and we'd come 74 miles in two hours when we steamed into Leonora and somehow, I rather pictured a reception committee, waving streamers to greet us - but no...

We reported to the Police, as instructed, then parked in the main street and Carmen washed the windows once more. The sun shone as we strolled around Leonora before gassing up, then going to the hospital out of town near the rubbish tip for Nita who wasn't too well. In the hospital grounds we had lunch while it was good weather.

Carmen's window cleaning was in vain as we forded sheets of muddy water repeatedly on the road going north.

From Leinster Downs with its beaut green paddocks, we could see mines in the distance. All this country has been extensively mined! At 5pm we pulled into Agnew Pub, notorious from our trip to W.A. some years ago. After some inquiries at the pub, some of the locals told us that the road we intended taking to Sandstone and Mt. Magnet was completely impassable because a drilling-rig was hopelessly bogged and nothing would get through for weeks in that direction, so we headed for Wiluna, a section new to us.

WILUNA, MEEKATHARRA & CUE   Saturday 9th June, 1973
Magpies heralded a foggy dawn. The road had dried out extra well and only the newly cut creek beds across the road caused caution while crossing.

We cruised into Wiluna, virtually a ghost town with three pubs still standing and three shops still operating, a police station and half a dozen homes in use. It was a quaint, well-cared for town and many Aborigines came to wave as we prepared to leave heading for Meekatharra. The surrounding country hadn't had rain since 1968 but had received tons since January.

Before long we stopped for a Native family who'd done the clutch in on their car heading toward Wiluna, so Bill promised to ring the mission in Wiluna from Meekatharra, asking for someone to send help. Tim passed a packet of biscuits out for them while they awaited rescue.

Meekatharra had certainly changed in the past four years. It had grown beyond recognition! It boasted a drive-in theatre, hotels and motels, new cafes, a TAB, lovely Council Chambers, War Memorial, swimming pool, etc. Four hotels stood in the main street along with a big supermarket. Bill had the brakes adjusted while we bought ice creams and goodies. The reports on the "closed road" which by this time we'd anticipated would be opened, was bad and was remaining "closed". We checked with the cops who were hopeless and who sent us in search of the Shire Clerk who was out of town at the Stock Car Race Meeting. This took us on an unscheduled trip to the Stock Car Racing. Eventually we found the gentleman who told us the hopelessness of our road, and that we would have to go via Geraldton which meant a good few miles more than planned. Clouds were again gathering after a perfect day, as we took the road to Mt. Magnet instead of that to Gascoyne Junction.

A very brief stop was made in old Cue for photos of the unique stone buildings (we'd also been here before). The poorest country we'd seen to date, surrounded us after Cue. Into the dark we drove to make up time and miles, a 300-mile detour, singing old songs. Bill insisted that the further we drove West, we should get out of this confounded rain - Alec concluded "It'll stop raining when we reach Africa!"

MT. MAGNET & CARNARVON   Sunday 10th June, 1973

It tried to rain a bit in the morning as we were pulling down tents, but we were grateful to get everything away dry for a change and on the way by 7.30am.

Between Mullewa and Geraldton there were howls of excitement over some Banksias and Hakeas by the road-side, so Doreen was forced to call a morning tea break which made everybody happy, as with cup in one hand, and magnifying glass hanging round the neck and a camera in the other hand, our excited botanists buzzed from bush to bush.

There were signs of cultivation everywhere now as we came nearer the coast, even traffic (Sunday drivers) appeared on the roads.

At 10.55am we sighted the ocean - from coast to coast. Soon we were in Geraldton with white sandhills, not red ones. On one side of the road were wheat silos, the other oil refineries. We briefly took a look around town, to which some of us had been before, and it being Sunday, nothing was opened so we went upon a great hill from which a grand view of the city was to be taken in.

The miles rolled by all afternoon. The bush changed very little and a small band of us were reminiscing when we passed the turn off to Hamlin Pool, very close to our hearts from the 1969 trip. In no time we were in the caravan park at Carnarvon, cooking our tea, showering and catching up on washing.

CARNARVON TO EXMOUTH   Monday 11th June, 1973

We were given an extra hour which wasn't hard to take with all the rushing the past couple of days, to make up time - now we were on schedule. 8.30am and we were taken into Carnarvon while Bill took the bus to be serviced.

Just after 11.15 we were travelling past banana plantations by the Gascoyne River which usually flows underground, but was now on the surface, being in flood. As usual, after the buggy's been serviced, something happens, and this was no exception - something to do with the oil this time, so while Bill looked for the trouble, we went down to the river and looked over the plantations.

Although the weather forecast was for "clearing" we ran into torrential rain all the way. At Minilya we dined at the gas station, taking cover from the insistent rain. From this point onward, when we'd left the bitumen, the muddy road was a nightmare, sending us slipping and sliding, pulling and shoving our way along while it continued to rain. There was over seventy miles of this and up the back of the bus we were really thrown around and nobody could see through their windows covered with mud, and maybe, just as well. With eighty miles to go we reached the bitumen again but had to forfeit a trip to Coral Bay.

Nearing Exmouth, the big towers from the US Naval Communications Station loomed into our dark vision and soon the sea in Exmouth Gulf could be seen on the right, its dingy grey water blending with that of the matching sky. Our road passed only 100 yards from the coast where we saw the prawning factory which looked like a caravan park.

After a quick look over the tiny town, we were in the caravan park which was under water, and when the attendant opened the office door, water flooded in. They reported that since we'd probably be flooded out tonight, the Civil Defence had offered us a hall for the next night. In the drizzle we erected tents and snatched a little to eat under the tarpaulin as best we could, then showered and hit the hay. We found out that the road on which we'd travelled all day was "closed". It didn't rain much more at night.

EXMOUTH   Tuesday 12th June, 1973

This town is mainly a fishing and tourist haunt with sample shops, motels, Tom the Cheap supermarket and the most scrumptious bakery. Just out of town the road took us past VHF (very high frequency) transmitting stations then the VLF which detects submarines under water. At Pt. Murat, right up the top of the peninsular, we stayed over two hours at the beach collecting corals and shells and having lunch.

At 2.30 we were at the Navy Communications Base, jointly run by the USA and Australia. Here we took aboard a charming American guide who explained the workings of the project. The base consists of three VHF receivers for receiving messages from ships and subs above water and also from other communication bases throughout the world. The second area is VHF transmitters for transmitting messages to ships and other communication bases and the third is VLF which sends messages to subs under water. Messages are received from various parts of the world by VHF radio and these are decoded and sent to either ships by VHF or to subs by VLF. Another system of receiving messages is via satellites with a dished receiver and this is fed into their communications network. The large mast tower of the VLF system is 1271ft. and the small ones 961ft. The length of the Antenna is 1mile long.

Our guide showed us a film in a luxurious theatre, then took us around the gym, hospital, recreation centers, and was most informative.

EXMOUTH TO DAMPIER   Wednesday 13th June, 1973

With just a brief stop at the Post Office, we were going by 7.30am, not knowing, not even enquiring if the road had been re-opened. We took the Charles Knife road off the bitumen to the Cape Range Oil Well No. 2 which was 15,186ft. high in the range. The scenery of the Shothole Canyon of limestone formation was spectacular and worth the trip. As the morning mist cleared, the ocean, or rather the Gulf beneath our high vantage spot, sparkled in the warm sun. We found our way down off the heights and back on to the road then stopped at the prawning factory to buy some prawns.

It was gratifying to find the dirt road on which we'd had so much trouble coming in, had dried out marvelously, enabling us to travel at a good speed. At 12.45 we rejoined the main road heading for Roebourne where, along the sides, sheets of water remained. After lunch we crossed the Tropic of Capricorn.

A flooded river presented a problem to many vehicles, but we went through easy enough to the roadhouse of Barradale, which was a beehive of activity where a dozen semi's lay, some stranded for seven days and the reports on the road ahead was pretty terrible - still flooded and blocked by a couple of vehicles. The only place of promise to camp was a "truck bay", so this had to do. The prawns smelled good cooking, so we wished we'd bought some. Another car and trailer pulled in to the bay for camping and later a Grace Bros. truck, and he told us that a cop at Exmouth had been booking every vehicle using the road out which certainly had no "Road Closed" sign on it when we used it - and the fine was $100 per tyre. We remembered seeing the cops at the prawning factory.

DAMPIER   Thursday 18th June,1973

Not a cloud could be seen as we packed up, gave the boys a push to start their car and were on the move. Water still lay in lakes and many times our eyes caught sight of the beautiful red Sturts Desert Pea. A new bridge across the Robe River which is usually dry, but now flooded, sped us across but we all piled out to inspect the rushing Robe.

It was gratifying to see a brand-new bridge across the Fortesque River which Doreen said was being built last October and certainly not expected to be finished yet. At the new town of Karratha we were informed that all the roads into the Hammersley Ranges were out for at least 48 hours. The road to Dampier passed close to the salt mine and once in town, we did our shopping, then dined in the park by the coach while the fire brigade filled our jerrycans and cleaned the windows. After speaking with an influential friend, it was quite apparent to Bill that there wasn't a hope for about a week of getting through the Hammersleys, as the Fortesque crossing was still six feet under water so we had to be content to take the alternative.

After lunch, as arranged, we went out to Dampier's Hamersley Iron Co. where we took on board Nev. Bailey, who capably showed us all over the iron ore works. Nev. guided us to the new loading plant on Intercourse Island. This plant can load up to 150,000 ton ships at the rate of 7,000 tons per hour. (The royalties Lang Hancock receives is $13,000 per train load and they can fill six or seven trains per day.

ROEBOURNE & SHERLOCK RIVER   Friday 15th June, 1973

Morning tea was in the main street of Roebourne where we were sweating on the information that the road after many dry days, had been re-opened to Port Hedland. A new road had been made recently, with the other alongside like a great irrigation channel, then transforming into a complete bog. Our road was a "corker" and sent heavy mud all over the windows so that we could see nothing except down the aisle. After slushing through some deep, messy bogs, we lined up, waiting for a convoy of trucks approaching, to take their turn through the major bogs. Cars, Landrovers, trucks and people were stopped everywhere. We bit in and squelched through, enveloping the whole buggy in red mud. And the next bog was equally as bad! Then the final test came when we had to cross Molly's notorious Sherlock River. A big sign said, "Reduce Speed". Already there was a queue of three or four cars, a couple of big trucks and a car pulling a caravan, stuck on the poor excuse for a causeway, which a grader was trying to pack with sandbags, but in vain. The tractor tried towing the car and caravan from the great hole into which he'd driven and wedged, but of course, the rope snapped, and Ma commented, "Wouldn't pull a billy-cart". Water was all inside the car and up over his wheels. The river was too deep to wade through! People were going up and down the queue trying to find more rope, so after a long wait, Bill had to reluctantly give them his big wire rope and with this the tractor pulled him to safety, so letting the mob get going again. We went in next, ahead of the others and went through very well without mishap and from a high bank on the far side, watched the rest while we took lunch break. All the cars had water coming up past their headlights. Bill retrieved his cable without a word of "thanks" and after some laughs and speculations, we were on our way again ready to take the rest of the "horror stretch" which definitely should have been "Closed Road". It was reported a semi bogged up ahead!

The semi was certainly bogged, but had tried his own detour and had gone right down just off the road. We all vacated the ship (all the water we'd come through must qualify us as a ship) and Bill took it easy and came through without any trouble, but on the other side was immediately confronted by the semi's driver who asked for the tow rope everyone had told him was coming on a bus. About half hour later we were still waiting and watching, but the tractor, in vain, tried all kinds of tricks to get the semi out, but to no avail. Ultimately, our cable snapped because of the stupid way it'd been used, and we set off leaving them to it. The driver, who was still running around in the spinifex in his bare feet assured us that his company would replace our cable.

The remainder of the road presented bog after bog all the way to Whim Creek, then Peawah River after which the country changed to red sand and the road improved.

One more bog had two girls stuck, but they were soon on their way and gave us little delay. The rest of the road wasn't too bad and about 4.0pm we crossed the main arm of the Yule River with lovely clear water over its causeway. The banks were lined with paper-barked Melalukas of a great age, so Doreen decided it was too late to go on to Pt. Hedland for shopping, so we made camp in this picturesque playground where everyone had a dip in the river. The water was just the right temperature.

PT. HEDLAND   Saturday 16th June, 1973

Today finds us half-way through our trip and hoping the latter half doesn't go as quick as the former. Yet another big semi-trailer was bogged a little further on, but needed no help as a grader was already on his way to assist and this grader we met on the West Turner River, a wide, sandy river similar to last night's camp spot.

For three hours we were in Pt. Hedland shopping while Bill took "Susie" to get new batteries and we were ages waiting while Dunlop's incompetent staff messed around.

We crossed the De Grey River and took the turn off to Mt. Goldsworthy, but came across a completely flooded section with a detour taking the traffic up onto the railway line, 25ft. higher than the road, but on driving on the latter, found it not wide enough and very risky for the little reward of Mt. Goldsworthy. We returned to Highway 1 and found a nice camp spot in a thick grove of Melalukas and palm trees.

TO BROOME   Sunday 17th June, 1973

Another glorious morning and the birds were singing. At 11.30am we came upon the first roadhouse in 350 miles, Sandfire Roadhouse, so took the opportunity of its lovely cool couch lawn, flowering shrubs and facilities to make lunch.

At 5.00 we were in Broome, Doreen's favourite place and after being introduced to the township and highlights, were driven through streets of giant Boab trees to our camp area on Roebuck Bay where the tide was half out. Everyone made use of the facilities, then had tea watching one of the most remarkable, unforgettable moon-rises, which only appears a couple of days a year. The moon rose full and orange on the water's horizon, and being very low tide, sent its long beam in a straight line, just highlighting the exposed sandbars, looking for all the world like a "stairway to Heaven". But to us Heaven was Broome.

BROOME   Tuesday 19th June, 1973

At 10.45am we were shopping in a few stores in town where Doreen had informed the cake and bread shop yesterday of the proposed influx, and they'd baked extra. Not long after we were running down to the white sand on Cable Beach where the rolling blue surf invited us in. (While surfing Tim caught a green turtle. He carried it out with its flippers waving madly, and rather shocked some of our crowd by asking "What is it? Is it good tucker?". B.H.)

On the track again, we continued around to Gantheaume Point, where the most glorious rock formations, ribbonned with an artists's paint brush, held our breaths. It was a real wonderland of colour, of quaint rock pools, one name Anastasia's

Pool. We lay in the pools and climbed all over the rocks, round to the imprints of Dinosaurs tracks, cast from their resting place a couple of miles out under the water, but are exposed on very low tides. We went around the coast a little further and explored the same kind of rocks in that area, then continued and had afternoon tea by a big wharf where again, folk spread in many directions, exploring caves, natural arches and strange formations of rock.

There was a rush for the showers on returning to camp as taxis were already waiting to take us back to Mrs. Kim's where again, we dined in style. It was an experience to watch the whole population gather ready for the movies - they came in truckloads, on foot, carrying pillows and queued up to get in. Carmen walked home with us and we sat around lapping up some of that beautiful moon.

TO DERBY   Wednesday 20th June, 1973

Another glorious morning after a dew and we were leaving, and I doubt if anyone wanted to be leaving at all. The bitumen road led us East through not-so-interesting land, stunted with dry scrub and small anthills which looked like the grave markers in the Japanese cemetery. We took the loop into Derby, passing Mowanjum Mission just this side of town, as well as a great cattle drinking trough, 393ft. long on Myall's Bore. From here we wandered to the famous big, hollow Prison Tree, an old Boab reputed to have held prisoners. It is 46ft. in girth and we crowded into it and had photos taken, naturally.

There wasn't much in Derby, but what there was, is spread out with Boabs scattered everywhere, a nice park by the swimming pool and Library-Art Gallery which provided us with some entertainment after lunch. Then we were on the Mitchell grass plains and at Leonard River turned off to Windjana Gorge, which is regarded as one of the most beautiful locations in W.A. It is walled by vertical cliffs of dark limestone from 100 to 300 ft. high. These cliffs are mirrored in the still, muddy water, still until a Johnson River crocodile launches himself off. We watched their tiny nose and eyes, the only visible part, drift motionlessly in the muddy water. Excitement was high that night as we armed ourselves with torches and lined the river bank, picking up the red eyes of many crocodiles on the far bank and cruising in the still water. All night long cattle bellowed, and donkeys brayed their blood curdling noise.

WINDJANA GORGE TO GEIKIE GORGE   Thursday 21st June, 1973

Only a couple of miles from Windjana we came upon the old ruined walls of Lillmooloora Police Station, silent reminder of the Kimberley's pioneering past. It was here that the notorious Native, Pigeon's first victim, Constable Richardson, was murdered in October 1894.

Approximately 24 miles from Windjana, a stream flows through the Napier Range in a large natural tunnel eroded through the limestone by my favourite place on the trip - Tunnel Creek. It was really magnificent, and our adventure took us, carrying torches and wearing gumboots, through the great gaping mouth of the cave from whose jaws hung long vines and tree roots. It was total darkness inside and the first section was like quicksand and one had to keep lifting the legs quickly to prevent rapid sinking. The Tunnel was about half a mile long and varies in height from ten to forty feet high. Its average width, about 50ft. A collapse in the centre of the Tunnel has caused a cave in leading to the top of the range and this often festooned with large numbers of flying foxes. Permanent water comes from springs inside. The outlaw, Pigeon, hid in the Tunnel for long periods whilst recovering from wounds inflicted by the Police and it was here that he finally met his death in a running gun battle with troopers. I could have gladly stayed a week at Tunnel Creek, but other such beautiful spots awaited us.

Brolgas were a star attraction on the bulldust road leading to Geikie Gorge, approximately ten miles from Fitzroy Crossing. It was about 3.00pm when we arrived, and we joined a boat trip - eight small dinghies fastened together, with a tiny outboard motor to propel us slowly through the scenic Gorge. Geikie Gorge is nearly 200 miles from the source of the Fitzroy River which winds its way through the limestone cliffs, which are white, ten feet above water's level, then change to gold, red and brown in layers. A couple of crocs eased their way into the still water, a lovely Jabiru, Australia's stork flew from feeding by the banks, while a lovely long tailed Rainbow bird swooped within feet of our noiseless craft, to catch a moth as Sulphur Crested Cockatoos noisily launched from limb to limb, squarking. The giant cliffs mirrored in the waters and it was impossible not to take photos of this magnificent place.

TO HALLS CREEK   Friday 22nd June, 1973

Fitzroy Crossing, or the remainder of it, which is two miles from the pub and store, seemed to be just a hospital run by the AIM and Post Office and perhaps two other buildings, boasting a population of 35 people. At the end of the town, the infamous Fitzroy Crossing, a cement pre-cast slab bridge which, in flood time is impassible and a flying fox has been put in to transport people. Norm McDonald who'd shown us the slides last night, had presented his eight-boat punt as a means of ferrying cars across for $10 in the "wet". Everybody walked across to photograph "Susie" racing down the steep bank, along the bridge, and up the other high bank. At 2.30pm we steamed into dusty Halls Creek, another town where one has to walk a mile between shops and here we strolled around in the heat eating ice creams or sipping drinks, or both. Even the locals said it was hot for this time of the year!

On rejoining the buggy, Bill confronted us with the worst possible news which dampened the best of spirits - the Tanami Track is definitely "out". Closed for the next three weeks! This, the locals had told him and was confirmed by the Police. It was beyond my comprehension as the ground around Halls Creek seemed dry and dusty.

Afternoon tea was in the following mountains in a well-timbered creek bed. Spirits were low and Gunga Din (another Bill) dismally proclaimed "Here we are, dying of thirst while the rest of the country's drowning!" Suddenly the anthills and Boabs re-appeared and we called a halt to radio our friend and contact, Bruce Farrands, the only civilization for the 750 miles of the Tanami Track and who runs the gas station and tent-motel at Rabbit Flat. Bruce seemed more optimistic than the cops at Halls Creek and said that the good weather was drying things well and may be right in five days time when we would arrive there... Wow...eee. (Bruce suggested taking a run up to Kununurra and Wyndham and back to Halls Creek to give the track three or four days to dry out. B.H.) The afternoon shadows lengthened on Durack country, well timbered and grassy. At 5 pm we crossed the Ord River and made camp shortly after. Spirits were revitalized!

TO WYNDHAM Saturday 23rd June, 1973

At the Kununurra-Wyndham signpost, we turned left, heading for the latter which was 38 miles from that point. Some beautiful gums, Euc. miniata, a brilliant orange-red blossomed in the bush all the way. We passed a Native camp, then could see Cambridge Gulf which appeared as a big lake. At Wyndham, the only town of importance for days, we did our shopping in its dozen or so stores, then headed out to Wyndham Port where two boats were tied up.

At the Ord River Diversion Dam we took group photos as Jean was to leave by plane tomorrow.

Our camping area was right by the water at Kunnurra where many birds had made their homes by the permanent water. The grass had been freshly mown and our allotted area very nice. A Centralian coach with only seven passengers, a cook, driver and courier pulled in nearby. I did the washing in a washing machine while Bill and driver Bill located the cause of some minor trouble we'd been having. I came back to find a little frog dancing over our tent.

ORD RIVER AND KIMBERLEYS Sunday 24th June, 1973

The Centralian crowd were called "everything" as they noisily rose at 4am and didn't even leave till just before we did. But I'm sure we'd have been awake anyhow, as the birds in their increasing millions, were deafening at dawn and for many hours later.

Just before the NT border, we turned off to go 22 miles into the Ord River Dam. From the top of the mountains was the most enchanting view of Lake Argyle, dressed in sparkling blue, drifting in and out the red and green hills and mountains enclosing it. A detailed map, erected on the mountain, clarified the distance and landmarks around. Desert Kurrajongs in flower added tangerine-pink, while the desert cotton glowed gold blooms. The colour was magnificent.

A stop at Kununurra's hotel was really something. The bar inside is built in the form of a cave with the counter made entirely of Zebra stone.

We crossed the great Ord River and travelled back as far as the Durham River and here everyone took to the water for a lovely swim. Even though we were traversing the same country, things looked different because it was afternoon instead of morning and even Pompey's Pillar looked different. It was most exciting when Bill radio'd Bruce at Rabbit Flat and confirmed that "we'd give it a go" after Bruce has casually said "You might just make it be the skin of yer teeth!" He arranged to meet at a very special bog and Bill promised to contact him again on the morrow.

WOLFE CREEK CRATER Mon 25th June, 1973

After a colder than usual night, we were ready and waiting early but since it was no use getting into Halls Creek before the gas station opened, some spent time looking for native implements. Tim found some "fair dinkum" ones.

Since our arrival at Halls Creek was premature, we took the tiny road through the mountains to the old gold mining town, 12 miles away. Old Halls Creek, "Durack's Folly" like all old ghost towns was most interesting but the only walls still standing are those of the Post Office and Police Station. We rummaged around for about 15 minutes, had morning tea, then returned to (new) Halls Creek where we bought bread and ice creams and kept our mouths shut concerning our assault on the Tanami.

The road became hazardous due to vehicles having been bogged recently but in most places blooming wattles lined the track.

At Carranya a "crater" sign was pointing, and we took the left fork and soon could see the 100ft walls of the Wolfe Creek Meteor Crater above the flat plain. We climbed its slopes to gaze in awe at this ancient masterpiece of nature. Funny, but it just looked like meteor crater!

At 3.20pm we came to the junction of the Canning and the Tanami Track so pulled up to take a photo of the shoddy signpost and decided to call it afternoon tea. Once on the Tanami Track, we came upon a series of creeks, the last one fairly deep with water, so we backed back and charged. Water splashed up the front and came down the open front roof hatch. (This was Sturt Creek which I knew had a solid causeway bottom, but I had forgotten just how deeply it went down. It really scared the living daylights out of me. The coach simply dropped its nose and headed steeply down into the water and it completely enveloped us with the water right to the top of the windscreen. I sat petrified, then in a few moments we were heading up hill just as quickly as we had done down. The coach shot up like a fish leaping out of water. I pulled up to sit and get over the shock and I don't think most of the passengers had really absorbed what had happened, particularly the darned fool who requested a repeat run for a photograph. B.H.)

At 4.30pm and we were at the turnoff to the Balgo Mission, and making radio contact with Bruce. He arranged to meet us at the bog about 10am, but advised us not to go into it before he got there. "Morning tea at the bog! "Sierra, Whisky, Oscar." The roos showed up around sunset which was very pretty, but we could only look at it from the bus while travelling and trying to find a suitable spot to camp. That we never found, but "made do" with a small clearing in the spinifex at dark.

TO RABBIT FLAT   Tuesday 26th June, 1973

It was bitterly cold when we woke, and a rather pretty sunrise appeared in the east, but it was no consolation against the cold, which we're not used to after all the hot weather.

On coming to a very bad bog we approached with caution, parked, then all walked a half mile or so in the spinifex by the bog. (Bruce told us this bog was 50yds. but it was more like 300yds. The boys heard, then found Bruce bogged up ahead just off the road. Many hands had Bruce out quickly and he took many of the suitcases and swags we'd unloaded onto his Toyota and drove off with them. We'd had no time for introductions. Bruce was quite good looking young man with blonde curly hair and very capable.

The buggy revved up and went carefully on but... down "Susie" went. Everyone laboured at different jobs! We filled up the deep bogs with spinifex while the boys put sand tracks under the wheels and Bruce worked like a Trojan, but we only gained a few yards each time we tried.

Lunchtime came and went, afternoon tea, the same and the work went on. A 3.50 the winch was tied to the Toyota, getting synchronised was very difficult, but we gained a little more ground each time, filling the ruts with ant-hills and spinifex. Before long a queer old codger from Billiluna came by, only he got bogged in front of us, and time was spent getting him out. (Jan is being a bit tough on poor old Bill Wilson who heard us on the radio and came to help. B.H.) Bruce's wife Jackie came up with an esky full of beer and soft drinks which gave the men new vigour and soon Susie was struggling through the last lap of the confounded bog, using ant-hills and spinifex for a steady base. Great cheers arose from the Tanami!

As we drove to Rabbit Flat, guided by Bruce, a glorious sunset brightened the close of day. Then the lights of Rabbit Flat could be seen, 350 miles from any civilization. Quickly our tents were erected, and hot showers and flush toilets were in good supply and once clean, we invaded the big tin dining room which would have been as well set out as the greatest Chevron Hilton dining room.

Everything was immaculate, lovely orange tablecloths graced the tables on which were more implements to eat with than we could remember what to do with (too long in the bush), serviettes and a bar at which we could obtain any liquor of choice. A three-course meal was served up, Bill and Doreen helping out as waiters, and we enjoyed our first and only baked meal on the trip.

In the dining room sat three Aborigines, stockmen brought in to recapture the herd of cattle which had been released when the road-train on which they were travelling, was hopelessly bogged. In a nearby room were hand-made souvenirs of quality, photos of the old days and folk around the adjoining properties, along with some funny poetry.

After tea, some of us hung around the dining room with Jackie and Bruce and Dick, a boozed-up road-train driver, with whom I danced to a tape recording.

AFTER RABBIT FLAT   Wednesday 27th June, 1973

We were able to sleep in till 9.00am. A cool wind flew up but soon quietened again. After breakfast we went off to see slides Bruce was to have shown last night. During the screening, my dancing partner, Dick came in to announce that there was a bad bog on further and he would wait with his Kenworth till 1.30 to pull us out if needed.

We leisurely strolled round the billabong which has semi-permanent water holes and teeming with bird-life, around the tent-motel, and into the most unique sunken vegetable garden which supplied all those baked vegetables for last night's tea. There were big watermelons, citrus trees loaded with fruit, climbing beans, enormous cauliflowers and a host of other things most of us can't grow. These were irrigated, and if rain should fall, none was wasted but sank into the troughs.

After lunch we headed off but only made it three miles, when down went the back wheels into a deep bog. Everyone knew exactly what to do this time with yesterday's experience, so down came every ant-hill and clump of spinifex while the men worked like fury digging and jacking the back wheels. To make matters worse, one of the inner back tyres was punctured. After a long delay, changing tyres and getting things just right, "Susie" reared into action and bulldozed her way out of difficulty and we hikers on the way.

Then another bad stretch loomed up (probably the one Dick had informed us about) so we called afternoon tea break and unloaded the gear again and looked the bog over, its detour as well. Ahead we walked once more past the bad stretch, then dived for cover as Susie snorted and ground her way, billowing dust which blocked our view. "Ah, she's stuck again", then Susie came bouncing round the bend at a pace while we breathed a sigh of relief. We climbed aboard our trusty steed when she pulled up on a more "stable" part of the road, then went like the wind through another dicey spot to wait for the rest of the Israelites.

A couple of miles went by OK then it was the same story - ant-hills fell to the axe and were thrown into the ditches that probably the Kenworth had made. Strangely enough, although it looked a bad one, we hurtled through like a bucking bronco and I stayed inside and rode Susie all the way.

The road improved all the way to the Granites, a deserted gold mining area worked round the turn of the century. It was dusk and long shadows threw an eerie light on the great boulder outcrops sitting on a couple of hills in the wilderness. The rusty remains of an old crusher from Halls Creek and some adobe mud and rock walls remained, along with the new-looking windmill pumping water to a trough.

Susie had to labour through deep sand just past the Granites and we were hoping we'd not be bogged near this ghostly spot, or we'd be forced to spend the night. We drove and drove and after many long hours of no wood, but plenty of spinifex, we came to a new road being made, and there made camp at last after a BIG day.

TO ALICE SPRINGS   Thursday 28th June, 1973 It was funny to find only a mile from our camp spot, a road-gang with lots of vehicles and men all out along the road waving to us. It was their generator we could faintly hear from our camp last night. Bill told the boss of the lousy road we'd been on and he said casually, "I'll go up and give it a lick!"

At 8.45 we came across a Kenworth road-train driven by Dick's son who had the road blocked while he pumped a tyre, so Bill yelled "All out". We walked (we really should be refunded for all this walking) while Bill took the buggy up on the bank around the cattle train.

On Yuendumu Reserve we were greeted by a group of skinny dogs, so assumed Natives weren't too far away. In no time they appeared, waving and laughing. The Mission was very tidy and those living on it, very well-dressed. Lunch was in the campgrounds and the "privileged men" were once again invited to go off for "man's talk", with a man called Darby. They were away far too long, but I enjoyed watching the zebra finches at play around some puddles. (I thought this was the strangest routine as Darby showed us all the sacred artifacts relevant to men's business. The amazing thing being they were stored in filing cabinets with the appropriate labels on the front. B.H.)

The road improved and widened and strips of water skirted the sides. We could see the MacDonnell Ranges in the distance and at 6.00pm we reached the bitumen on the Stuart Highway and in no time we were in Alice Springs and putting up tents at Carmichael's Caravan Park, settled among the hills and run by a couple of ex-Sundowners."

Well, that's the way Jan saw the trip and one diary comment she makes about the trip back to Sydney reminded me of something. Jan wrote "After leaving Soulia our narrow dirt road detoured around every bog hole, through to the Hamilton Hotel, a lonely outpost which serves mainly semi-trailer drivers, especially in the wet when they inevitable become stranded there". Yes, we made a stop there and I was amazed to see this notice in the Toilet. "Please conserve toilet paper by making use of both sides".

Jan wrote about the nice Aboriginal Ranger who found us in Fort Mueller way past our permitted distance. Well, she was wrong, he was more like a snake in the grass. We arrived home to receive a letter from the W.A. Department of Aboriginal Affairs listing our transgression. They asked for any reason why we shouldn't be prosecuted and have all future permits revoked.

This was very heavy stuff and required some quick action. A number of our passengers were botanists and had collection permits, including Alec Blombery and Betty Maloney, so I rang Alec and suggested that our deviation was essential to collect some rare specimens. Alec agreed and drafted a letter to that effect. The Western Australians accepted this, and everything was OK, except that on all future permits, as well as all the usual dos and don'ts, typed across the bottom was "no plant material to be collected".

It was a rare Gunbarrel trip that we didn't have to help Aboriginals with broken-down cars, even though our permit stipulated that we must not talk to Aboriginals, and I'll bet they weren't even aware of the fact. We carried a lot of general purpose hoses as blown hoses were often the problem, also it was necessary to have everything in the way of a complete tyre service on board.

It doesn't matter who the people are, who is broken down, we are all obliged to help each other. After repairing a car one day, the elderly driver asked could our mob push start him as the starter motor had gone missing. His ten or twelve passengers piled aboard and I looked in to make sure he was in second gear. There was no gear shift lever anywhere. I pointed this out and the old fellow just laughed and said "yeah, that fella fell off long ago, but no problem, we stuck in second gear".

These Aboriginal people are just amazing, could you imagine city people, or any white people for that matter, setting out to cross outback deserts in a car with shot radiator hoses, no starter motor, and no gear shift, but with complete nonchalance.

The cook at Giles had a thing going with one of the Nurses at Warburton and asked could we take him across and he would fly back with the transport plane. He told us a brand-new road had just been opened straight across the desert to Warba. that would cut a third off the travelling time, and he referred to it as the "cut line".

This proved to be true, except that it hadn't been graded and finished. A bulldozer had pushed through to Warba. and back leaving soft patches littered with broken mulga roots. We bogged once and had to fix two flat tyres, and another hazard was the track was not wide enough for a coach. Although we were travelling right through the Great Victoria Desert, there was a fair amount of timber and I didn't want to scratch the bodywork, so the axe and bush saw were used many times.

Today this has become the main road, in fact the only road and it is called the Great Central Road, or something similar, although many people still refer to this as the Gunbarrel. It really is a whole new system of roads plus realignments with very little of Len Beadell's original track still in use, and there is talk of it being bitumenised!

DAVE SIMPSON In 1973 we had royalty in Sydney with the official opening of the Sydney Opera House by Queen Elizabeth.

Meanwhile we felt a bit like royalty ourselves as we were regularly chauffeured around Alice Springs in a 1928 Packard that looked like Al Capone's personal transport.

It began when a young mechanic set up in business under a mulga tree at Ayers Rock. Dave Simpson also sold fuel in 44-gallon drums, so to help the cause we bought from him. In time a lease was advertised and as Dave couldn't compete, B.P. built the first service station at Ayers Rock.

Dave was a genius at restoring old vintage cars, and started building a motor museum to house them in Alice Springs, only he ran out of money. We did a deal, we bought the pride of the fleet, the magnificent old Packard at market value, with the agreement that Dave could buy it back in twelve months, which I'm sad to say he did. Apart from anything else, it would have been an excellent investment. I never did get to drive it as Dave always insisted on driving us. Later it became a wedding hire car, before going back on permanent display.

Dave is the only person I have heard of who has driven the Canning Stock Route with two-wheel drive, and without an accompanying vehicle. He and his then wife first drove the Gunbarrel Highway about 1970 in a two-wheel drive Ford F 100 Ute and then did a survey down the Canning in the same vehicle. They carried everything they needed for the whole trip including fuel. They considered running tours, but never did, probably because hardly anyone had heard of the Canning Stock Route in those days.

Our house in Sydney had become a regular stop-over for many of our outback friends, and Dave was no exception, but I don't think he appreciated the size of Sydney.

After driving him up to the northern beaches to buy a hard-to-get motor part he said another thing he wanted to checkout was in a place called Liverpool - "Was that nearby"? He was collecting parts mainly for model T Fords and was considered an authority on these cars.

Dave's wife, a pretty Aboriginal girl had two teenaged daughters from an earlier all Aboriginal marriage, and the elder, Jennifer was sitting for her final school exams in Alice Springs. Dave wanted to offer her a prize to work for, and we suggested she join our Tasmanian tour and she duly joined the tour in Sydney.

The Richmond Vintage Car Museum was on our Tasmanian itinerary, and I took Jennifer to inspect a beautifully restored T model Ford, labelled 1924. Jennifer took one look and said, "What a mess, 1922 headlights, 1923 radiator" and she went on and on. The owner was dumbfounded staring at this young black girl, and finally said "How would you know?" "Oh, my father is the expert on model Ts" she said. That brought another dumbfounded look, and he asked "Yeah, and what is your father's name?" "Dave Simpson" Jennie said. Another astonished look - Dave is blue eyed and blond. "Not David Simpson from Alice Springs?" he asked. This had the Sundowners and Jennifer chuckling along for days.

After all his work it came as a surprise in 1983 when Dave sold up the Museum and the dozen or so restored cars to the Territory Government.

He then bought Cane River Station in N.W. Western Australia, but after battling through two summer heatwaves, sold up and moved the family further south to Carnarvon.

He told us his grandfather's brother had started the banana growing along the Gascoyne River in Carnarvon in 1928 when he brought banana suckers from Queensland. Today there are over 400 growers.

Dave and his wife Belinda bought a banana farm of about ten acres and with his usual flair turned this into a tourist attraction. It became one of our favourite stops on West Coast

Tours and he always made sure we left with enough fruit to last the Sundowners at least a week, courtesy of the house.

Central Australia however has a powerful appeal that lures people back, and Dave sold up in Carnarvon and returned to Alice Springs in 1993, no doubt to find a new challenge.

1974. Bill floating in the buoyant waters of flooded Lake Eyre

1971 MOVIES, NEW ZEALAND, BORROLOOLA
1974 LAKE EYRE, CYCLONE TRACY

This was the year that McDonalds arrived in Australia. We predicted they would never take on, but we came to use them, if only for their toilets.

Also, crocodile shooting came to an end and many waterholes where we swam and knew to be croc free became too much like playing Russian roulette.

Our wall map of Australia was gradually being covered with a spiders web of black lines, but there were still some gaps, such as the East Alligator country, later called Kakudu, and Borroloola. Both these were added in 1971.

Around 1971 two movies were shot largely on Angas Downs Station, one was *Burke and Wills Story* by Lord Snowdon and the other *Walkabout* by Nicolas Roeg and won acclaim. *Walkabout* wasn't strong on dialogue but made almost mystical use of the outback scene.

It began in an apartment overlooking Sydney Harbour, with naturally a view of the Harbour Bridge. John Meillon was packing a lunch hamper, then accompanied by 14-year old daughter (Jenny Agutter) and 6 year old son (Lucien John) they drove their VW Beetle to the Flinders Ranges for lunch. (Not a bad effort on the roads in those days.)

Father John is totally inept at fire making and manages to incinerate both himself and the VW. Naturally a band of nearly naked Aboriginals arrive to inspect the fire, causing the terrified children to run for the hills, and the Aboriginals lacking any tracking skills, lost them.

Next scene they are tramping across the salt desolation of Lake Eyre, while at the same time a team of foreign scientists led by Noeline Brown, are carrying out experiments on the salt. The men spend their time staring at Noeline's legs instead of their instruments and the wind keeps lifting her skirt. This has nothing whatever to do with the children or the story. Next, we find them wandering on the red sandhills of Angas Downs where every type of Australian animal manages to cross their path, even a lonely looking wombat, and why not seeing he was nearly 1000km out of his territory. Jenny's school uniform was in tatters and they were starting to get hungry, having missed out on the cut lunch back in the Flinders Ranges.

Over the sandhill and about to meet them was David Gulpilil, dressed in a pocket handkerchief and a dead goanna. This meeting was rather traumatic for David as he was on walkabout after his first initiation and mustn't see or be seen by any female. (This could have been better explained in the film.) But being a good natured young fellow, David says, blow his future he'll save the children.

Tim Lander told us while working with crew he and Laurie Liddle dug a hole at the foot of a Quandong tree and lined it with polythene and filled it with water, then lined it with reeds. They trapped birds and tied their feet with thread to the branches.

After they drank at the pool and dined on Quandongs, David then led them to Reedys Rockhole near Kings Canyon. Then came the controversial bit when he cast off the pocket handkerchief and goanna and dived into the pool. Then Jenny threw off what little was left of her school uniform and also dived in. They behaved quite well and just carried out a sort of graceful swimming ballet around the pool.

In another absolute change of scenery, they managed to walk to tropical country out of Darwin where David found an abandoned house. A bit of soul searching showed him that he had bombed out with his initiation business, and maybe he had fallen for Jenny, so he painted himself up, performed a dramatic dance routine and hung himself. This left the children in a bit of a spot, so they walked out to the Stuart Highway and were lucky enough to flag down a road-train that just happened to be going to Sydney.

Tim and Laurie had fallen in love with the wombat and by the end of the filming had pooled their resources with an offer to buy him, but unfortunately for them, he of course was "professional" wombat and not for sale.

The other film on Burke and Wills was filmed by Lord Snowdon (then husband of Princess Margaret) for television. Snowdon first looked at the authentic Cooper country but found it too expensive and settled for Angas Downs instead. He recruited locals to play parts. Laurie Liddle became Sepoy One, Noel Fullarton-Dost Mohomet the camel driver, and Tim Lander the horse breaker. Arthur Liddle, being the son of an old camel man, was technical advisor on camel gear.

Tim told us to watch for the funny bits when we got to see the show, like River Gums referred to as Coolibahs, and thick stands of small River Gums as mangroves in the Gulf. Also, when Mr. Burke is dying, he opens one eye to check the camera angle before he croaks.

Being away so much of course we missed the show on TV, and this was a time before we had videos. But one night when we were camped in the caravan park at Bright, Victoria, Doreen and I decided to eat out in town. While waiting to be served we perused the local paper that carried an ad. for Snowden's *Burke and Wills* on the local TV channel that night.

While walking back to camp we passed a motel with a neon sign advising that colour TV was available in all rooms. Doreen grabbed my hand and propelled me toward the lobby. With the Italian tobacco farmers selling up and moving into town businesses, we were met by a pretty young Italian girl at the desk. She was not up to Doreen's request for a room for an hour or two, and said we would have to ask Father.

I tried to hide behind an Aspidistra as Doreen tried to explain to the Italian gentleman that we needed to watch TV. He suggested we take a room that hadn't had the bed made up and we moved in. My mother-in-law was on the trip and as she loved Angas Downs, Doreen decided to run back to camp and collect her to see the show. While she was away, the proprietor looked in to check we were OK and asked, "Where is the woman with you?" I answered, "She's gone to get her mother". He just looked at me as though I was raving mad and quickly left.

On the next knock I opened the door to Doreen, her mother, and about twenty Sundowners who insisted on coming as they had all been to Angas Downs. The motel room was absolutely packed, with someone even sitting on the toilet and watching through the open door. After the show the mob sneaked off into the night and we checked out with the proprietor and assured him that the TV was excellent, and there was no charge! At last we were able to tell Tim we had seen and enjoyed the show.

NEW ZEALAND While sitting around the campfire one night on the Birdsville Track we were asked where we intended to holiday at the end of the season (although some people insisted our whole life was a holiday), we answered possibly New Zealand. "Good, we'll come with you", the whole coach load replied. Although our private holidays were something of a safety valve to get away from groups, what could we say.

So, it was agreed, and we had to do a great deal of research to plan a satisfactory tour. Taking our coach to Tasmania we felt was essential, it was simply impossible with New Zealand, so we looked for a small, experienced company who would give personalized service and came up with Len Jenkins of Jenkins Coaches in Gore, South Island. Len was an old-world type of gentleman who would go to any length to satisfy his clients. Our only problem (and a small one at that) was Len, along with everyone else in Gore spoke in a sort of dialect of English.

Up to that time I had never heard a New Zealand accent, and later realised that it is hardly noticeable in the north, but the further south you go, the more distinct it becomes. Someone remarked that in the far south, people suffered from loose vowels. Our driver, said his name as Lus, and I called him that for a day or two before I realized it was really Les. One day he spoke of the view of the "Per Suffolk" which turned out to be the Pacific Ocean. There were language problems with little things like Les handing me a jug and saying "Ful thus wuth the Zup" and I finally realized he meant hot water from the Zip hot water service.

Les gave a detailed commentary but it required come concentration because of his accent. One day he was explaining the Maori had wiped out the original wildlife including the Moa - "The Maori ate every one of them" A passenger asked "Gee, were the Moa the original inhabitants?", not understanding they were big flightless birds.

The "Chullie Bun" was an esky, or perhaps it was a Chilli Bun, like a savoury sweet bread, and John Jackson, our mechanic told of ordering a tub of chips at a take-away. Jacko had no idea his order was ready when the girl asked, "Who ordered the pottie of chops".

Laurie our cook, was a retired shearers' cook and had a van fitted out as a kitchen, drove ahead and had meals prepared when we arrived. Dairy products were ridiculously cheap, and Laurie would insist on pouring a cup full of cream on all breakfast and desert dishes. New Zealand was certainly a weight hazard.

We came home with memories of Les's excellent driving, snow covered mountains, cable car rides, swimming in thermal pools, Maori concert, helicopter ride over glaciers, spouting geysers, and of course the ever-present strawberries and cream.

Apart from all that I have one indelible memory. At the Fox Glacier Camp, we arranged an evening at the local Pub. This required walking around three sides of a large paddock, and when Doreen required something left behind, I decided to take a short cut back, straight across the paddock in the misty rain. I forked my leg over the fence, having no clue it was electrified. I have no idea how many times I shot up and down, or for that matter, how I got off, but I lay for at least ten minutes on the wet grass before I could stand up and take a step.

After the New Zealand tour, I suppose it was inevitable that the returning Sundowners would spread the word. With the number of inquiries, we had to schedule two New Zealand trips a year, and of course as we couldn't accompany them all, we had great faith in Len Jenkins.

Only a small amount of currency could be transferred out of New Zealand in those days, and as new vehicles were nearly unobtainable, young fellows were forced to put their speed stripes on old Ford Prefects. Len wisely banked all the tour money in Australia which allowed him to holiday here with us. The new Valiant Charger had just been released in Sydney and when he saw it, Len just had to have one. "It ul be the only one in New Zuland," he said. The Valiant Charger had been *Wheels* magazine car of the year in 1971, and rather expensive at about $3000. Many years later when we had a brand-new Denning Coach, Len fell in love with that and worked out a deal with Alan Denning whereby he had the first

Denning in New Zealand. Len was thrilled with the Aussie Denning, "Passed all those Bedfords going up Coronet Peak" he told us.

We invited Laurie the cook on a Central Australian trip, but I don't think he was happy out of his environment. One night he was cooking sausages on the fire and said, "You know, Australian sausages are awful". I checked, and they were Sanitarium brand out of a can. I explained that they were vegetarian and contained no meat, and this upset Laurie greatly. "That's what I mean, un New Zealand we putt meat un our sausages." I hate to think of the stories of privation in outback Australia that Laurie took back to New Zealand.

On hearing of our successful New Zealand tours, Ian Campbell asked could we arrange a Barker College trip in the August school holidays. (Our regular trips were in summer). This is a copy of a letter sent to Ian at the time of our final Barker Reunion in 1994:

> "Just a short note to thank you for an enjoyable evening with Doreen and Bill. Watching the slide presentation, how lucky I was to take part in the 1973 New Zealand tour, and how unlucky not to have been part of a Central Australian Safari or a Tasmanian trip. Bill will remember, as we did on Monday night, using the old-style toasters with fold down sides in the hut at Lake Pukaki to warm our freezing feet. I've told that story hundreds of times. By the way it was great to hear the Hands say that they would never consider taking a tour with school children unless Ian Campbell was in charge. So many people owe you a lot Ian. Signed Bruce Davis, Manager, Application Services, Unisys Aust. Ltd."

Unless you are a ski nut, I can't recommend winter touring in New Zealand, and I remember well Bruce's story of that freezing night at Lake Pukaki. Like most lakes in the South Island, Pukaki was man-made by the building of hydro-electric dams and these dams seemed to be forever being raised to retain greater volumes of water. As the Cabin Village was about to be flooded and replaced by new buildings on higher ground, the manager, Pegleg, had stripped things like heaters and let the cabins run down. It was a bitterly cold night, way below freezing, and our only heaters were a few open side toasters. It ranks among the most unpleasant nights I have ever spent.

A remarkable engineering feat on the west coast was the Homer Tunnel, and this was to cause us a great deal of trouble. We were about half-way through when a coach ahead lost traction on an ice sheet on the tunnel floor and finished up jammed against the wall on both sides. This blocked traffic both ways. We all piled out to help and I was amazed at the length of the tunnel, we could just see a spot of light at each end. Les conferred with the driver and it was decided that the back wheels would have to be jacked up and chains fitted, as apparently the wrong tread pattern tyres had been fitted. We were to strike this years later in North America, where they usually fit different tyres in winter.

While they were working, traffic started to build up both ways and many drivers kept their motors running, claiming that if they had to wait too long, their motors might not restart, and of course they had their headlights on to illuminate the chain fitting operation. The air became increasingly dense and with the increase in temperature, ice stalactites started dropping from the roof, like knives. It didn't require much imagination to see that if it went on too long, this could become a life-threatening situation. Thankfully with Les's help the driver finally had the chains on and seesawing it back and forth straightened up and drove forward. It left me with something of a dread of driving through to Milford Sound.

At Coronet Peak we were outfitted with Army surplus great coats to go up in the chairlift, a good thing too, as halfway up the chairlift came to a standstill. I was sharing a chair with a Barker boy and our teeth started to chatter as we swung back and forth in the freezing wind.

We were calculating if it was feasible to drop to the snow bank far below, then thankfully the gadget started up again.

Later Ian Campbell and I were standing on a small level area at the top of Coronet Peak, when Ian moved forward his feet slipped beneath him. He shot forward trying to keep his balance on the icy ground, but couldn't stop with his army greatcoat flapping. Ian looked like a giant stork as his arms waved wildly - meanwhile on a lower level, a group of elderly women looked up to see him advancing. He crashed into the women and instinctively threw his arms around them. This was definitely not Ian's normal behaviour and I have never seen him so embarrassed. For all this, on his return he was pleased enough to start planning another New Zealand trip.

We continued with New Zealand tours for a period of ten years until Len Jenkins passed away and his family chose to sell out rather than stay with the business. The new owner failed to live up to our standards and we felt it was pointless to continue. This was a shame, as we felt that it had been a service to our regular Sundowners and we regarded it as something we enjoyed doing, and really only charged enough to cover our expenses.

There were inconveniences of course, the worst happened while we were on tour in Western Australia. We received a call from my mother in Sydney to say that Qantas had rescheduled a flight due to leave in four weeks' time, to two days later. Doreen set about writing and posting letters to every passenger, explaining they would leave two days later than planned. She then wrote to Len Jenkins and he rearranged the itinerary and bookings throughout New Zealand. About five days later another message came from Qantas, it was all a mistake and we would be leaving on the original date. I won't go on with this story, I think enough said.

BORROLOOLA

Our mate, Ted Egan wrote a song about the characters of Borroloola, and although those he spoke of had largely passed on, new ones had taken their place, as it was that sort of "town".

Willy Shadforth would top my list. Willy was a coloured man who owned the local Seven Emus Station and was obviously of Chinese and Aboriginal descent. On one trip we had a passenger who spoke with a thick Scottish brogue. Willy asked what was her accent and when I said Scots, he said "Might be related, I had a Scots grandfather".

I believed about half of what Willy told me, like how he acquired the Station - he described how he had a dream of the horse that would win the Melbourne Cup. It was so real, he raised all the money he could to back it, and of course it won, long odds as well and Willy used the money to buy the Station from his boss.

He used to complain that the pub was only allowed to sell beer (to try to overcome the Aboriginal drinking problem) which meant he had to drive to Tennant Creek to get a real drink.

I asked if Borroloola was an Aboriginal name, and he said "No, I'll explain - when that fella Leichhardt and his party reached here they were starving and the local blackfellas took pity on them. Among them was a girl called Lulu who was a famous cook and she cooked them a meal. When they were hungry again they asked, "Can we borrow Lulu." I put the story to Max, the publican and he said, "Perfectly right, except it wasn't because Lulu could cook".

Although everyone called the station Seven Emus, the correct name was singular, Seven Emu. It really was named by Leichhardt when his party shot an emu and seven ate it.

Willy invited us out to the Station, but didn't explain that the track was nearly impassable. There were numerous creek crossings and at one stage I fitted the half-tracks on the back wheels to cross a section of soft sand. The Station was a real Aussie bush sort of place, just a few bough sheds, and the bathroom was open air. The bath sat on a rise under a Tamarind tree with a view down to the river.

Willy introduced his wife, Bess, who was a powerfully built black woman, and then the crowd asked for a photo. Willy put his arm around Doreen and Bess put her arm around me, I couldn't breathe and thought she cracked at least two or three ribs.

She had cooked a huge Johnnie cake, a sort of damper, full of dried fruit for our lunch and Willy offered us a slab of corned beef. It was one of a number of pieces that were floating around in a drum of what appeared to be green slime. We declined, explaining that we had already taken too much advantage of his generosity.

The *Sydney Morning Herald* ran a full-page article on Willy after he gave some land for an Aboriginal Reserve. I took it back to show him, and after he perused it for a while, I realized that he couldn't read, so read it out to him. As I read, Willy kept having hysterics and finally said, "What a lot of bull, I must have been pissed out of my mind when I spoke to that reporter". Makes you wonder why we read the paper, one thing was true though, with less land, he started calling it Six and a Half Emus.

Willy had a large family, boys and girls, and the girls were quite beautiful. One day he announced he had saved up and was taking the whole family to London to meet the Queen. In Darwin they all bought new clothes, but got no further. I know that Willy couldn't resist a gamble and he reckoned that Darwin was a town full of crooks. For all that, Willy was a good mate, and most certainly a character.

Another mate from Alice Springs, Ivan Wiess ended up in Borroloola when he sold his business and inevitably became another of the local characters.

We had come to rely on Ivan flying parts to us on a few occasions and it was our loss when he sold up in Alice Springs and moved to Borroloola. I honestly believe there was something in the air up there as the strangest things used to happen, like Ivan normal one day and putting a gun to his head and blowing out his brains the next.

Some of the toughest men I know told me they would never attend the Borroloola Rodeo as they reckoned it was just a riot waiting to happen, and I'm sure our Sundowners were perfectly happy when we left after attending one.

When talking to Ted Egan about the Borroloola country he spoke about Mallapunya Springs Station (he had incorporated a verse about George Darcy, the owner in one of his songs). He said it was a pity we would never see the wonderful tropical fruit trees and the Springs as the Darcys would probably shoot tourists on sight.

Determined to try, on one trip I left the mob in the coach on the main road and rode our trail bike into the Station. In the garage I came upon a Toyota and sticking out from underneath were the biggest bare feet I've ever seen. The fellow came out and introduced himself as Wogga Darcy, and I stated my case. Wogga listened and then said, "I reckon you better git mate, we don't want no tourists around here".

There was a large Aboriginal population on the Station and the Darcys themselves were part Aboriginal. A few years later the ABC decided these people would make a great documentary.

A rather patronising reporter interviewed Wogga and asked, "You have never married, Mr. Darcy, so what do you do for female companionship?" Wogga looked nonplussed and answered "Easy, I just run the buggers down".

Fiona came to Mallapunya as a school teacher and finished up marrying Norman, the youngest of the Darcy boys and later set up a clothing shop in a van and travelled around the Stations selling her wares. We kept meeting up with Fiona along the road and the Sundowners gave her a lot of business, buying jeans, rodeo shirts and such like.

I worked on Fiona to allow us to camp on their fabled Springs, which ultimately, we did and Fiona and Norman arranged that we be welcomed rather than shot.

Years later one of our Sundowners, Olive Murphy was travelling on the QE2 to Singapore when it stopped to pick up passengers in Darwin. Olive was talking to one of the new arrivals and asked where she came from, and got the answer "Oh a place no one has ever heard of, Mallapunya Springs". Olive replied, "Never heard of? Why, I've camped there". Of course, it was Fiona, and she said, "Well you must have been with Doreen and Bill". Just another instance of what a small world it is.

1973 Between trips we managed to see a little of TV and they were screening a daring new show called *Number* 96. Also, due to rising cost, the price of our three-week Central Australian trips had risen to $140.

Arthur and Bess Liddle from Angas Downs finally came for a holiday in Sydney and as this was their first big trip out of the Territory, they marvelled over many things. One thing Arthur asked almost straight away, "Where do the trees grow for these huge telegraph poles?". I had never given this a thought, but in South Australia and the Territory the poles are all ferro- concrete and are called stobie poles. We took them up to the Hawkesbury River, and Arthur said, "In flood, ay", I said "No, it's always like that" and he became thoughtful, turned to Bess and said, "Fancy it never runs dry."

A great attraction at that time in Sydney was a show called *Les Girls* at Kings Cross, so we took them along. It was all singing and dancing with what appeared to be beautiful, shapely girls. The rather perverse attraction was that they were all men. After the show I said to Bess, "You know they were all blokes". She looked at me and said, "Don't be silly, as a little girl I was brought up in a black's camp, and I can tell you I know a bit about the difference and those certainly weren't blokes." Although I felt she had missed the whole point of the show, I decided not to argue.

Then it was off to the Blue Mountains where Bess was quite afraid of the landscape and wouldn't venture anywhere near the lookouts, saying, "Take me back to the nice flat country".

The late Barry Morris was a good bloke and a mate, regardless of what some reporters may have written, and we arranged for Arthur and Bess to meet Barry and his wife Annette. Over afternoon tea Barry got a bright idea - his next door neighbour bred prize cattle and would Arthur like to have a look. Yes, he was more than happy and in his new Mercedes we drove around the paddocks admiring cattle. Then suddenly we stopped when the motor overheated, the long grass had wound around the pulley and snapped the fan belt, and we had to walk back. Arthur loved telling this back home, "You know the grass in New South Wales grows so long..." Arthur did even better after a trip to America with Noel Fullarton, and could intersperse a conversation with "When we were in the States..." Noel was invited to America to contest camel races, and of course upheld our reputation by winning, and Arthur went along to give him a hand.

1973 was the Centenary year of the discovery of Ayers Rock, well by whitefellas that is. Derek Roff (Senior Ranger) planned a re-enactment and the boys from Angas Downs carried it out.

With a string of camels and Tim rigged out as Mr. Gosse, they rode around the Rock looking very authentic. Arthur had arranged all the right equipment he believed Gosse would have used.

I can only list 1973 as a no hassles year, the coach performed superbly, and all the trips were booked-out well in advance, even though we had ceased all advertising years before.

1974 With Tasmania the first trip of the year, we arrived to find Hobart divided with a span missing on the Tasman Bridge, and this required a long detour up river to get around. With the high arch of the roadway some car drivers never saw the gap (caused by a boat hitting a pylon) until too late and went straight over the edge. What a way to go, then of course there was the photo of one car that just stopped in time and was teetering on the edge. After it was repaired, I'll bet that I'm not the only person who's had something of a phobia about driving over the bridge.

There was another trap to Tasmania that I had never anticipated. We normally refuelled in Tasmania when we arrived there, but this time topped-up in Melbourne before sailing.

We drove up to Cradle Mountain and did all the usual things, and on the morning we were due to leave it was bitterly cold. The coach, which normally started immediately, refused to start. I tried and tried, but it wouldn't fire. After nearly flattening the batteries I turned to the locals for help. The first question they asked was "Where did you pick up your fuel?" When I said Melbourne, they told me the problem.

Bass Strait Crude contains an excess of wax which separates at very low temperatures forming crystals that block fuel lines and filters. It appears B.P. produce summer and winter fuel for Victoria (it is costly removing the wax) and 100% winter fuel only for Tassie, and I had a tank of summer fuel. They advised me to wait a few hours, then with a boost from a couple of extra batteries it started. It was a lesson well learnt and I topped up with the local winter fuel at the first opportunity.

1974 was one of the wettest years on record and in Alice Springs the Todd River was in flood most of the year. We, along with about half the townsfolk spent most of a day being entertained by watching the effort to retrieve an Australian Pacific Coach that had been swept off the river causeway.

I asked one of the APT fellows later about the fate of the driver - "I think he's probably selling pies on Flinders Street Station," he replied. One of our passengers, Ron Dorman was a freelance photographer, and regarding it as a photo opportunity, sold the shots to a popular magazine. What didn't help was the prominent "L" plate someone had attached to the front of the coach.

It was a year when we swam in rivers and creeks where we had never seen water before and that included Lake Eyre.

LAKE EYRE In 1964 Sir Donald Campbell attempted and broke the world land speed record for a wheel driven car at a speed of 648.5kph on Madigan Gulf, Lake Eyre. This was on Muloorina Station owned by the Price family, and Elliot Price became involved in back-up and support for the attempt. It was about three years after this that we decided to take a party out to see this site, so being on private property, we contacted the family. Elliott Price had passed away, but he left a married son and two married daughters to carry on the property. The elder daughter Hazel, was married to Bill Mitchell, and over time Hazel and Bill became our friends. We were allowed to camp on the Homestead lagoon and shown great hospitality at no charge.

The track out to Madigan Gulf was four-wheel drive, but with a burst of speed across the bad patches the big coach never had any problems. The Gulf at the south-eastern end of Lake Eyre was like any sea, after parking the coach in the coastal dunes we walked down to the beach, but instead of water there was a sheet of white salt stretching to the horizon. Straight ahead was the course where Campbell established the world speed record. It was hard to believe that standing there we were 21ft. or 6.35 metres below sea level.

On our living room walls are two prized paintings by regular Sundowner, George Nash. One showing the coach parked in the coastal dunes with the Lake bed stretching into the background, and the other across the beach with Sundowner passengers strung out from the beach to the far distance across the Lake.

This was drastically changed in 1974 when the Lake was flooded to the highest level in recorded history. Apart from the different colour, we might well have parked in the coastal sand dunes at Cronulla beach, as we looked out at an inland sea, with surf crashing in on the beach. The water was eight to ten feet deep and I was able to get some good shots of Doreen doing what we had though impossible, surfing in Lake Eyre.

When camping in the bush it doesn't pay to move too far from your tent if you have to get up during the night. We had one fellow who did this, and with no one answering his calls, he had the good sense to wander no further and simply lay down and went to sleep where he was. He had no trouble finding the camp again come daylight. The Sundowner crowd took pity on him and bought a bell to hang around his neck.

Getting lost in the bush is no joke and with experience you automatically stay aware of which way shadows fall, even the shadow of the vehicle you are driving and know which direction you are heading - although I couldn't make much sense of the chap who told me that he would never get lost as all he had to do was face north, and east was to the right and west the left. I didn't bother to ask how he knew where north was.

One night after leaving Alice Springs we camped off the Stuart Highway just south of Central Mount Stuart. It was an old road camp clearing completely surrounded by thick mulga and in this sort of country the mulga trees all look identical. Around breakfast the following morning we found one of our crowd missing. Bob's tent was empty and no sign of him anywhere. That morning there was an unusually heavy fog and before we could do any sort of tracking, the whole group were tramping all through the bush calling out Bob's name.

The bitumen road was to the west, but if he walked in any other direction, he could walk a hundred miles into nothing, so I finally decided to drive back to the village of Ti Tree and get police help.

Bill the cop rounded up his old police black tracker and his wife. The old chap looked a bit shaky and I asked some Aboriginal kids if he was any good. "Na, 'ees nearly blind, poor bugger, but 'is missus is real good, ay," they answered. Bill followed me back to camp and sat down to have a cup of coffee as the old couple trotted off into the bush. Bill assured us they would find Bob with no problems. At this stage the infernal fog started to break up and the sun began shining through.

Later a car pulled up and Bob, looking absolutely deadbeat staggered out of the back seat. He told of how he had got up during the night and although knowing he was lost, made the mistake of continuing to walk around thinking he could find the camp. He then lay down and went to sleep only to wake up dripping wet in the fog. It was time to get smart and he sat it out until the sun broke through and knowing he had not crossed the bitumen he simply walked with the sun on his back to the bitumen and flagged down a passing car. He did not know whether we were north or south, but he soon found us.

I thanked Bill and pointed out that we were OK as we had our bloke, but he had lost his trackers. He just laughed and said he would just cruise down the road as they would come out right on Bob's footsteps. Bob was going to book with us the following year but was talked into joining an adventure holiday in New Zealand where we were told he lost his life in a fall.

At many places diesel fuel was only available in 44-gallon (200 lt.) drums, and as the drums were reused, it sometimes happened empty drums lost their filler caps and water or dirt would get in before they were refilled.

On one trip we made it into Alice Springs with the motor misfiring, having picked up water in the fuel. A slab of beer soon activated our old mate German George to "do" our injectors and clean out the water in the system. With everything fixed, we were all set to head south only to be told that South Australia was flooded and all roads were closed.

The only alternative was back through Queensland and with bitumen right through to Mt. Isa we should be OK. At Cloncurry more bad news, with heavy overnight rain closing all roads in Central Queensland. Another detour, the only way across to the coast was to drive north to Normanton, then east across the Atherton Tableland to Innisfail.

It was all easy going until sometime after leaving Normanton when the oil pressure light started to flicker. I checked the oil level thinking that it must have dropped perhaps due to a leak, but it was OK, in fact it was slightly over full. Then the rain caught up with us at Croydon, but in an hour or so we had reached the brand-new bitumen of the Mt. Surprise Beef Road which meant a sealed road to the coast and all the way home.

One worry ended, we had made it all the way around the flooded roads, but our other worries were far from over. With plenty of oil in the motor and no oil leaks, I reasoned that either the pump was failing or more likely an engine bearing was on the way out. Shades of the very first trip with the Austin that cost us a new motor in Adelaide.

From Mt. Surprise to Ravenshoe its mostly uphill all the way as the road leaves the savannah plain and climbs to the Atherton Tableland, so in driving rain and poor visibility I was trying to monitor the low oil pressure and praying that we wouldn't be doing an engine rebuild on the side of the road. To cut a long story short, we made it to Ravenshoe and coasted downhill to Innisfail, then rather than turn left for the hour and a half drive to Cairns, decided to turn right to Mourilyn for a very good reason.

Immigrant Italians dominate much of the commerce in far North Queensland and I knew the Cali brothers, Johnstone River Transport's maintenance workshop and factory was situated there. I had a great regard for Joe Cali, and although they normally didn't take in outside work, I threw myself on his mercy. He asked if any work had been carried out on the motor recently and I told him about German George doing the injectors in Alice Springs.

He nodded and told a mechanic to drain the oil. Then he put his finger in the oil and lifted it to his nose and told me to do the same. "Diesel eh?" he asked. Then went on to explain that "When the bloke in Alice did the injectors I doubt he replaced the sealing washers, probably didn't have any. In any other diesel it wouldn't have mattered as the injectors are on the outside of the motor, but with a Detroit they are under the rocker covers, then cruising at about 2000 revs per minute the tiniest leak drains into the motor and gradually builds up and dilutes the oil".

They resealed the injectors, renewed the oil and the oil pressure returned to normal, and to my great relief, Joe's opinion that no harm had been done to the motor proved correct, but that had certainly been one hell of a trip.

Joe Cali arrived in Australia in 1928 (the year I was born) from Sicily, landing in Brisbane with a suitcase, a mandolin, no English and 10 pounds in his pocket. He settled in Innisfail and although only 16 managed to get a drivers licence. He learnt English talking to, and carrying supplies to, cane-cutting gangs. Four years later he bought a taxi, then a second. Extortion was rife with the Sicilian Mafia at this time and when Joe refused to pay they blew up both his cabs. Undaunted Joe bought a gun, showed it to the gang leader, and told him if anything happened to his next cab he would be a dead man.

He started again, and no vehicle was ever touched. In 1937 his brother Len, then 16, came out and joined him.

After the Second World War the Cali Bros., under the name Johnstone River Transport expanded into the bus business. Their problem, as I was to find in later years, was they couldn't buy buses, so they simply went ahead and built their own, earning a Certificate of Excellence from the Italian Government, which promoted the work of Italian craftsmen abroad.

In 1948 they received a letter from Reo Motors, America, "We wish to compliment you on this splendid bus body that compares favorably with any American bus". C.S.R. opened their huge bulk sugar terminal at Mourilyn in 1960 and Johnstone River Transport won the haulage contract. Joe went heavily into debt to buy a fleet of A.E.C. trucks that came with no cabs, so he set up an assembly line to make and fit cabs made from wood to meet the contract deadline.

I was sad to hear some years later that Joe Cali had passed away. We need people like Joe, a loss to us and to our country.

1974 ended with one of the greatest disasters that our country had ever seen. On Christmas Day 1974, Darwin was almost wiped out when hit by Cyclone Tracy. As a declared disaster area, it was many months before we were allowed back in, and the state of the city was beyond belief. Somebody had cleaned up selling hundreds of "T" shirts emblazoned with the words "Oh, what a night I had with Tracy".

On our first visit to Darwin after the cyclone we camped at Howard Springs with Ivan, a driver for one of the big coach lines. Ivan had been having numerous problems, one being motor overheating and he was driving around with the back engine panel up to try and get more air around the motor. In those days there was an extensive camping area at Howard Springs and people could swim day and night in the pool formed by the warm spring water. Also, there were two gates that were locked at 10.00pm, one about half a km up the road, and one at the entrance of the camping area and we were all issued with keys.

That night as a last thing I lifted the rear engine panel up on the coach when I disengaged the main power switch and we all went to bed. Later we were awoken by someone pounding their fists against the side of our coach, screaming, "Come out Ivan you bastard, I'm going to kill you".

This fellow was puffing as he must have run from the gate about half a km up the road. climbed out of the tent demanding to know what was going on, and he put his head down and charged me. I jumped to one side and he kept going straight into our small lightweight tent. The tent was wrecked, and I prayed for Doreen who was wrapped up in the wreckage.

He wheeled about and waving his arms like windmills, charged me again and missed again as I did the Spanish bull fighter move. He turned and fell to the ground exhausted and muttered something about "My daughter told me all about you, and you are going to pay". I have no idea what this meant. Then he pounded the ground with his fists.

Finally, he said "You're not Ivan, are you?" I said, "No, why did you think I was?" He pointed to the rear engine panel that I had left up, the same as Ivan's.

Doreen had crawled out of the wreckage of our tent, and I went to the coach and got a couple of cold cans, opened them and gave him one.

"Is Ivan here?" he asked. I lied and said "No', but in fact he had set up camp up the back out of sight. He finally trudged off and after some running repairs, Doreen and I went back to bed.

Then we were awoken by the noise of Ivan's mob packing up and breaking camp. It was scary as he floodlit our tent driving past and out in the dark, on high beam.

Over breakfast I asked why no one came out to back me up during the night, and everyone freely admitted they were scared out of their wits by the madman and they hid down in their sleeping bags.

The manager then came around and asked where was Ivan. I gave him a brief resume and he said, "He's taken off with his key, I'll kill him". I suggested he had better get on a queue.

It was a well-accepted fact that with Cyclone Tracy and its aftermath, many people were deeply traumatised, and many people were acting like nut cases for a long time after.

I had known Ivan quite well until that night, but was never to see or hear of him again.

GO-ANYWHERE COACH

Specialist outback safari coach operator Bill Hand, of 'Sundowner Coach Tours', has to face formidable obstacles on occasions. This selection of pictures taken by his wife Doreen and coach party members shows the situations the coach has faced and overcome on recent trips. The Denning-built unit has a Detroit Diesel 6V-53 coupled to an Allison AT540 automatic driving a Detroit Locker No-Spin drive axle.

HUGE bow wave is pushed up by the coach as Bill Hand crosses the South Alligator River between Jim Jim and El Sharana, in the Northern Territory, while passengers watch from the bank. It emerges watertight at the other side. At right (below), Sundowner passes what is believed to be the only camel wagon in use in Australia. Here Aboriginal contractor Bobbie Nailen supplies food to muster camps on Anna Creek Station between Oodnadatta and Maree, in South Aust.

SPECIALLY developed half-track belts assist the drive and trailing axle in de-bogging the coach in soft conditions. Drive wheels can also be fitted with another kind of wrap-on traction assister for heavy going.

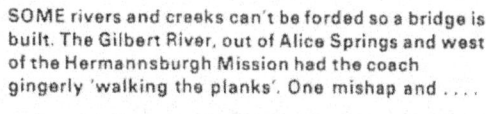

WASHING the coach in a river is a chore gladly undertaken after having traversed bulldust and mud. Passengers saw alligators in the river that night, though. River is the Robinson, east of Borroloola in the N.T.

SOME rivers and creeks can't be forded so a bridge is built. The Gilbert River, out of Alice Springs and west of the Hermannsburgh Mission had the coach gingerly 'walking the planks'. One mishap and ....

1975 FIJI

The year that Sir John Kerr dismissed the Whitlam Government. We were in Fiji and couldn't make head nor tail of the garbled radio reports filtering through.

Len and Dorothy Webb were regular Sundowners and had travelled on many of our trips and had just returned from a tour of Fiji. We could run tours to New Zealand, so why not Fiji? After all, they had been there and would act as advisors. They told us how all those foreigners, Indians and whatever, were running everything and the poor locals were missing out. But they had been impressed by Tommy (not his real name for obvious reasons) who had acted as their tour guide. The Government had had enough of these other mobs controlling all the business activity and wanted to promote native Fijians into running things, particularly tourism.

The Fijian Government told us Tommy was the perfect example of this new breed of tour managers. He could take us off the beaten track, see things the tourists never get to see, and experience true adventures. Well, Gus Williams was an Aboriginal and a most honest and reliable tour operator and it sounded like Tommy would be exactly like Gus.

The Webbs knew many Sundowners and even before we had decided, people were queueing up to join the trip.

Sun. 9 Nov. Well it was on, we flew into Nadi (Nandi) and spent the night at the Coconut Inn. Mon. 10 Nov. Tommy arrived with two girl cooks, Nancy and Anisia, and we boarded an old bus. We bounced along a pot-holed road for hours and I was expecting someone to eventually call for a toilet stop, but they must have crossed their legs. We finally stopped on Mt. Victoria for an extensive view of the Island, then drove on to Pt. Ellington. This island was called Viti Levu and tomorrow we would take a boat across the channel to the island of Vanua Levu.

We were to stay the night in the house of a sugar plantation, but on arrival found the house occupied and we were relegated to the verandah. Everyone put their sleeping bags in a row, but we had spied a small shed in the garden and moved in there. This was fortunate, as we weren't woken by the screams during the night. It appears the locals had caught coconut crabs and left them in baskets on the verandah. The crabs apparently weren't stupid and worked out how to open the lids and on their way, crawled over the faces of the sleeping people.

Tue.11 Nov. I was awakened by a bright light and a strange voice, and all I could see were two great hairy black columns. When I focused, I realized they were legs belonging to a giant Fijian man, holding a lantern. He kept saying "Get up, tides in". I looked at my watch, it was five o'clock. The ferry was an old sailing boat and we were told that the channel was really a sea trench, and one of the deepest in the Pacific, which wasn't at all reassuring. We had breakfast on board. The smell of food and the exhaust fumes didn't go well for Doreen who spent a most uncomfortable time leaning over the side, wishing land would come quickly.

Our boat couldn't land as there was no wharf, and we had to transfer into dinghies, this was done with a great deal of confusion, but we were to find this was normal. There was a toilet where we landed, and everyone queued up only to find it locked, so it was a matter of hold on while a kid was sent to the village to find the key.

We transferred to a bus assuming we would drive to the next village, but when we got there, found the road cut with the village on the other side of about half a mile of water. Our gear was taken by boat, but as the water was only knee high we walked, or trudged across.

Tommy had been giving me lessons on our expected behaviour. The villages we would stay in would not have dealt with tourists before. There would always be welcoming ceremonies that would be 100% genuine, conducted in the Fijian language, and as guests we must know what to do.

When entering a village, we would be conducted to a bure where the Chief (Toroga) and some senior men will be waiting. They will sit at one end, and we at the other, all cross-legged. The white chief (me) and their chief each through a spokesman (Matinavanua) will exchange gifts of Yaqona (Yangona, or Kava). First up I present my gift. If the chief accepts it, he reciprocates by offering us mixed Yagona. I will be the first to drink, then his Matinavanua, then the Chief, then our eldest male passenger, then the likewise Fijian, then one after the other until all have drunk. Also before accepting, clap once, then drink and clap three times. Whew!

To refuse to drink is a great insult. In the evening there is always dancing. It's normal for girls to ask you up, except they don't ask, but tap you on the knee, it's extremely rude to refuse.

Tommy impressed on us that this was no joke and had to be carried out properly, or it would reflect very badly on us, and him in particular. After we arrived Tommy conferred with an old fellow and came running back, this was going to be even more complicated - a special ceremony.

There were two parallel rows of cowry shells with the Chief sitting cross-legged at one end. had to crawl between the rows up to the Chief, then sit, and he removed a whale's tooth (tabua "tambua") from around his neck and put in around mine. Then we had the hand clapping and drinking bit. Apparently, this was very significant as the tabua can only be worn by the Great Chief.

Tommy said later that I did well by not touching the shells when I was crawling, as this would show great disrespect and people have been killed for less. The problem was, I don't think he was joking. We then sat cross-legged on mats and had a great feast, all using our fingers.

This was followed by a crashing of drums and the men put on a warrior dance. They had bunches of leaves tied around their legs and ankles, and their arms and wrists. They were painted up and carried long spears. These fellows were absolutely fearsome, as they leaped and yelled and twirled their spears.

After supper it was a "Tralala" or normal dance. We found this could go on all night, and was fuelled by constant helpings of Yaqona which kept you going. But grey hair warrants great respect, and Doreen pointed out that the grey hairs (nearly all the Sundowners) had to get their sleep. We were allocated four bures (huts), pit toilets and open showers. We just settled in when the rain came down and it rained all night.

Wed.12 Nov. We carried the gear back across the bay at low tide to our waiting bus. The bus was air-conditioned as it had no windows. Then the rain came, and we dropped the blinds. This had the effect of being in a submarine. The blinds not only kept out the rain, but also the sheets of flying mud from the wheels.

We finally reached the town of Labasa (Lambasa) where Tommy's brother was a local medical officer and had arranged a feast in the hospital grounds. Straight after this Tommy and Anisia totally vanished, never to be seen again, and thank heavens Nancy stayed with us, or things would have become impossible.

I had learnt all the essential routines, including my lavish thank-you speech, and at every opportunity we purchased Yaqona roots for the necessary gifts. From then on, someone would appear with a message advising on what we must do and where to go. It became like an elaborate game of *Survivor.*

Thu. 13 Nov. The village of Nasekula, this came as something of a relief as there were no official duties for me as the men were all away loading sugar. It was most relaxing with only women and children. Then back to the bus to drive to Saivou village. On the way the bus became bogged, and people appeared from out of the fields to help. I found it rather satisfying to sit back and watch someone else having to de-bog a bus.

We had to go through the usual ceremonies on arrival, but we felt a little on edge, as these seemed strange and moody people. They advised us to watch our belongings as evil people come out from the hills and steal everything. We were starting to miss Tommy and his advice.

Fri. 14 Nov. We were handed a missive that said, "Today we walk across the island to Nabalebale Village, horses will carry luggage". What it didn't say was the distance was 12 miles (about 20km) and there was a mountain range in the way.

Before we could leave, some of the locals got into a fury claiming one of our ladies had bought a hat and not paid for it. It was all solved when it appeared she had given the money to the wrong person.

The horses were loaded up and plunged down into a river and climbed out on the other side, but we had to walk a tree-trunk that had been felled across the river. Some of our folk found this very daunting, not being trained tight-rope walkers.

After walking about four miles through the jungle at the foot of the mountain range, we came on an old man selling fruit, and called a sit-down break. He made up fruit juice for us and I bought a watermelon for later. (This I was to curse, as I had to carry it up the mountain.) We climbed and slipped on the red clay track through showers of rain, and the horses found it difficult, often slipping back. At the top of the range we called a halt while our strung-out group came together. We cut the watermelon on some big leaves and divided it up. Then the strangest thing happened, some children arrived from out of nowhere selling drinks and sandwiches.

It became obvious that many of our folk were not travelling well, apart from being exhausted, they were having tummy problems, probably from the food and water. I was looking forward to just going downhill, but the wet red clay was treacherous, and the showers turned to steady rain. At times the horses with their loads couldn't stop and slid downhill with their legs held rigid.

Suddenly the track widened out and there were teams of men clearing and widening the track. They said they were building a road across the island, and suggested we should come back next year. At this point one of our fellows collapsed, and it was agreed they would take him in their Landrover. They took off with Reg in the back, and the last we saw was the Landrover sliding sideways downhill in the mud. We could see Reg's face looking terrified enough to forget his illness.

Next Dorothy collapsed, and the workers cut poles and made a stretcher and carried her down the mountain. When we got down to sea level the rain stopped, it became excessively humid and we were totally exhausted. Just before the village we saw what looked like a crowd of kids playing in a lagoon, and I threw off my coat and fell into the water. There were deafening screams as a mob of naked girls leapt out of the water and hid in the bushes. If you could be killed for touching some shells, I hated to think what the penalty would be for this.

We were to stay the night in the village of Nabalebale and if we offended the chief or anyone else, it was just too bad, we were totally beyond any ceremonies, dancing, or any activity at all, and Doreen pushed the "old grey hair" story all the way. There were no showers, only the river, and it required sloshing through the mud some distance to the pit toilet.

Sat.15 Nov. We caught a bus to Savu Savu where there were boiling springs and some quite good shops. Then on to Dromuninuke, this was a very pretty place, and was the most civilized village we had visited. Instead of the kava business, we shared a cup of tea with the chief. They showed us red prawns in the creek, organised a fish drive, and a kid climbed a coconut palm and threw us down fresh coconuts.

Just the same, that night they insisted on the Tralala dance. I couldn't face it and sneaked off. I sat on the beach, my back against a palm and watched the moon come up over the sea, then heard giggling behind me. A couple of young girls jumped me...... and dragged me back to the dance.

Sun/Mon.16/17 Nov. Everyone went to church, no escaping this one, and our more knowledgeable people explained that it was part Roman Catholic and part Wesleyan. I had to crank up my practice thank-you speech and someone produced Tommy's daily missive with future instructions.

After lunch it was a one-hour drive to the ferry, then about another hour to Kioa Island. With no wharf and a shallow sea, the ferry stood off some distance and we had to jump overboard and struggle ashore with our gear. A tall rather tough looking fellow waded out to meet us. I smiled, put my hand up, and shouted "Bulla" all in the approved way. I waited for the usual reply, but instead he said in a loud voice "We don't speak Fijian here". (Well there you go, I've blown it again.)

These people we found were Ellice Islanders and certainly not Fijian, they were possibly part European, part Chinese, well I don't really know, but certainly different and even had their own language, although with an English teacher at the school, the kids all spoke English.

We were led into the long house where we were marched in pairs onto a platform and auctioned. At first, I thought we were part of a local slave market, but it was only families bidding for whom they would accept as guests.

We got Alfred, the chiefs son, who didn't say "Bulla". The huts were built high up on poles, with rickety ladders up to the front door. Alfred said we would have afternoon tea, and he produced a couple of rather disgusting looking chipped hospital kidney dishes, and poured hot liquid into them. Whatever it was, it certainly wasn't tea, but it was hard to identify after the four spoons of sugar he added.

Alfred had gone to school in New Zealand as we guessed from his accent and lived alone in his hut. He had a pile of New Zealand religious magazines and hidden under them a few "Playboys", which seemed to suggest he was widely read.

As befitted guests, we were to have chicken that night. Alfred instructed some kids to catch one of the chocks that scratched out a living pecking at coconuts under the hut. By the time they caught it, I think the chock had died of exhaustion.

All meals were held in the long house, and we were instructed not to stand up during the meal, unless you wanted to make a speech. The guests sat on the floor, with the food laid out in front of them, and the family sat behind and waited while the guests ate. If you ate everything, your family had nothing. Our chicken looked more like a dead pterodactyl and was as tough as plastic. I chewed and chewed and finally gave up.

Alfred asked, "Are you finished?" and we swapped places. His great jaws crushed the chock, I'll swear, bones and all.

The community toilet was the local beach, and Doreen and Daphne (one of our women staying in a hut nearby) were proceeding down in the dark, when a gentleman intercepted them and asked did they require the toilet. They admitted they did, and he offered his services as a guide saying, "The beach is the place, the tide comes in and the tide goes out".

Alfred took pity on us and arranged for us to use the school teacher's "flush toilet". This was a toilet bowl mounted over a long drop, and flushed by dipping into a 44-gallon drum that was filled by runoff from the roof.

They drank a rather fearsome grog called Toddy, which was made by cutting off a coconut bud and sealing a bottle to the stalk, the palm dripped juice into the bottle where it fermented.

Some of the folk amused themselves swimming and paddling around in dugout outrigger canoes. Our second evening meal in the meeting hall proved not a lot better than the first and was followed by a western style dance.

Tue. 18 Nov. After breakfast in the meeting hall we were to be met by the boat and the all metal band gave us a rousing send off, except the boat never appeared. This happened again, and then again, before the boat finally appeared. Then it was time to pick up our gear and wade out to the boat. No special speeches required, just a wave and a shouted goodbye. It took 90 minutes to reach Lamini village by boat. This was a village of women and kids as all the men were away working somewhere, and thankfully this meant no speeches or ritual.

Wed. 19 Nov. We chartered a bus to the Somo Somo shops and swam at a beach famous because Prince Charles had swum there, and the coral was very good. I was fascinated by the banging under the front of the bus, and got under to look. It had broken front springs and every time it hit a bump, the front axle bashed the sump. Sooner or later the axle and crankshaft must meet, probably breaking the crankshaft, but you don't get smart with bus drivers, so I didn't comment. As he had no handbrake, the driver used to leap out and chock the wheel with a lump of wood.

Reg was playing with his little radio trying to find some English, but no luck, it was all in Fijian. We heard them say Australia, then Whitlam, then Frazer, then Kerr, and kept on repeating them, but we had no idea what was happening, and it was only when we got home that we found that the Whitlam Government had been dismissed.

Thu. 20 Nov. Waited for boat that never arrived. As we had some sick people, we were directed to the hospital outpost. Pills were dispensed wrapped in old newspaper, and ointment also in newspaper. To fix an upset tummy, medicine was supplied in a "Fiji" brand beer bottle with the label still on.

People in Fiji cook with kerosine and everywhere there are little tin shed purveyors of "Karosin". Seeing one of these I walked over to see what else might be available, and the only other thing for sale was a small slightly rusty tin of Cottees jam. Someone else had come up with a loaf of bread (all that was available). The bread was carefully cut into the exact number of pieces, and each smeared with a small amount of jam. It was the best afternoon tea we could imagine.

Dinner that night was very bad, not much and poor at that. The main course looked and tasted like green bootlaces. The problem was we were there an extra day as the boat had not arrived. Tommy was supposed to be with us to settle the account with the women and they seemed to think I must have the money and I was not handing it over.

Fri. 21 Nov. The boat arrived and stood off at sea and sent in a dinghy. It went back and forth transporting the group. It was returning for the last of us when a huge Fijian armed with a machete walked up to me and demanded payment for our stay. I tried to explain about Tommy, but he would have none of it. He flew into a temper and slashed around with the machete, and where we had plants all around us, we were now in a clearing. Meanwhile Doreen was loading the last of the mob on the dinghy.

I felt like Horatio holding the bridge outside Rome. A fellow came sprinting down the beach all dressed in white, like Darwin rig, and he looked important. He shouted at the big fellow in Fijian and the two of them proceeded to have a heated argument. The newcomer signalled me to go, and he didn't have to do it twice, I ran, jumped into the boat and we were off.

The boat was a clipper ship, skippered by an Australian, Robbie Lepper. He apologized for being a day late, no one had told him we were white people, and Fijians don't worry about being a day late. Someone asked about food, and Robbie put on a magnificent fish barbeque. This was utter luxury, blue sky, white sails, blue sea, good food, magic!

Sat. 22 Nov. Went ashore on the Island of Karo for the day and saw the locals calling up turtles in the lagoon. We were given large seed pods which resembled turtles.

Sun. 23 Nov. After breakfast aboard, everyone thanked Robbie over and over. We then disembarked at Levuka on Ovalau Island. We proceeded to Viro village which was very quiet as it was Sunday. They housed us in three bures, and there were good showers and toilets. These people hadn't been paid, and wanted a cheque, so Doreen and I paid them, which left us flat broke. We explained this to the group, and asked them to hand over all their money, as we might have to pool it to get to Suva, where we could get a transfer from Australia.

Mon. 24 Nov. After breakfast picked up by boat (the owner was Ernest, a Frenchman) for the journey back to the main island of Viti Levu. On the boat, a very gentlemanly old chap came up and introduced himself as Tommy's uncle, and had our secret instructions for the rest of the trip. Also, he had a handfull of cheques to cover us from then on. I explained about our money problems and he assured us that all would be fixed up. After landing we waited the regulation hour or so for our pick-up bus that finally drove us to the village of Dakuivuna and the chief spoke to us through the school teacher, who acted an interpreter.

For some reason, there was a church service and it was expected that we would all attend. When the plate was passed around, our folk were embarrassed as they only had a few coins left. The money was counted, and it was announced how much the locals had contributed, and then how much the visitors. A murmur went around the Church, and I thought that we had blown it, but then realized that they were amazed we had given so much! There was very little flat land in the village and it was necessary to brave a slippery red mud slope to move around. Thankfully the Tralala ended at 11pm, as I think they were disappointed at our lack of enthusiasm.

Tues. 25 Nov. We left at 8am by bus to Wailotua No. 2 Bridge on the Rewa River, and waited the normal hour for long boats. Then down river to Vatukarasa village to a welcome lunch. These people were great weavers, they made all sorts of baskets and mats. A good evening meal was followed by lots of dancing.

Wed. 26 Nov. Left again in the long boats down the Rewa to Virea Landing, and this time waited two hours for the bus to Suva, reaching Suva at 1.15pm.

While our people explored Suva (with empty pockets) we went straight to Tommy's bank and met the manager, Mr. Khan to arrange a money transfer from Australia. This wasn't easy in those days and took a great deal of time. While we were waiting, I passed over one of Tommy's cheques and asked if there was money in the bank to cover it. Khan looked most unhappy and finally said "I can't tell you that". I persisted and asked again if there was any money in Tommy's account. Again, he said, "I can't tell you, but I'll draw you a little picture". He drew a zero and pushed it over the desk.

Our money came through and we were given a bag of cash, then we headed downtown for a meeting with the group. Doreen had a list of the people's accounts, and reached into the bag and handed out the money - they could go on their buying spree now. We were in rather sleazy surroundings, and it's a wonder someone didn't snatch the bag.

With money in the pocket, we marched into a cafe and triumphantly ordered "T" bone steaks. Not one person could finish their meal, and we decided it would take some time before our bodies could accept real food again.

We stayed at a hotel on Duncan Road run by a Mr. Prasad, who asked me how we intended to pay and I put him off.

Thu. 27 Nov. Spent the morning at the Fiji Visitors Bureau and requested they find the Minister for Tourism. First up we asked that they guarantee the cheques by contacting Mr. Khan at the bank, and they told us this had been done. Then they proposed the Police pick up Tommy and we could take court action against him.

We discussed it and decided it was as much our fault, we had given Tommy more money than he had ever seen in his life, and it must have gone to this head. It was also partly the Tourism Office's fault, accrediting someone who had no idea of handling money. No, we didn't want to see Tommy in jail, and we would just have to wear the loss and put it down to experience.

The Sundowners wouldn't get any bargains today, the "Oriana" was in port and Suva was crawling with Australian tourists.

I gave Mr. Prasad Tommy's cheque and he flew into a rage and wanted cash. I asked why, and he said, "I will not accept a cheque signed by a Fijian, not even our Prime Minister". I told him it was the best I could do, and he rushed off in his car to the Bank. The Tourism Minister was as good as his word, and the cheque didn't bounce.

Fri. 28 Nov. At the bus depot we went through the same routine while Mrs. Ramdass rushed off to the bank with the cheque, and we had to wait in the bus until she returned. Again, the bank cashed the cheque and we were on our way. The main road along the south coast was a shocker, boggy sections, landslips and detours and we were happy to reach the Man Friday Resort at Korolevu. This was the first example of pure tourism we had seen. They had displays of dancing that were so "touristy" I was afraid the Sundowners might boo.

Sat. 29 Nov. Back on the bus and drove along the coast to Sigatoka, where a duty-free shop did good business. We had a good lunch beside a shady creek, then back to Nadi and the Coconut Inn.

Sun. 30th Nov. Qantas flight to Sydney.

Back home we sat down and did a serious study of the whole Fijian exercise, and came up with the following conclusions. Tommy supplied what we asked, off the tourist track and true adventure (almost to excess). The amount he charged fell well short of the actual cost. It seems he had no skills in costing and handling large amounts of money, and panicked when he realized the money had gone and the cheques would bounce. Maybe he thought it better that I get killed for passing a dud cheque than him.

At the reunion of the trip everyone agreed that the fare they paid couldn't have covered the cost and we were obviously well behind the eight ball, and they were all happy to make a contribution. To sum up, in the end we managed a slight loss, but put it down to experience and an absolutely unforgettable three weeks.

Although it was obvious we could never rely on Tommy again, we kept in contact with people in Fiji and early in 1976 we received a letter from the Fiji Visitors Bureau quote "Tommy ran afoul with another group from New Zealand and he's a dead pigeon as far as we are concerned."

To sail around Fiji in Robbie Lepper's boat was considered, but without being racist I could appreciate Mr. Prasad's point of view, and admit that the Fijians we dealt with couldn't run a chook raffle.

A bit of unrelated trivia - Nadi is pronounced Nandy, because D is pronounced as ND. Yaqona is pronounced Yangona, because Q is pronounced as NG.

On the subject of Yaqona/Kava, I have heard it described as an addictive drug, which I doubt very much. Having drunk gallons of it in those three weeks, I would be happy not to taste it again!

Back home in Australia we found the Government was becoming worried about the increasing consumption of Kava (or Piper Methysticum) among Aboriginal communities because of its alleged debilitating effects.

Kava is big business, and one of the few export products that can be completely produced and processed at village level. This brought Kava under the National Food Code and made it illegal to sell in Australia, the only country in the world to ban the substance. This has made the Fijians less than happy as they are struggling to find viable export commodities, and it seems certain such a ban could contravene G.A.T.T. free trade provisions.

At present, only the Aboriginal population in the Territory and the Islander community in Sydney have been big users, and in the other states there is no use for Kava at all.

1975. Fiji - Travelling between villages.

1976 OBIRI ROCK & MISSING FINGERS

This was the year that the North Australian Railway was closed down, with the result that we no longer had the problem of many rail and road crossings between Larrimah and Darwin.

At one time, trucks operating from Alice Springs unloaded at Larrimah and the goods were railed on to Darwin. The North Australian Railways Union pressured the Whitlam Government to upgrade the line and Larrimah was upgraded with gantry cranes and floodlights and thousands of steel sleepers were stock-piled to renew the line. Then the Fraser Government declared this was a waste of money and the operation was closed down.

The steel sleepers gradually disappeared to be seen again in the form of stockyards and fence posts all across the North.

Continuing the rail line from Adelaide, through Alice Springs to Darwin seems logical, but the old line going less than a quarter of the distance to Alice Springs seemed to make no sense at all.

For a number of years, we had been driving into the country now called Kakadu - it could be hazardous after a big Wet, with only dirt tracks and many creek crossings without bridges. There were both crocodile and buffalo shooters camps and we used to swim in many of the waterholes along with crocodile shooters who assured us the crocs were shot out.

On Jim Jim Creek, Tom Opitz and his wife Judy had a General Store, it was completely built of palm trunks, and elevated above the floodwaters. We used to camp behind Tom's Store and swim in the lagoon.

About 15 years later we were doing the tourist boat tour on Yellow Waters and the name of the boat was *Tom Opitz*. I asked the Ranger running the tour (who knew everything) did he know who Tom Opitz was, and he answered, "wouldn't have a clue".

At the end of the track by the East Alligator River there was a grog shanty, run by Terry Robinson called the Border Store. As the local Aboriginals had little use for money, Terry mostly traded in bark paintings, and we made the mistake of putting little value on them in those days.

The first time we saw the Dance of the Seven Sisters was at Terry's Border Store. Seven rather elderly ladies went off discretely and hid behind some rocks to take off their tops, then came out and danced topless. The dance is more of a shuffle.

A big fellow wielding a spear rather half-heartedly chased after them, causing one of our young fellows to remark he couldn't imagine why the big fellow would bother, and if it was required to be topless, why couldn't it be with some nice young ones.

I have seen this dance a number of times since as it appears to be the number one women's dance across the outback. It seems it requires long pendulous breasts to get the body painting correct, and there is little variation in footwork.

The Seven Sisters refers to the seven stars of the Pleiades in Orion, and in Greek legend were the seven daughters of Atlas and a nymph who were pursued by the wicked hunter

Orion and transformed into the group of stars bearing their name. The Aboriginal legend is strikingly similar and is also found in ancient beliefs all around the world.

Terry told us of the wonders of Obiri Rock (later called Ubirr) but there was no road access. Four-wheel-drives found a way around the edge of the flood plain on tracks that often varied after each wet season. I asked Terry, seeing this was such a wonderful place, if he could act as a guide and see if the coach could make it. We drove back up the main road a distance, then turned off to the right and into an Aboriginal camp, then kept going to the edge of the flood plain. To our left was water and to the right thick scrub.

He explained, too close to the water and you break through the crust and bog, then you are limited on driving to the right by increasing heavy scrub. It was a bit like the old story of driving along the beach with the tide out.

Terry guided us along and we finished up parking under a couple of magnificent Leichhardt trees, at the foot of a high sandstone cliff face. We climbed up a valley into an area of cave overhangs where there were wonderful ochre paintings of crocodiles, fish and spirit figures. Then climbing higher there were more cave paintings and we looked out over the flood plain and down on the coach parked at the bottom of the cliff below. This was an absolute highlight and we determined to include it on all future trips. Terry suggested that to keep the Natives on side we should ask for and pay an Aboriginal guide, and suggested asking for "Old Jim".

The access was more difficult after a big Wet and it was necessary to force a way through the edge of the scrub with mixed results, and it was still possible to break through the hard layer and bog.

Once, I felt the front wheels sink and pulled up immediately. A local tour operator showed up and tried to suppress a bout of hysterics at our predicament. When he stopped laughing with his passengers, he said "I'll pull out in no time with my four-wheel drive bus". He tied a rope from the coach onto the base of his bull bar and reversed. This ripped the bull bar straight off his vehicle. He stopped laughing and flew into a foul temper, stowed the bull bar and drove off saying "You can get your own bloody self out", which of course with time and labour we did.

The 1976 trip however was different, it was after a severe Wet season. Trying to find a way through I bogged the coach really badly, and it was obviously going to take a great deal of work to get it out.

Even "Old Jim" wrote us off and walked off back to his camp. We had broken through to greasy black mud and we would have to lift one wheel at a time and get Marsden matting

under them. As the wheels were down to the axles it was a huge jacking job and was taking hours. I must have been getting tired and careless because when some blocks fell under the coach, I rolled under in the mud to retrieve them. Just then the jacking blocks gave way and the coach crashed down. I rolled out and thanked my stars I was OK, then felt an intense stinging in my left hand.

I looked in disbelief at my fingers, half the index finger, one third the next, and the tip of the third were totally crushed. I have no idea what happened and in retrospect can only say I was lucky, as it could have been my head.

In the distance ahead, a fellow with a Toyota had set up a camp and some of our people ran down to get his help. Bing was a Works Surveyor planning a new road straight through the scrub to the Border Store. Another example of "You should have waited till next year". He agreed that I was a hospital case and proposed we drive around to the new mining camp at

Jabiru where aircraft were constantly flying back and forth to Darwin. We drove on to the strip at Jabiru to find not an aircraft anywhere and no staff to speak to.

Bing said to hang on, we would drive to Darwin. It was now dark, the dirt track was rough and winding, we came around a bend and a buffalo was standing in the middle of the track. I could see we had no way of stopping in time and in a flash I could see the buff flying over the bonnet, through the windscreen and crushing us to death. With an incredible bit of driving, Bing threw the wheel over and stamped on the brakes, with no buff we would have rolled over, but instead slammed into the buff side-on. The buff bellowed and charged off into the scrub. Bing sat for a moment, lit two cigarettes and put one in my mouth. I was using this trip to give up smoking, but decided that this was hardly the time.

My hand felt as though the Spanish Inquisition was trying out some of their equipment, and every half hour Bing lit another two cigarettes and put one in my mouth.

He told me they had some heavy equipment coming out from Darwin and he would use it to pull the coach out the following day.

We reached the old Darwin hospital just before dawn (a big new one in the Northern suburbs replaced it some time later) and Bing helped me out and asked was I OK. I said "Of course", passed out and woke up in a hospital bed.

Bing was as good as his word and Doreen drove the coach into Darwin several days later to make sure I was still alive. They amputated what was left of my fingers and I played host to an endless stream of tour operators and coach drivers. I couldn't believe how the word spread, and how many people could be concerned on my behalf. One was Jack Maddock, in Darwin researching for a book on Roadtrains. Others offered help and did we need a driver, but I thanked them all and assured them that I had faith in Doreen carrying on.

A week later Doreen rang from Alice Springs to say she had made it. She had driven across to Halls Creek and down the Tanami Track, and had had a few adventures. After leaving Halls Creek, the cable gearshift started to jam, and she couldn't access reverse gear, which makes you extremely careful with a vehicle like a tourist coach.

The Track divided and which way should she go - a wrong decision and there was no reverse. We carried a stripped down trail bike, so she got it out and asked if anyone could ride a motorbike, no answer, so she explained she would ride out on one track to check it out. Then one fellow volunteered.

She asked why wait till now, and he replied "Well it just occurred to me that we are in the middle of nowhere, you are riding off over a sandhill, and if you don't come back, none of us know how to drive the coach".

I still had dressings on my fingers, but I told Doreen that I would fly straight down to Alice Springs. When I told the doctor he said, "Forget it, you will be here for a week or two at least".

Darryl Tutty was a local tour operator and a good mate, so I rang Darryl and asked him to pick me up. I grabbed my gear, walked out of the hospital and Darryl drove me to the airport.

Driving down to Alice Springs there is time, well some, to acclimatize, but it's all a bit sudden when you fly. From balmy Darwin I found it seven degrees below zero in Alice that night.

I drove back to Sydney on the Oodnadatta Track and had the hand dressed at the old Leigh Creek Hospital, then at Broken Hill Hospital. Back home it was a matter of working flat out preparing for the next trip, and ignoring the pain in my hand. It was important to get everything right as this was an Around Australia trip.

I thought my hand would settle down, but this wasn't the case, and for the sixty-five days it never let me forget. There was nothing for it, back in Sydney I went straight to the doctor, he was astonished, and said that I required another operation, something about fixing nerve endings. He said that they must be rough in Darwin as they never finished the job!

Due to a mixture of sheer good luck and abject fear, I've managed to live life almost totally free of dealings with the medical profession, and never take such things as cough medicine. I'm crossing my fingers, or what's left of them and hoping it stays that way. So, I will blame this attitude, combined with the obligation I felt to Doreen and our Sundowners for what turned into a rather stupid decision (or maybe it was just my pride).

It is difficult with a big crowd of people to remember names and one method is using an association of ideas, so Doreen used to suggest that we were going to a party, and each person would speak their name and what they would bring, starting with the same letter as their name. So, I am Bill and I will bring the beer, and it really was a help.

As our trips were usually fully booked, mainly with repeats, we always interviewed new passengers and if there was any doubt about their compatibility we suggested they book with some other company. Anything or anybody who interferes with the enjoyment of a tour effected the four-eleven principle, where if a passenger is happy he will tell four of his friends, but if unhappy will tell eleven. However, sometimes odd people slipped through the net, and it's safe to say Louise was one such. So, with Doreen's little game, she said I'm Louise and I'll bring the Loganberries", only to be referred to from that time forward as Loganberries.

At Mt. Isa we used to take a side track and camp in a lovely setting by the Lake, and on one trip some young, rather wild looking young fellows followed us in. I went over to their car before they could get out (it is an advantage to look down at them) and asked what they wanted. The leader said, "We've come to join the party". I assured them there was no party and suggested where they could go. They had a short conference and took my advice.

Later that night one of our fellows told me that they were back. "I just saw them sneaking through the trees over there" he said. We had some pretty fit fellows on board, so I proposed that we grab these blokes and throw a scare into them. We spread out and crept into the trees, and sure enough I saw a figure crouched down hiding. In a moment of sheer recklessness, I jumped the figure and threw him to the ground. There was an unearthly scream that just went on and on.

I had just bowled over Loganberries with her pants around her ankles.

She ignored me for the rest of the trip and I think she believed that I was some sort of a sex maniac. She never booked on another trip, so I must have used the ultimate deterrent.

At the end of our season Doreen found time to join our New Zealand tour and was amazed at the standard of cabins they were building in Motor Camps since last we were there. With their backdrop of lakes and snow-covered mountains, she reported that it really was a luxury "camping" trip.

Trivia section - in New Zealand they don't have Caravan Parks, they have Motor Camps.

1977 NEW DOMINO COACH & FIRE
U.S. TOUR

This was the year that Elvis Presley died, although a lot of people claim that it never happened.

The year started with the dreadful Granville train smash, where 83 people died, and we nearly lost a good Sundowner mate. Jack Maddock lived at Springwood and like many locals, always sat in the same seat on the morning train, but this day some ladies came aboard and one took Jack's seat. Ever the gentleman, Jack said nothing and spent the trip wandering through the train. The carriage he normally occupied was totally flattened when the Granville bridge came down on top of it. Such is life, to quote Ned Kelly.

We had been badgering Dennings (Alan Denning had sold out to J.R.A.) to build a coach on air suspension, but they were not interested, saying that steel springs did the job perfectly well. Then a new company, Domino Coaches let it be known that they had developed coaches using air suspension. Athol McKinnon, who we knew from Dennings was working with Domino, and I felt that Athol would look after us, so we placed an order.

The first trip of the year was one of our popular Mystery Tours (where people were happy to pay good money and not know where we were taking them)

When Domino informed us that the coach would not be ready on time, it became a mystery for us too. I had to run round and borrow a coach from Ron Deane, as we had sold the current coach to Western Safaris in Perth. (A year or two later a woman came up to me in Central Australia and said, "You are Bill Hand aren't you, you sold my husband a coach", I cringed, expecting the worst, but she went on, "it was the best thing he ever did, the presence of that coach in our fleet increased our business no end.")

Came our second tour and still no Domino, so it was back to Ron Deane to borrow another coach. I hesitated to show Ron a blow up photo that Doreen had taken of me driving his coach across a flooded causeway with the water halfway up the side. He looked at it amazed and asked for a copy to frame and put on his office wall. Ron was a mate and a thorough gentleman.

The price quoted on the new coach was $95,000, but when we went to pick it up they announced the cost had blown out to $102,000. I was furious, I had never heard of anybody being treated this way, and when I checked it over, instead of the specified Michelin tyres, it had some Asian tyres I had never heard of. They would never have tried this on a big operator, but they must have figured that a two-bit operator like Bill Hand would just have to wear it. Of course, they were right, but it's a small industry where we all know each other and I felt I had done my bit when Domino finally went out of business.

Later in the year on a Gunbarrel trip we were banging away on a really rough stretch and there shouldn't have been as much noise, after all we were on air suspension. I stopped to check and found the treads peeling off our much vaunted Asian tyres in streamers and hitting inside the wheel wells. There wasn't a thing we could do about it and just drove on, hoping the tyre casings were better than the treads. (These were steel cord tyres). The noise finally ceased when the last of the treads had thrown off and we made Carnarvon on the West Coast with no treads and driving on the steel wires.

I phoned the tyre people in Perth demanding a refund. They said, first they would have to view the tyres, so send them down to Perth, and second they don't refund but would be happy to replace them.

It was no time for temper but I couldn't help myself. I told them that first they were like porcupines with broken steel wires sticking out everywhere and I didn't think any carrier would touch them, and second, I didn't want replacements, as I wouldn't fit them on a billy-cart.

Bell Bros. the Michelin people in Carnarvon fitted a new set all round and suggested in future I try not to save money with cheap tyres. Letters, photos, phone calls were all to no avail with Domino - they just stonewalled us.

On returning home, the coach had to be serviced at the authorised dealership, C.L.A.E. Engineering at Bankstown. That night we were watching TV and about 8.00pm they phoned and requested I come over to Bankstown. I said it could wait, but they insisted. I arrived to see the coach sitting in a sea of foam between two fire engines and was told that an electrical fault had started a fire and half the coach was burnt out.

The electrical fault story was ridiculous, and the manager and I exchanged some pretty heated language, with the result that I called him an idiot and a bad bastard to boot, and asked what they intended to do about it. He retaliated by telling me to tow it off their property or they would charge parking rental.

In desperation I turned to the C.S.I.R.O. at North Ryde, as suggested by some of our Sundowners. Their engineers discovered the foam sound proofing in the motor compartment was soaked in used automatic transmission fluid, and put the story together. They said that the coach had been running on a Dynamometer when someone disconnected a hose on the automatic transmission, probably to fit a pressure gauge. The hot transmission fluid sprayed everywhere, including the extremely hot exhaust pipe and acted like a flame thrower.

Of course, they were right, it was the only possibility, but we nearly came to blows again when I put it to C.L.A.E.'s manager. The coach had to be returned to Domino in Brisbane to be rebuilt, and we had to go back to Ron Deane to borrow coaches once again.

Perhaps they thought we little people were of no account and couldn't afford to fight them, but fight them we did, although it took two years to come to Court. For good measure we threw in every cost we could think of, including a very satisfactory reimbursement for Ron Deane. Only two days before the Court case they made an offer which we rejected, and then they paid up in full.

More trivia -C.L.A.E. began on the waterfront at Balmain under the name Central Launch and Engineering I believe about 100 years ago. Try as I might, I can't say anything good about C.L.A.E., Domino, and certain Asian tyres, except that they are all out of business.

November, 1977. Ron Deane had no use for automatic transmissions, so driving a Queensland National Parks Tour including Carnarvon George, I got more than enough practice double shuffling a crash gear box, and I have trouble believing people who tell me they prefer a manual gearbox.

December, 1977. Tony Mccafferty of McCafferty's Coaches invited us to join him and some friends in the industry on a study tour to the United States, with tours of inspection to various truck and bus plants, plus a few general interest tours.

Overseas touring is a great pastime and we have travelled widely in our retirement, but still have trouble coming to terms with the fact that pretty well every second person you speak to expects a tip, although I shouldn't complain as we were entertained quite lavishly by General Motors in Detroit. This had to be the right time to go to America with the Aussie dollar being worth 112 cents to the U.S. dollar. Those were the days, and it was to be over 20 years before we returned to American soil and found you needed a swag of Aussie dollars to get a cup of coffee.

In our coaches we always left out a row of seats to spread the remainder wider apart, only to find airlines don't use the same system. I thought the flight to Los Angeles was going on forever as I sat like a hunched-up grasshopper, aching in every joint. At least, Tony planned to break the journey home with a stopover in Honolulu.

After L.A. we had 3 nights in Seattle in the rather flash Olympic Hotel, and Doreen had a problem with the bathroom plumbing. There were all sorts of levers on the wall, but nothing produced water. One lever seemed to do nothing, until we noticed the plug went up and down. Then she leant over the bath and pulled two levers at once. A cascade of water came down all over her, and she looked like a drowned rat.

After seeing the wonders of Seattle, the Space Needle, Boeing Factory, and fifty different types of Hot Dogs, it was on to Vancouver. Here we knew all about the levers in the bathroom, just couldn't find one to flush the toilet, and ultimately found a button on the floor. A big thing to do in Vancouver is visit Queen Elizabeth Park where we saw a mob of Australian parrots.

A beautiful morning flight to Minneapolis with snow on the Rockies and breakfast on board - the choice being crepes and bacon liberally covered in strawberry jam and ice cream, or if you knocked that back, thinking it a bit odd, crepes, hot dogs and hot apricot jam etc. Reps from Thermo-King Airconditioning met us with drinks in the Airport Lounge. This was the start of a pattern, first the factory inspection, then the sales movie, followed by the gift presentation. (This was usually a classy pen and pencil set).

We were put up in the Radisson Hotel and taken to dinner that night in the Radisson Flame Room. The standard meal was a huge steak, charred on each side and raw in the middle, OK, I know this is considered the correct method, but I can't stand the sight of blood on my plate, so while everyone got stuck in with gusto, I sat staring at this huge slab of meat. Then one of the jewellery draped executive wives snapped her fingers and called "Waiter, take this away and cook it properly". Thank heavens! I called and said, "Here mate, take mine and do the same".

We were entertained by "The Golden Strings" an orchestra of nine strolling violinists, two pianists and one bass player. One of our party asked if it was possible to get a copy of the music, and a company rep. rushed out and came back with a presentation record for each of us. These Yanks go overboard for their guests. The following morning, they drove us to the airport, turned on farewell drinks in the VIP Lounge and saw us off to Detroit.

First stop in Detroit was the Rockwell Axle Plant, where after the usual routine and the pen and pencil set, I put my foot in it by criticising something. The Yanks are incredibly hospitable, but you criticise at your peril. I commented that on our outback roads we had snapped steering tie rods. The rep asked, "What the hell is a tie rod?" I pointed it out and he said, "What the hell are you talking about, that's a cross toob". Then he went on with "Had one of your Aussie fellows over recently called Lindsay Fox. He has a few vehicles (about 1000 I think) and he had no complaints, how many do you run?" I felt like lying and saying about 50, but finally admitted to 1 and noted his satisfied smirk.

The following day General Motors reps took us to their Detroit Diesel Spare Parts Plant at Romulus, where we were amazed to see humans were not allowed in the aisles, as they would be run down by the robots that raced around picking up and dropping off required parts.

We were presented with caps, belt buckles and writing pads to go with the pen and pencil sets.

That night Doreen and I decided to break away and walk the streets of Detroit. There were very few people on the streets, and seeing a place open, decided to have a drink and a late supper. We walked in and too late realised it was totally Negro and we were the only white faces.

We went to back out, but a waitress stopped us and asked, "Say where do you folks come from", we answered Australia, and she announced in a loud voice, "These folks come from Australia". The patrons looked up and gave us a cheer and the waitress led us to a table. A young black police girl parked her motorcycle on the sidewalk and came in for a cup of coffee. The waitress introduced us, and she sat at our table which I found very reassuring, at least we had the law on side.

She talked of going to Africa for four weeks to find her roots, and I asked did she get four weeks holiday, but she told us the City keeps running out of money and a number of cops are laid off without pay until they can afford to re-employ them. She asked about employment in Australia and had trouble believing our working conditions.

The following day I mentioned to some G.M. fellows about our interesting evening and they were horrified and said they wouldn't dream of walking around Detroit even in daylight. We spent the day at the Redford Detroit Diesel Engine Factory and to me at least, this was the highlight of the trip.

Tony had arranged with Greyhound for our own coach, which left plenty of room, there only being sixteen of us. We drove the mile-long tunnel under the Lake to Windsor, Ontario in Canada, where Ford make their famous Windsor VB engines. After the Canadian Customs check it was across Canada to Toronto on Lake Ontario in overcast weather.

No wonder we saw so many rusted cars, as trucks were laying a mixture of salt and sand on the road. The scenery couldn't be more bleak, the ground was white with snow as we passed leafless orchards, and it would be a waste using colour film as everything was black and white. On to Niagara Falls and that night back into the U.S. at the Niagara Hilton beside the Falls.

I opened our room door and walked in to find a beautiful blonde girl sprawled across the bed. She just waved, but I mumbled an apology and backed out. A couple of bell boys came past and I told them there was a bird in our room. One said, "Don't worry, someone has left the window open". The other said, "I think he means a chick" and turned to me and asked, "You a limey or something?" We were led down to the desk, the matter sorted, and we were given another room. Seemed a pity in a way. That night regardless of the freezing weather we walked across the bridge back into Canada and had tea in the Observation Tower overlooking the Falls.

After spending the next night in Buffalo, we caught an early flight into New York and spent the day flat out sightseeing. Although it was Sunday, you would never guess. All the shops were open, and they were preparing for Christmas. Talking with a sales girl in Macys, I asked if they get double time working on Sundays. She had never heard of such a thing, and said "No, I get Wednesday off". They work people hard in the States.

After managing to see everything from the Empire State Building to Central Park, we were running out of time and had to catch a cab back to the Airport. This proved to be the most difficult thing imaginable. I took to literally throwing myself in front of the cab, but Doreen would be pushed to one side by the locals who would get in the cab and leave us. Finally, in something of a panic about missing the flight back, we took on the locals at their own game and fought them off and just made LaGuardia Airport in time.

The next day it was around the Southern shore of Lake Erie to Cleveland, Toledo, then down to Dayton and Indianapolis. This is certainly not a tourist route, even the Yanks refer to it as the Rust Belt, and we passed endless factories, steelworks and slum housing.

Although we kept the same coach, they had a regular change of drivers, who were mostly Negro and excellent drivers. Just after Cleveland a blizzard swept in across the Lake, it reduced visibility and a number of cars simply slid off the road. I couldn't imagine driving in these conditions, and thought we would have to stop, but the driver just took it in his stride and ploughed on.

Having changed countless flat tyres, I examined all around the coach and couldn't find the spare wheel, so asked the driver where it was hidden. He laughed and said, "I have never changed a flat, there's a bunch of dimes on the dashboard and a phone call brings a service guy straight away". After our talk he must have thought we were primitive in Australia.

Indianapolis was home to General Motors Detroit Diesel Allison Division, where they made automatic transmissions (gear boxes), light aircraft turbine engines, and tourist coaches. We were each assigned a company rep. as a minder. While we blokes were driven out to the Allison Factory, our girls were taken to check out Department Stores and Hair Dressers.

At Allison we were allowed to drive the "most advanced coach in the world". It was powered with an Allison aircraft turbine engine that weighed nearly one ton less than a conventional diesel. It was whisper quiet and needed no muffler, no radiator, and caused virtually no air pollution, not even odour.

After all the ra ra and us shouting "When can we have one" we were very quietly told the downside. "Miles per gallon wise, it's still only half as good as a diesel, but we're working on that." Apparently, it never happened as we have heard no more about it.

The next day our group was to visit the Cummins Engine Plant at Columbus, 45 miles to the South, but when I told Chris Verla, our minder, that I used to race cars, he suggested I might prefer to do a few laps of the Indianapolis 500 Speedway in a racing car.

The first of the winter snow fell that night and Chris picked me up in his "winter car", a Chevy four-wheel-drive. On the way to the Speedway we saw cars stuck and pranged and as we should have guessed, the snow had closed the Speedway and I missed my chance of a lifetime. The day was not a total loss, as we enjoyed the Motor Museum, the best I have ever seen.

Chris then took us out to Greenfield to see their huge western gear clothing emporium, where we couldn't resist a few items that were well styled and remarkably cheap. I was wearing the New Zealand sheepskin coat I bought on the Barker College winter trip, and at the payment counter, the checkout girl asked, "Is that real sheepskin, where did you get it?" I pointed out that her store had racks of them, but she said they were fake, synthetic and mine must have cost a fortune. I suggested she try a New Zealand holiday where sheepskins are fair dinkum.

We were presented with the inevitable pen and pencil set at a send-off dinner at the Hilton that evening.

Driving up to Chicago in a blizzard was hair raising, seeing cars and trucks off the highway, and on arrival in Chicago we were told it was 38 degrees below zero, wind chill temperature. I had thought New Zealand on our Barker trip was cold, but this was seriously cold. Even the cops on the beat wore balaclavas beneath their caps, and looked like bank robbers.

The big deal here was the Greyhound Bus Maintenance and Reclamation Centre where coaches were stripped and rebuilt. They certainly got good use out of their Detroit Diesel Motors as they were being rebuilt after completing a million miles on the road.

Among our group we had Ted Rolls, the Manager of A.B. Denning, the bus manufacturers, and also Kev Kirkland of Lismore. Kev noted that all these American coaches were on air suspension and asked why Denning couldn't do the same. We added our two bob's worth as we were thoroughly browned off with the Domino people and would prefer a Denning if they would change from steel springs.

While Ted Rolls was deliberating, Kevin took a sheet of paper and wrote out an order for a new Denning coach with air suspension and signed it on behalf of his company. The upshot was that the coach was built, and Kev took delivery of the first Denning that rode on air. It was used in Denning advertising twice, first as the first of its type, and second after it had completed one million kms on the road. And of course, thanks to Kev's order we later replaced the Domino with a new Denning that rode on air.

We walked, slipped and were blown around by the freezing wind as we tried to see the sights of Chicago. The Sears Tower at 103 floors, the tallest building in the world at that time was a must. The lifts were like a theme park ride as they shot up a quarter of a mile in less than a minute, and no doubt the view would have been great had the observation windows not been coated in ice.

The Americans must drive up the price of oil in winter as they seem to need all building interiors to be hot boxes. Our hotel room was so hot we had to open the window to cool it down and in the process watched as slabs of ice broke up in the surf on Lake Michigan. The radio and TV ran programs warning people not to try to travel home, and in the morning the hotel lobby looked like a refugee camp as hotels had opened their doors to allow people in off the streets. Then out to the airport where there was doubt about getting out, but after much delay finally flew out and on to Las Vegas and incredibly bright sunshine.

After what had been a serious study and information gathering exercise, we became tourists, taking in everything from the Grand Canyon to Disneyland.

On a tour of Hollywood, our coach driver listed all the no-nos, saying "Company regulations state that you don't bring food or drink on board, and my name's Bill, and my regulations state that you all shut up when I'm talking". How many times have we all been tempted to say that!

The flight home was made much easier with a three-day stopover in Honolulu for some relaxation after the heavy itinerary thus far. During this time, we became friends with Adrian and Joy Goddard from Parlorcars in Perth, and this friendship became invaluable later, when on two occasions in Western Australia calls to Adrian solved some desperate problems. (More of that later).

I must give high praise to Tony McCafferty for his organisation of this tour and if there was any fault at all, perhaps it was the month chosen, but if it had been any other time, it would have been impossible for us with our work commitments.

I came home with masses of specifications for building a super coach and thanks to Kevin Kirkland, Dennings were going to change from steel springs to airbags.

There was a general belief at the time that steel springs were simple and air suspensions were too sophisticated, but this is not true, and it's extremely dangerous working underneath changing a steel spring, whereas replacing an airbag is simple, with no need to get under the vehicle.

When I was in Darwin Hospital I heard the bad news about two Centralian drivers ending up in Alice Springs Hospital, one with multiple fractures to an arm and the other broken ribs, after being crushed under a coach while trying to knock out a broken spring.

**1977. USA Tour near Niagara Falls.
Kevin Kirkland, Dick White of Dennings
and me in New Zealand sheepskin coat.**

1978/79 MARLA, CRAIG SOUTER, DESERT BREAKDOWN, COOPERS CREEK

Holden ceased production of the Kingswood and released a new model called the Commodore selling for the premium price of $5600.

Meanwhile we were trying to get a handle on this blessed metric system that most people, and particularly those in the outback were trying to ignore. The English were not interested, and the Americans wouldn't have a bar of it, believing it to be an attack on the American way of life by the sneaky Europeans.

Instead of a few inches we had hundreds of millimeters, and what the devil were kilojoules or kilopascals. As well, everything became smaller, miles shrank to kilometers, gallons to litres etc.

We didn't even know how to pronounce kilometers, and in fact still don't know to this day, but I'm certain of one thing, towns were definitely further apart in those days.

Sadly, in March my mother Susan passed away and apart from our personal loss, this complicated our office routine as Mum handled this work while we were away on tour.

Also this year, a mate, Greg Oakley, dragged a mob of demountable units up the South Road and set up a Roadhouse called Marla, about seven km south of the old Afghan well called Marla Bore.

Greg was a Pioneer coach driver on the Alice to Adelaide run who mostly drove the northern leg, changing over at Welbourne Hill Station with southern drivers who drove back to Adelaide. The South Road, or Stuart Highway, was simply a track linking up the station homesteads, and as it was mostly in a shocking state of repair, it was usual for coach drivers coming the opposite way to stop and compare notes on the road conditions, and particularly after rain. So, we came to know drivers like Greg quite well.

He had an obsession about a roadhouse being needed at Welbourne Hill as it was about halfway on the long stretch between Coober Pedy and Kulgera in the Northern Territory. On his stopovers Greg worked on Ernie Giles, the owner of Welbourne Hill Station to form a consortium to build Greg's roadhouse.

Then a problem arose when it was announced that a new train line and a new highway would be built further to the west and with the road being built straight, and no longer zigzagging from homestead to homestead. Greg took a big gamble by siting his roadhouse on the western side of Welbourne Hill Station where the new highway should cross the old and adjacent to the new railway.

It all worked out exactly as planned and when Granite Downs became Aboriginal land, the Oodnadatta Road was diverted to the south to meet the highway at Marla.

Doreen and I managed later to drive out to Marla (by way of the Simpson Desert) for the official opening and Greg invited us to stay on as long as we wished as his guests. People don't come much nicer than Greg Oakley.

Although he is now retired and living down south, Greg's dream has become a township with a rail siding, police station, supermarket and houses, as well as a greatly expanded roadhouse.

1979 Rod Laver, probably the greatest tennis player of all time won everything including Wimbledon. Then most people have probably forgotten or maybe didn't know that this was the year that open road speed limits were introduced. Until 1979 there was no speed limit outside built up areas and the Northern Territory is the only part of the country where this still applies.

I recall back in the 1950s a racing driver friend was booked at over 100 miles per hour (160km), the charge being dangerous driving. He pleaded that under the circumstances, and with his ability there was no danger, and the judge agreed. Of course, there is no chance of ever returning to those days, the government has become too dependent on the revenue from fines.

This was also the year when the huge space station called Skylab crashed back to earth. We were camped in outback Western Australia and by all accounts in the path of where it was expected to crash. After tea we listened to the radio for progress reports as it circled the earth coming lower and lower. In the early hours of the morning we were still staring at the sky and being sustained by endless cups of coffee when news came through that it had come down in pieces on Balladonia Station to the south of us. Later the folk at the station, who were friends and one of our regular stopovers, donated the parts to a dedicated Museum in Esperance.

I can't recall that Doreen or I have ever taken a sick day off in our lives, although I had a close call. We had just returned from a trip, walked in the door and I fell to the floor hit by the most dreadful pain. I was carted off to hospital and diagnosed with kidney stones. What a problem, with a week between trips and the gear had to be sorted and cleaned, the coach had to be driven across Sydney and serviced, but with me lying in a hospital bed, Doreen did it all. Finally, on the Friday I was given the OK, left the hospital and started the tour the following day.

Although my timing was impeccable in this instance, I started worrying about the ravages of age and wouldn't we be better served with some back-up.

The Souter family had lived in our street for over twenty years and we had watched the kids grow up. Young Craig had served his time with Ron Deane's Bus Company and was available. We required someone without family ties, a trained mechanic, a competent coach driver and the ability to be affable among older people. As Craig had an adventuresome spirit and wanted to travel, he jumped at the offer.

Many operators had found it necessary to pull trailers to carry all their equipment on camping trips, but we had felt that this severely compromised where a coach could operate and had somehow managed to cram everything onto the coach.

Around this time Weighing Stations started popping up all around the country, with as usual, each state having different regulations. This brought more problems as the Domino coach when fully loaded and with fuel and water tanks full was always marginally overweight on the back axle. We learnt to shuffle the big people around before a Weighing Station, and while most people co-operated with our luggage weight allowance, I was sometimes tempted to ask if they were coming on tour or moving house.

We had recently bought a Ford F100 light truck and employing Craig as another driver, considered the Ford could become a fully mobile trailer, and it would be a great benefit to have two vehicles.

In theory this was a brilliant solution, but in practice, the Ford proved to be such a thirsty beast we couldn't afford to take it, and to get the necessary range it would have to be converted into one huge fuel tank. So, it came down to Craig sharing the driving and helping Doreen, and then servicing the coach between tours.

We had now been operating for eighteen years and had overcome and beaten hundreds of problems, bogs, breakdowns, and I thought just about anything that could happen, but the worst was in 1979 and thank heavens we had Craig with us.

It was a Gunbarrel trip and we had driven across the desert from Ayers Rock and were leaving the boundary of Warburton Aboriginal settlement when a dreadful bang and crashing noise came from the motor. It sounded as though it had blown to pieces, but for some reason was still going, so we turned around and proceeded slowly back to the Settlement and conferred with the local management.

Across a dry creek bed, on the edge of town there was a slab of concrete that apparently had been the floor of a building, and they suggested we park the coach on this slab and set up camp there.

Well, first things first, we drained the oil and removed the sump. Lying in the bottom of the sump were dozens of smashed and broken gear teeth. I just went into denial or shock, or something and sat staring at them. It was obvious that these were timing gear teeth, but what had smashed them. Then among the wreckage we found a couple of 3/8 inch diameter socket head bolts also severely smashed.

OK, it was becoming obvious, the air compressor was bolted to the back of the motor by internal bolts - these had come loose and dropped down into the timing gears, crunched into them and snapped them off.

It was quite amazing that the motor kept running, but there must have been enough friction between the gear faces to keep it going, for a while at least.

I think it was starting to get to the passengers that we had an almost impossible problem. Here we were, in the Warburton Ranges, sandwiched between the Gibson and Great Victoria Deserts, and about as far from anywhere as it's possible to get. Someone suggested that it felt a bit like landing on the moon, only to find the rocket home didn't work.

For starters, the gearbox must come off to get to the timing gears on the rear of the motor. This was a daunting task, assisted by a trolley jack loaned by a helpful local. After many hours of hard work, the gearbox was out, and the motor stripped, showing the mess of stripped timing gears which reminded me of corn cobs, and in the meantime camp had been set up. A fire was going, and the Sundowners had created their little home from home.

Hordes of Aboriginal kids had descended on our camp, I think under the mistaken idea that a circus had come to town, and I impressed on everyone to be very nice to them as the tolerance of their people toward us would depend on the stories the kids took home.

With electrical storms around I tried to raise our mate Ivan Weiss in Alice Springs, but got nothing but static, so went into town to find the local radio operator. Ivan Weiss and his partner Ian Lovegrove owned a trucking company and a small charter airline and looked like being our only lifeline.

Fortunately, we always carried a Detroit Diesel Parts Book that listed the part numbers for ordering replacements, and armed with these, and using the local powerful radio, we contacted Ivan in Alice Springs. Thank heavens for mates, he noted the part numbers, and said he would get them jetted up from Adelaide and flown out to us at Warburton.

In the meantime, we were entertained by the local Aboriginal young men racing around in cars having what appeared to be demolition derbies. When one car wouldn't start, a second was brought up to push start it, but there was nothing fancy about this operation. The second car was driven at speed into the back of the first which then started and drove away. The pusher car then stopped, and its grill and headlights fell off onto the ground, this was greeted with delight by the onlookers and must have been the funniest thing that happened all day. Seeing the exhaust pipe and the muffler seemed to be the first thing to fall off, sleeping became a bit difficult when the fun went on rather late some nights.

A delegation of Aboriginals arrived, led by an old man with a long white beard, and a young boy as an interpreter. The old man made a speech which I couldn't understand, except for a word or two of Pitjanjara. Then the boy spoke up "Dis old man says you mob can't stay here and you gotta go cos this is proper blackfella country". So, I explained that we would love to go, but look here, and showed the old fellow the broken gear teeth and the stripped timing gears. The old man was no fool, he obviously understood, and he found it quite amusing. He laughed, patted me on the shoulder and we parted the best of friends. It's understandable I suppose that Aboriginals often delight in the white fellas clever technologies dumping him in the proverbial.

Warburton had been a Mission run by a religious sect and was in the change-over phase to Government, or Aboriginal control, although the Missionary people were still there. With time on our hands, waiting to hear from Ivan, we walked the town and talked with the locals, and some of them were a strange lot.

We spoke to the Mission lady who lamented that her car had broken down and she could no longer drive around the camp and collect the kids to be brought to Sunday School. We offered to look at her car, but she said "No, if the Lord wanted me to continue, He wouldn't have allowed the car to break down, we must abide with His plan". It made me wonder, here I had been blaming Detroit for our breakdown.

About this time, it started to rain, and it simply poured down. In a short time, a gully between us and the Mission became a small river that flooded above our knees. A Missionary man waded across the creek waving a key, and invited us to use the meeting hall to get out of the rain. The hall was built for the Aborigines, but as they "didn't appreciate it" it was kept locked.

The Hospital nurses enjoyed the company of the Sundowners as a couple of them were near breaking point from the pressures of the job. One, Sister Sue, was even debating leaving with us, when and if we did get away. About a year later we ran into Sue in Oodnadatta. I asked, "How does this compare to Warbo?", and she replied, "Like Paradise". She was working at the local hospital and in love with the local Policeman. A year or two later, while shopping in New Leigh Creek we ran into Sue once again. She was pushing a double pram carrying a beautiful pair of twins and she looked transformed from the girl we first met in Warburton.

Just when the mission mechanic was telling us that with the rain, they were officially closing the airstrip, a call came through from an aircraft requesting permission to land. It was one of Ivan's pilots and it was the messiest landing I've ever seen, he threw up sheets of mud and water and the Cessna slewed all over the place as he fought for control. He had our parts and I thought he would elect to stay, but after quickly refueling he took off in another shower of water and mud that was even more dramatic than the landing.

The Mission Ladies asked the Sundowners to join them at Church on Sunday night. On a head count basis, it seemed the Missionaries were slightly ahead on conversions with the camp dogs. When the hymn singing started, the dogs raced up to the church and joined in, moaning and howling along with the singers.

Although we had the parts to rebuild the motor, it was obvious it would be days before the roads dried out enough for traffic to move.

If someone had offered me triple time to do this job in a workshop back home, I would have walked away, but here there was no choice. But I need not have worried, as Craig rolled up his sleeves and got into the job. With everything back together came the moment of truth and with my finger hovering over the starter button, I pushed, and it burst into life and ran perfectly, to wild applause from the Sundowners.

There have been many occasions on tour when disasters have occurred, and things have looked hopeless. This causes some people to panic at the time, but when they get home, can't wait to tell everyone who will listen about their great adventure.

All up this holdup took five days, but being a six-week trip and a flexible itinerary, we still managed to cover all bases for the rest of the tour, and of course the experiences at Warburton were only possible with the breakdown.

We could just about fill a book with stories about Gunbarrel trips alone, but one stands out in my memory. We made camp at a regular stop about a half-day drive west of Warburton. It was off-road and had a series of deep, dependable water holes. Just on dark a couple of cars pulled in carrying a group of Aboriginals. Assuming they were locals I walked over to make friends, but they said they were out of their country and just passing through, and would we mind if they camped near us.

I thought this was a bit strange, and after tea joined their camp to ask where they were going. They explained, "We gunna see Australia, them goldfields, and that big city Perth, and the Nullabor Plain, we like your mob, we tourists". It turned out they came from Indulkana Aboriginal Settlement at the foot of the Everard Range, north of Marla. (We had been to Indulkana, but that's another story).

We were talking with their radio going in the background, when an old fellow suddenly said, "Shush, shush, it's da noos". This was the time of uprisings against apartheid in South Africa and the news was about a street battle in Johannesburg. This made the old chap most upset and he shouted, "I always reckoned them Hermannsburg mob was a mob of bad bastards, ay". A young fellow tried to explain, but the old man would have none of it. Well the radio had a bit of static.

I spent the rest of the trip wondering how they went, how would they go in the whitefella world in places like Perth, and what help would people give them. After a bit of a yarn I walked back to our camp to find our crowd had all gone to bed, so I was warming my hands when the fire blew up in front of me. I would have to give another lecture about putting batteries in the rubbish box.

Later that year we had to borrow a coach from Ron Deane (that is another story).

On picking up the coach I pointed out to Ron that it had a brand of Asian tyres and he said they were getting a good run from them. Travelling up the Birdsville Track with Craig behind the wheel, a front tyre blew out. As Craig was fighting for control, the other front tyre blew, and he brought it to a stop with the front bumper almost scraping the ground. With only one spare, we had to rob one of the duals, and switch it to the front. Would a single at the rear carry the weight? Well, we were lucky - it did.

Knowing Birdsville would be of no help, once again we radioed Ivan in Alice Springs to fly over a mob of Michelin tyres to Birdsville. The plane was just landing as we drove into Birdsville and Ivan had pulled out the seats to make room for our tyres.

When I returned the coach to Ron Deane in Sydney he walked around it and then smiled a bit ruefully and said, "You had better bill me for a set of tyres".

Around this time Peter Barnes, who managed Brockie's Garage in Birdsville featured in a TV ad for Ford light trucks. On asking Peter about the ad he said "Yeah, I'll say anything for money". One day I needed a tyre from Barnsey (as everyone called him) and he explained with the price of new truck tyres, they only stocked re-caps. The tyres had been stacked on top of each other which is a big NO NO as they squash flat and being tubeless, won't expand to meet the rim. A tube would have helped, but as we had none, we tried every method to inflate the tyre with no success. Peter then got a crate of toilet rolls and soaked them in water until they became papier-mache. Then with half a dozen kids holding the papier-mache between the tyre and the rim, the tyre inflated.

When it was finally changed in Sydney, all the tyre fitters gathered around slack jawed in amazement at the material jammed between the tyre and rim, as they had never heard of such a thing. I didn't bother to explain that people in the outback like Barnsey never let a problem beat them.

This was also the year of the Coopers Creek Lilo Expedition from Cullyamurra waterhole to the crossing at Innamincka. We had travelled up the Strzelecki Track to Innamincka and Mike Steel's Trading Post Store. We knew Mike from the early days when he ran "Red Rover' four- wheel-drive safaris specialising in Coopers Creek and Burke and Wills country. At that time there was nothing at Innamincka except the ruins of the old A.I.M. Hospital and a vast bottle heap behind the ruins of the hotel. Many of these bottles were collectors' items and I guess everyone who passed through collected some, although ultimately most floated away on a flood. The town had closed in 1954 when the publican refused to comply with licensing regulations.

Mike fell in love with the old ghost town, gave up the tour business and built a store, then a new hotel was built and finally the old hospital was restored and became the Ranger Station. Innamincka is no longer a ghost town.

Coopers Creek was in flood and we could not cross to the other side in the coach to explore the historic sites, so we had time on our hands and Doreen came up with one of her brilliant ideas. We would use our lilos to float downstream to Innamincka - it didn't seem all that far when we travelled by coach!

Eleven explorers set off late morning on the exciting expedition. The water was fast flowing past our camp site, but we soon came to areas where the water had spread out into tree lined channels and we had difficulty keeping track of each other until we came to another large waterhole, then the current slowed and we had to paddle, and so the pattern continued all afternoon. The paddling was hard work, and we were relieved to see the buildings at

Innamincka in the setting sun. The new problem was to get back to dry land before we headed off to Lake Eyre, then we walked up to Mike's Store.

Mike looked on in disbelief as a mob of sunburnt, exhausted, half-drowned people trooped into his store. We downed some drinks and sweets - all on IOUs as we had no money, then I loaded everyone into one of Mike's trucks and drove back to camp. The rest of the group had the fire going and were relieved to see everyone safely home.

Mike Steel was a great mate - on our holidays he had flown Doreen and me in his Cessna up to and over Coongie Lakes and then onto the Walkers Crossing Track between Gidgealpa and the Birdsville Track, which we incorporated into some of our later tours.

Mike has a really dry sense of humour. When talking one day I asked, "Do you remember when no traffic ever came through Innamincka?" Mike "Yeah, that was last January", then I said, "But with 200 cars through last Easter there is no sign of the recession". Mike "Yeah, but did you notice they were all last years' models".

One evening we had a phone call from a girl representing someone called Michael Edgely telling us we had been recommended to act as technical advisors on a major film about Burke and Wills, starring Jack Thompson and Nigel Havers. At first, I thought it was a joke, but anyway suggested Mike Steel was the bloke they should talk to. The film was produced, and a number of luxury trailer homes were dragged out into the desert during filming. On completion of the film, rather than take them back, Mike was able to put a price in for them and they became part of his Trading post.

With administration of Innamincka transferred to the National Parks and Wildlife Service, tourists are now required to pay a vehicle entry permit. A whole new set of rules and regulations have been introduced. Mike, sixteen years after resurrecting the town, saw it as a death knell. "I came here to get away from all that. When I arrived, we could do as we pleased, build what we pleased, and the town was self-regulating. I feel it is the end of my era, so I'm moving on."

1980. Craig Souter, Doreen & Bill at Sundowner reunion.

1978. Washing the Domino Coach in Coopers Creek crossing to the Dig Tree.

1980/1 NEW DENNING BOGIE DRIVE COACH
FRASER ISLAND, DEATH

This was the year SBS came on air as a TV Station, but the big story of 1980 was Azaria Chamberlain, and the question, did a dingo take the baby, and of course people we knew became involved in all sorts of ways.

But at last we took delivery of a new super coach. It was built by Denning in Brisbane with bogie drive, that is eight driving wheels across the back and riding on eight air bags. Power was a 71 series V8 Detroit motor, driving of course through a fully automatic transmission.

During the life of this coach we upgraded the motor to a fully rated 92 series V8 turbo which at 475hp was probably the most powerful coach in Australia. Apart from the size of the vehicle, it was just like a car to drive, but I can't claim all the credit for the design.

It started when talking with a couple of Centralian owner/drivers. Eric Blizzard intended to build a coach on an Army six-wheel-drive chassis. It would have been the ultimate, but Centralian went belly up, and it was never built. Kevin Bryant however saw many problems with Eric's idea and suggested that bogie drive with two back axles and eight driving wheels would be an excellent compromise, and we fell in with K.B.'s design.

Also, Ted Rolls and Dick White from Denning along with ourselves had learnt a lot of things on our American trip that were incorporated in the build.

Of course, it was the newly allowed length of forty feet, but at the Motor Registry they insisted it was 100mm (or some such damned measurement) too long, so we pulled the bull bar off, registered it, then put the bull bar back on.

We could no longer travel to Tasmania as they claimed their Tassie roads couldn't cope with 40ft-long vehicles, but after a year or two they fell in line with the mainland and we returned to the Apple Isle.

Also, this was the first of many years of including Fraser Island on our touring schedule.

When I was a little kid, Mum used to tell me of how I was called after her brother Bill who as a Naval Officer died in the English Channel in 1916, and of her other brother Alex, who was General Manager on Fraser Island for MacKenzie's Timber Mills. So, it was interesting to see Central Station on the Island where Uncle Alex had had his head office.

Somebody once said, a society that has been denied is probably most prone to go on binges, and no doubt they were thinking of grog. It certainly applied to the changeover in the running of Hermannsburg. For around one hundred years the missionaries were the authority, then suddenly they were gone, and the Aboriginals were supposed to run their own show. The grog flowed in, old paybacks were settled, and all sorts of strife took place.

We hadn't realised this was happening and took a group to Hermannsburg, only to have them abused by a crowd of drunks. I was furious and fronted them and gave them a blast, causing them to back off and some of them were quite humble in their apologies.

The troubles caused a lot of people to leave, Gus Williams being one. He went to live with his mother's people at Warrabri, half way between Alice Springs and Tennant Creek. We made this a regular stopover as we were anxious to keep in touch with Gus, and as Gus's friends, we were made welcome at Warrabri. This name incidentally is an amalgam of two tribal names, Warramunga and Warlbri and these days is better known as Ali Curung.

Our Mate - Gus Williams

The local Aboriginal men told me they used a short cut when driving across to Queensland to attend such events as the Mt. Isa Rodeo. By using station bore tracks it was possible to drive east to Lake Nash on the NT/Queensland border and save a couple of hundred kilometres as opposed to using the highway.

I was intrigued by this and decided to incorporate it in our next East Coast, Gulf and Kimberley Tour. This was a popular tour that followed the East Coast as far as Laura on Cape York, then west to Dunbar and around the Gulf, following around the top of Australia into Western Australia, along the Gibb River road to Broome. The return trip went via Halls Creek and down on the Buntine Road to Top Springs in the Murranji country, continuing through to the Stuart Highway, where we camped on Morphett Creek, just south of Bank Banka Station.

After morning tea in Tennant Creek and a stop at the Devils Marbles, we had lunch with Gus at Warrabri. The locals explained it was about 500kms to the Queensland border, the first 50 through the Davenport Ranges following the old track to the abandoned Hatches Creek Mine.

The advice was - if the track forked, always choose due east. On the map there was not even a dotted line, although it showed two Stations, Annitowa and Argadargada out in the middle of nowhere.

Crossing through the ranges we came on a number of jump-ups, or wash-aways where we would hang the tail and it was necessary to cut down the banks with shovels, and it became obvious that no big vehicles had ventured through this way. After some hard going through sandy river beds we started coming out onto flatter country and the track became easier so at the first suitable spot we made camp.

The following day we were on lightly treed sand plain country, roughly following the Elkedra River which was only a series of dry sandy channels when the inevitable happened and the track ended at a bore. This mean driving back for miles to find a fork in the track which we finally achieved. After an hour or two we saw what looked like a mirage in the heat, as a dry channel turned into a river gum lined lagoon or water hole, so we declared a swim and lunch time.

This brought on a total crack-up of one of our passengers. He seemed dead set on creating a mutiny, and suddenly I knew exactly how Captain Bligh must have felt. He told the rest of the passengers they were in the hands of incompetents, they were lost in the wilderness, and now they were going to waste time having a swim. It didn't help when I pointed out that we weren't lost, for if we kept going East we must come to Queensland, after all it was a pretty big state.

Dear, oh dear, how did we ever let this nutter through our screening process, but as the rest of the group ignored him, he finally quietened down and sulked.

After lunch and a beautiful cooling swim we finally reached a bore and from there onto a well- used track to a Station homestead. There was no identification and not a person anywhere, and I concluded this must be Annitowa. Driving east on a well-used track we came to another dead end at a bore, so it was back to the Homestead and try again. Second time lucky and we came onto the Sandover Highway. How did we know? Well, at some time it had been graded, it was the only line (dotted) on the map, and the terminology "Highway" is very loosely used in the Territory. I assumed the mutiny to be over when I announced our track was on a map.

A couple of hours up the Sandover we called quits and declared camp after what I'm sure most of the crowd considered a fun day.

Lake Nash was quite a Station, more a township really, and situated on a waterhole of the Georgina River and had a large Aboriginal population.

From here the main track or continuation of the Sandover road went north to Camooweal, but as we wanted to go south to Soulia, was there a track? There was none shown on the map. The locals assured us, regardless of our map, that there was a well-used track south to Urandangi, but to be very careful if driving off the track as it was heavily lined with empty bottles. In fact, you couldn't get lost, for if the track forked, simply follow the line of bottles.

The story was that Lake Nash was a dry camp and getting a drink required driving to Urandangi, this being over one hundred kms, so naturally you bought grog to sustain the drive back and cast out the empties along the way.

The large letters spelling Urandangi on the map hardly seemed justified as there were only a couple of houses, a small general store, and as expected the most important building, the pub.

Here we had an alternative, either follow down the Georgina by Linda Downs to Cliff Donahue's Highway, or take the graded road east to the Mt. Isa/Boulia bitumen. We considered we had had enough excitement for a while and chose the bitumen.

Just after this Gus was prevailed upon to return to Hermannsburg to lend his authority to a law and order campaign and it became a hassle to obtain permits to cross Aboriginal lands like Warrabri so we never repeated this trip, although the next year we drove from Camooweal to Urandangi and via Linda Downs to Boulia.

1981 This year saw the ultimate disaster when one of our passengers died on a tour, but first a bit of background.

During the early 1960s, when driving north of Woomera, we came upon a coach stopped on the road with all the passengers grouped around a figure lying on a lilo. Ray the driver explained the chap was very ill and asked if I had a two-way radio and would I call the Flying Doctor in Pt. Augusta. He was a very old man, and his face looked like white wax and he didn't appear to be breathing. An elderly lady was crying over him and chewing on a lace hankie.

I took Ray aside and said, "Mate the bloke's dead". "No no," he replied, "Please get on the radio".

I got onto VNZ Port Augusta, who in turn transferred us to the RAAF, Woomera who arranged for an Air Force helicopter to come out. With this arrangement we left them and drove on.

About a year later I caught up with Ray and heard the rest of the story. "Well of course he was dead," he said. "But say that he is dead and you're on your own and no one will help you". He explained how the RAAF helicoptered the body to Woomera, and then being stuck with a body supplied an aircraft to fly it back to Sydney.

Then there was the story of an early coach trip up the Tanami when a passenger died 24 hours out of Halls Creek. The driver radioed Halls Creek Police, but they didn't want to know and told him to wrap the body in a tarp and drive on.

As he explained to us it was difficult to maintain a happy, enjoyable tour when the mob knew they were holidaying with a corpse.

We never anticipated anything like this, but it was to happen on a Gunbarrel North tour.

Nancy was one of a pair of women travelling together and at Ayers Rock became rather ill. The Nursing Sister checked her out, gave her something and everything appeared OK.

Mt. Augustus was included in this itinerary for a simple reason. For years everybody had been quoting Ayers Rock as the biggest rock in the world, then the *Guinness Book of Records* came up with Mt. Augustus (called after the explorer Augustus Gregory) as being the biggest, and more than twice the size of Ayers Rock, so we included it in our Gunbarrel North Tours from 1977 onwards.

Mt. Augustus is also the name of the local Station and the manager back in 1977 was a delightful gentleman called Dudley, who directed us to camp alongside the local swimming hole. He was amazed to find we were from Sydney and told of a few coaches that had come from Perth, but we were the first from the "Eastern States".

Dudley retired and in subsequent years new people took over the Station and gradually turned it into a tourist resort.

So, it was in 1981 that we were driving north of Meekatharra on the Great Northern Highway and getting near to the left-hand track to Mt. Augustus when a screeching noise came from the radiator fan. The fan had a Horton fan clutch that only came on as needed, but the bearings had collapsed, and the fan was starting to cut into the radiator. We drove off the road and set up camp and I walked back to a property we had recently passed to try for help. This was a place called Karalundi and run by Seventh Day Adventist people. Shades of Auntie Rose in the South West, these people couldn't do enough for us. They loaned me a car to drive back to Meekatharra where I felt sure we would have no trouble buying new bearings. But no luck and we ran up a huge bill phoning motor houses in Perth, all to no avail.

On standard coaches Alan Denning (being the smart fellow that he is) used Holden wheel bearings on fans, but by going up market and using fancy American gear we were in big trouble.

It was a Saturday and nearly lunchtime when I decided to ring Adrian Goddard at Parlorcars, Perth (our mate from our American trip). Adrian wasn't overjoyed to get the call as he was just walking out the door with his golf clubs. However, he could access the bearings and would put them on the Greyhound overnight express coach which should pass through Meekatharra at 1.00am Monday morning, so I gave him the directions to our camp site.

Back to camp and Nancy was rather unwell at tea that night, but she told us she had always had a thing about seeing Broome, and was determined to carry on to fulfill her dream. She went off to bed early and a little later her friend took a cuppa to the tent for Nancy. She came back in a state and said, "I think she's dead". It was obvious Nancy wasn't going to see Broome, and this gave us a horrendous problem.

There was no answer on the Police radio - we later found out it was the night of the annual Meekatharra Ball. We finally managed contact and were told to stay and wait for a Police inquiry. Did anyone murder Nancy?

About 11.00pm the Police arrived, thankfully accompanied by an ambulance. Photos were taken, and statements collected, and Doreen and I were requested to attend the Police Station, Meekatharra on Monday morning to sign affidavits.

Sunday was a very quiet day - we were invited to explore the Seventh Day Adventist property, Karalundi. We had showers, bought fruit, vegetables and drinks, and Doreen phoned Nancy's sisters in Sydney. The sisters arranged for a nephew in Perth to handle the next stage of arrangements for Nancy's body, which eased our minds.

Sunday night, everyone was in bed early and about 1.00am I took a stool and sat out on the highway. Not a thing passed on the road, but after an hour lights appeared in the distance. A Greyhound coach pulled up and the driver looked a bit amazed with me sitting beside the road, and not another thing in sight. He had a parcel for Bill Hand - beauty, good old Adrian!

Monday morning broke with a heavy fog and Doreen and I drove down to Meekatharra using the car still on loan from the people at Karalundi. We drove into the town to the sound of gunfire and were whipped into the station by Police and told not to move. It turned out that some young Aboriginals had got on the turps the previous night and broken into the sports store. They had stolen guns and decided to shoot up the town. They must have been pretty harmless as the police (wearing flak jackets) gradually rounded them up and the youngest turned out to be eight-years-old. Meekatharra certainly lived up to its wild west appearance.

We finally signed the affidavits, returned the car with a million thanks, and with Craig having fitted the Horton fan clutch bearings, turned off on the station track to Milgun Station, then Woodlands and finally arrived to see a beautiful sunset on Mt. Augustus.

Our trips were sold as adventure holidays rather than coach tours, and folk felt a little short changed if they didn't get at least something such as a decent bog, so they took all the aforementioned in their stride as typical outback adventure.

On another occasion I thought we were going to have a death on our hands. We were south of Kalgoorlie in an extreme heat wave when I blew a front tyre. I left the tyre changing tools on the ground for a few minutes, only to find they were too hot to be touched. The job had to be done using gloves and wet rags. Just as I finished, a woman passenger turned deathly pale and collapsed.

I drove like mad to Kalgoorlie Hospital where amazingly she came out right as rain after a little more than an hour. The doctor explained that she was on a salt-free diet and they simply filled her up with salt water. He explained that sodium retains fluids in the body and is necessary in very hot weather. He suggested she keep taking salt, adding that almost nobody is truly salt intolerant, and we had good reasons to be worried, as sodium is critical to the functioning of the nervous system, and lack of it can cause disorientation, convulsions, coma, and death. Perhaps we should not be too dogmatic about the do's and don'ts we are told.

Painting by Kevin Mann and signed by passengers (Road Wreckers of '81).
Donohue Highway 1981.

NEW ROAD CHALLENGES
DONOHUE HIGHWAY & GIBB RIVER ROAD

We had often routed tours through Boulia in Western Queensland and came to count Cliff Donohue among our friends. Cliff was Shire President and ran the local general store. He had long tried to raise the money to grade the tracks linking outback stations to enable tourists to travel from Boulia across to the Northern Territory Border and through to Alice Springs, and so create tourist money for his town.

In 1976 Cliff told us that the road would soon be opened, and it was voted that it be called the Donohue Highway in his honor, so from 1977 we began using it and the so-called Plenty River Road on the N.T. side of the border.

Due to lack of road base available in the country Cliff's road rapidly turned to bull dust and in places was miles wide as people drove out further to void the bull dust holes. I worried about what effect rain would have and in 1981 we found out. A cyclone came down from the Gulf, flooding Western Queensland, closing roads and bringing transport to a halt everywhere.

Our old friends Jan and Bill Trompp were on this trip and as usual Jan kept a detailed diary and she has kindly allowed me to quote from this.

So, starting after leaving Alice Springs, these are just the highlights from Jan's diary:

"The Road Wreckers of '81

Nora Martin	Beattie Smith	Fern Baudish
Gwen Bagot	Doug & Phil Pitt	George & Ivy Westwood
Doug & Zoe Tait	Len & Margaret Nuberg	George & Chris Gear
Craig Souter	Bill & Doreen Hand	Alan & Beth Brenchley
John & Marj Cradock	Kevin & Betty Hughes	Brian & Jo Long
Jan & Bill Trompp	Mike Young	Vic & Jan Cole
Bruce & Esther Herps	Paul & Sam Herps	Jane Herps
Kevin & Beryl Mann	Nicole Mann	Nancye & Darren Alderson

Tuesday 19th May   ALICE TO HARTS RANGES

Leaving Alice Springs at 12.00 we took off on the excellent bitumen Stuart Highway and ultimately crossed into the tropic zone at 12.30, then onto the Plenty River Road some 20 minutes later. The bitumen, after some time, gave way to a good gravel surface. From our excellent vantage point in the front seat we could see the Harts Ranges ahead.

Craig excelled, taking us for afternoon tea up a tiny, windy road in and out trees of supplejack, to a garnet mine where we had a field day fossicking on the surface for garnets or mica and anything in between. We located many in hexagon cubes and they were lying all over the ground - the easiest fossicking I've ever done.

Once back on the Plenty River Road, the rugged Harts Ranges loomed amongst gathering cloud and looking very photogenic, so we called for a photo stop. It was pretty late when we camped 20km this side of the actual Plenty River.

Menacing clouds and a gathering wind had us watching the sky. The full moon was hidden.

Wednesday 20th May PLENTY RIVER

It blew a gale all night, sprinkled on and off and became cold in the early morning (7.30am) when we were travelling. A quick photo stop was at the Plenty River which had one small puddle. Not much further, and the Marshall River was crossed where the turnoff to Jervois Station lay. The right, red road was smooth after being slightly wet.

A left turn took us into the Plenty River Mining Company about 19 km along a pretty decent road where substantial puddles were an indication of the ½" of rain last night. It was really cold when we were invited out to fill jerry-cans with water and fossick for Malachite and Azurite which looked its most vivid greens and blues in the wet. Returning along the road we ran into rain, then once back on the highway, found it very wet.

All the way through Jervois and Tarlton Downs we splashed, throwing red mud up all over our steamed-up windows. Just after 11.00am we crossed onto Manners Creek Station and saw a flock of corellas, numbering hundreds. The road deteriorated and was half underwater. At a rig we met a chap who'd ridden a motor bike and could go no further. I felt sorry for him!

Lunch break was a hilarious sight with the dining tables and all the stools beside the bus in the middle of the road in the wet. Our feet were plastered with sticky clay-like chocolate mud, elevating our size by a few inches.

At 5.00pm we crossed the border into SUNNY QUEENSLAND where it rained more. We'd go a few yards, then reverse, driving forward in our tracks to gain only a couple of yards. It was tough going and on reaching some hills eventually on a little crossroad (to where?), it was decided to make camp on the high ground where the bus could be safely parked. Darkness came down quicker than ever and by the time the wet-wood fire got going, it was raining, and our tent was wet before it could be erected. The gigantic tarpaulin was fastened to one side of the bus so we had a dry spot under which to eat tea.

Thursday 2 1st May STRANDED IN THE WET Donohue Highway

Next morning after unmerciful rain and wind, very little sleep too, it was wisely decided to stay put for the day. We tuned into the radio listening to chatting Station people and found the situation grim everywhere. The rain had ceased but the wind persisted which would be to our benefit. After breakfast, a brief meeting was held then we all dispersed to dig trenches round the tents, or dry off lilos and bed gear at the fire.

Friday 22nd May DONOHUE HIGHWAY

It was so nice to sleep in later after a lovely starry night with very little wind. The plan was to see how things looked, have the gear dry, get an early lunch and perhaps leave at noon.

At 12 noon in full sunshine we were travelling the hills quite well for a while, but soon came down onto the black soil plains and had to get out three times to do some walking. The pebbles were pretty, mostly glazed Jasper and some Agate in amongst the Mitchell grass which looked very dry, but when it had to be dug up for de-bogging, the roots were very much alive and tough. Not a tree graced the plain for miles and it was hard going for the bus. To the left, far off could be seen a lake. Again, we were forced to climb out in the gidyea country, so we used branches of the struggling wattle to pack the ruts and this was a great success.

Only a few hundred yards, and down she went into what didn't appear to be much of a bog at all, so out we got again and Bill said, "Oh, this is nothing, we won't be here long enough to get the cork out". (All our bogs are judged on how many bottles of O.P. rum it'd take to drink our way through as recorded in the Ted Egan song.) Into reverse, then forward, then reverse and repeat the performance several times but it wouldn't budge. The right front wheel was absolutely out of sight! Dark was approaching quickly so while the men laboured, most of the ladies erected tents. The men snatched a bite and continued to work to set the bus free, but all work was abandoned. Dingoes howled all night just to set the despairing scene.

Saturday 23rd May DONOHUE HIGHWAY

A glorious day, weather-wise, greeted our predicament and after breakfast the boys shovelled again and the ladies and kids carried and collected rocks which were stuffed into dug-out holes. Bill Hand tried the 8.00am radio and nobody answered at Glenormiston Station which was the closest and only hope for getting fuel. In desperation, he located the Flying Doctor in Mt. Isa who asked if we were an aircraft, and if so are you airborne. Bill answered "No, I'm a tourist coach and I am bogged". That brought some laughter! The Flying Doctor couldn't raise Glenormiston either, but suggested we try again at 1.00pm when Linda Downs and Glenormiston have their galah session. What a helpless lot we felt! So, we just kept working, digging, collecting rocks until poor Bill despairingly, with not much confidence, muttered, "Well, I'll give 'er a go". I continued my bucket collection, not even bothering to watch, then I braved a glance over my shoulder to see the buggy going backwards, first up in the air, then levelling out while everyone cheered madly - the 27-bottler was conquered! We filled the road with rocks then the road gang retired to watch while Bill raced her across the newly formed road.

We had lunch in the lovely sunshine, harassed by flies, then at 1.00pm the galah session went on the air. We listened as one property chatted with the other, Bill doing his best to "butt in" periodically, till eventually the Flying Doctor chatted them up, telling of a coach in distress who was trying to radio them. Then we connected, and Bill told them we were near a bore on our left and the casual voice reported that the bore was only 25 miles from Glenormiston Homestead.

A speck could be seen at the end of the road. It took ages to come and the chap who emerged was from Manners Creek Downs. He was carrying loads of helicopter fuel. Bill told him we'd take it and fly over the bogs. The helicopter fuel was to be used in a movie that was to be filmed here. We were also informed by Ross Hetherington that this was Martins Bore on Linda Downs and we weren't near any bore on Glenormiston. No wonder the Glenormiston fuel hadn't arrived! We had been using fuel up at an alarming rate with all the bogs and never getting better than first gear.

At 3.00pm we were again walking while Bill left the road in a big detour. Again and again Bill found it more successful driving anywhere but on the road. However, it didn't work all the time and again and again the buggy was bogged on the treeless plain where only the Mitchell grass came to the rescue. Doreen and Craig would walk way out, plotting the safest course on firm ground and posting sentries to guide Bill. He cut back onto the road until a big gate loomed up with a nasty wet muddy bog in front of it so while we afternoon tea'd the fence wire to the left was temporarily rolled back so Bill was able to drive through before it was replaced perfectly as before. The next person along that road would certainly scratch his head at that one! From there the chosen route was off the road again and as he resumed a path to the road, down she went again.

It seemed to be inevitable, a bog at the end of every day for the sun was fast fading and we weren't likely to get out of that one. So, in the dark, on beds of stone, but thankfully surrounded by a few trees of gidyea, we pitched the tents. Most went to bed early that night - I wonder why? I bet Sam would have checked under his lilo tonight, for this morning he found a snake under it.

Sunday 24th May TO GLENORMISTON

After a heavy dew, as expected, we were up early with the men shovelling and jacking up the back wheels. They were so proud of their neat hole they wanted to leave the coach in it. We packed and readied, departing just after 10.00am but before long we were walking again. In fact, we spent most of the morning walking, "See Australia with Sundower - and walk". Small lakes on the road had Bill driving out into the scrub and bright-shirted people were used as "markers", this working very well. At least each day found the road drying a little more and by today we were in second gear.

A vehicle could be seen miles up on the horizon. This turned out to be Jim Dwyer from Glenormiston with our precious 2x44 gallon drums of diesel. Did he receive a noisy welcome? "'Boof' the cross cattle and bull terrier dog never had so much attention. It was decided not to refuel yet so the kids were allowed into the back of the truck with Boof for a bumpy ride while these two chaps, Jim and Frank, reconnoitred in the scrub, our "markers" following their advice and experience and Craig took the coach way out, in and out trees, then returning to the road. The flies were bad in this cattle country and we had to be whisked before filing back into the coach. At a more stable part of the road, the first tank of diesel was put into the bus. By 12.45pm we'd reached the real boundary gate of Glenormiston and followed Jim's guiding wheel tracks to avoid a notorious bog.

We thought it was great when we'd sat in the coach for just over an hour. A fence went parallel for miles on our left and at 1.55pm we stopped for lunch. Although there were some dicey patches along our route, we were doing the best speeds for days. In fact, things were getting boring and some slept.

In the dark we travelled into higher country, using the road most of the time till at last a light in the distance brought cheers and we arrived at Glenormiston at 6.40pm, on the banks of a part of the Georgina River. It looked like a city with houses, fences, caravans and out-houses everywhere. "The promised land!" This property is a prosperous three million acres of 3,000 sq. miles. Steaks for everyone greeted us and Myrtle the cook produced miles of mashed potato, pumpkin and tomato which we devoured in relays while some showered.

Bill asked how much the diesel cost and Jim Dwyer told him "whatever you normally pay" and of course Bill wanted to include the fuel he'd used bring the diesel 150 miles, but Jim said "Oh, but you were in trouble, that's OK". He promised us more meat tomorrow. It was nice to wash my hair, accompanied by Jo, and eat such a nice meal. We drove back 5 miles along the road from which we'd come and camped in the trees and had a very good night's sleep.

Monday 25th May GLENORMISTON

A lovely day after a dewy night and we didn't have to dig ourselves out of any bog for a change. Doreen sent off telegrams via the Flying Doctor on the radio, telling friends of our delay. We had a nice time on Glenormiston but like a wild thing, didn't like being caged and we were chomping at the bit for the next bog. A radio message told us we should stay, that the road was impassable (like waving a red flag at a bull) but we took off at 9.00am. Jim and Frank had gone out real early, hoping to reach Soulia and bring back food for which Doreen had given him a list. We went into the "city" of Glenormiston, spent time photographing and enjoying the lake, then about 10.30am we were mobile. Only 15 minutes later the road ahead presented a horrible boggy lake, so our scouting party went head to step it out. All OK. We rounded a bend and up sprung an enormous bog around who's edge we flew at a speed because we couldn't pull up. Then, after a half mile, the Georgina River appeared with a terrible boggy-looking bottom, so we took morning tea on this side. After testing its bottom at the conclusion of morning tea, Bill had a good downhill start and raced the buggy full pelt down through the boggy bottom and straight up the other side. Cheers could be heard all over Queensland! Not much further and we all bailed out at a dicey patch, but all was well with no problems. At 11.40am we passed a sign announcing the Georgina Channels and Glenormiston mail box, used when the river is high and the mail can go no further.

We turned off onto the old road which was to go over rockier ground, however, about midday came to a steep river-crossing, thick with muddy sludge. Out we piled, picking our own dicey way across, then Bill drove it full bore and the bus almost came up, except the eight back wheels spun round and round and... It was well and truly stuck in the slippery black slush which clung to the wheels. This was, I thought, the worst of them all, the men worked up to their knees in mire, Doreen too. We collected Coolibah branches and rocks for many hours but try as they may, it wouldn't come out. Big skids were put in front of the wheels and Bill gave it another go, and it almost got out... more rocks... then out it came some 2 hours 10 minutes later. Our washing was out drying while we had lunch or afternoon tea... who cares. Brushing off the thousands of flies, we hit out about

3.45 and in only ten minutes it was "all out" to pack the next river base with buckets of agate before tackling it and this paid off for we were on board in no time. Our road sailed over nice, rocky patches before finally spreading all over the country so that it was difficult to pick the way. Before us was a great grassy plain which looked as though it could present more than a problem, so we walked. Doreen and Craig "hoofed it" far ahead, waving the bus on in the safe areas. We were back in the bus and could see a Father Emu with three babies, grazing in the Mitchell grass. All went well for a while until we arrived at a great expanse where not a blade of grass seemed to grow, and lakes of water lay ahead. This, as told by the Glenormiston crowd, was the "impassable section" so we found ourselves walking for miles on what looked like a dry seabed. Craig set up "marker-people" but, for the most part, the ground had hardened well, and we felt rather relieved to again be riding into more pebbly hills...

These hills petered out and once again, we were on the mud flats, following tracks of Jim and Frank's vehicle. These flats were certainly not "level" and the whole country, void of vegetation, looked like the remains of a battle field with potholes and corrugations. The inevitable bog section appeared at a creek, so Craig went ahead, or rather upstream, looking for a safe crossing and leaving his human "markers". What a horrible place - miles to the trees - potholes - and darkness advancing. But there we were for the night! The suitcases and camp gear were unloaded and the only place flat enough for a tent located about two hundred yards away, so the girls, in the dark, made camp, our tents all being very close together. The fellows dug, then we all dined on food which, by this time was "pooled" and meat from Glenormiston, all cooked by Beattie and helpers right near the bus. It was a long and dangerous hike back and forth to the camp and bus! We didn't get much sleep on Herbert Downs, the property on which we were bogged.

Tuesday 26th May HERBERT DOWNS

I really didn't feel too "jolly" on waking. Looking around, you'd swear we were on the moon, and just as helpless. Bill and I were totally out of tucker and had pooled our only packet of dried peas last night. A nice breeze had sprung up at night and this would aid the situation, surely. After community cornflakes, the men set to work, jacking up the monster. A great flock of Brolgas came over landing a short distance away.

At 9.00am we heard the excited cry from the river, "Vehicle coming". In drove Jim and Frank loaded with our provisions. They were received with ovations and Frank opened a carton of beer for he had to get some money to take home to Myrtle. They stayed and we all had a fun time yarning and laughing, forgetting our troubles briefly. When they left, we pulled down the dry tents, which was difficult for me in the strong wind and I was thoroughly pooped. A great flock of Pelicans cruised high overhead!

Not long and the boys freed the monster to more cheers, so the luggage was carried to a "depot" and stacked under a sign somebody printed 'SOULIA". The road over the back section was packed, but the front wheels went down in no time, so the bus went into reverse and even the Marsden matting skids didn't help. A fast run was made, and we cheered the coach through then packed the gear waiting at the depot and all proceeded to walk across the river for it luckily had a stony bottom. I fell into quicksand and fell backwards just as instructed by our captain on the mike some days ago. I pulled and pulled at my leg before I eventually sucked it out and Bill washed my shoes in the river.

The plains continued flat and lifeless with just occasional gibber patches of jasper. We walked a couple of dicey looking patches and Doreen scouted others, but miraculously, we kept going. On one "walking section" we investigated large round, grey boulders of silcrete. At 1.50pm after a few more walks and hole filling we lunched on our newly acquired provisions like gluttons. The jasper here was covered in white spots as though birds had done guano over them.

Everything went well till 3.00pm when lakes showed up in front of us and all vehicles had sought a different passage, leaving tell-tale tracks. Our scouts went in all directions, but nowhere looked good, so we all got out while Craig crouched over the steering wheel, and with fire in his eyes, drove like a bat out of hell straight through, spraying water, to safety. That Donald Campbell act was talked about all day and Craig, the hero.

Soon a gate had to be opened and at the other end, a horrible bog so we bailed out. Our hero did a repeat performance and gave her the guns, but it only went half way and stuck again. Out came the shovels, the ruts were packed and in only 15 minutes we were mobile. At 4.10pm a very long bog approached, fed by channels of water which our crowd dammed, then our scouts, finding no alternate way reported and Craig confidently made another dash for the middle. Luckily, there was a slight decline and the speeding coach went down with no hope of stopping and this bog was conquered. I couldn't believe my eyes when I saw him settling down safely on the other side.

The next river presented a problem, so our captain stripped off to trunks and slipped in up to his knees, testing the depth right through. It was slimy, but with everyone out walking, there was a good chance. People undressed, and all waded across. A very big Perenti Lizard about 4ft. long lay calmly on the bank. The crossing, although impressive with a giant bow wave gushing over the hydrofoil, was no problem and everyone played in the river, throwing buckets of water around. In the middle of all this, a utility driven by a coloured man stopped for a chat, but when he and the passenger, a white bloke, tried to go again with the handbrake on, it just wouldn't, and the back wheel jammed, so Allan fixed things temporarily and we set off again at 5.25pm, fording a smaller river then out onto another inhospitable plain just before Herbert Downs Homestead. Our scouts walked a lake, but the sandy bottom seemed OK.

Yet, two more horror stretches appeared, but the sandy bottoms saved the day. At this late part of the day, it seemed inevitable that we should get hopelessly bogged! However, we ran into a clump of trees, with no bindies and plenty of room to spread out. The only dampener was that we had a seat change. Beattie and helpers made a nice community stew and Johnny cakes with rice desert. As we finished tea, lo and behold, a vehicle with only one light arrived out of the darkness. It was Percy, the Aboriginal and Bill from Glenormiston, half-tanked and heading for Boulia to get properly sloshed before the pub closed. It was amazing how they'd got so far. Doreen coaxed us to bed early.

Wednesday 27th May   TO BOULIA

We no longer have a front seat, but at least have lots more room for our feet and rocks. Very early, the sunrise was a corker, reflecting in the water on the road. At 7.30am it was full speed ahead because there were clouds covering most of the sky and it'd been a muggy night. A rainbow arched from the direction of Glenormiston. After only ¼ mile we came upon a permanent lake and then stockmen, rounded-up horses, and a large herd of cattle being driven. The boggy parts of the road were all traversed at a good speed as we neared civilization - Boulia, the Promised Land. At 7.50am we passed through the dingo fence. We maintained a good speed on the straight road and Bill told us about the magic Min Min lights of Boulia until we hit the bitumen at exactly 8.39am. To our right, the sky was black and filthy, the sheep, the first sighted in weeks, grazed on the Mitchell grass. The most-awaited Boulia loomed up along with large sprinkles of rain. The mob invaded the Min Min store, then the Post Office for emergency telegrams, announcing our new arrival date. (We should have been home tomorrow). Everyone was laughing and happy and by 9.55am the sun was once again shining - what a country."

Well thanks to Jan for her story, it seemed that we could expect all sorts of trauma when Jan and Bill booked on a tour, and I have to admit that without the help of a number of practical and fit men on this tour we could have been in a critical situation. Also, the passengers' enthusiasm and sense of humour was indispensable.

Fortunately, we had made a friend of Jim Dwyer (he pronounced it Duhwire) on earlier trips and we regularly brought up papers and magazines in Alice Springs for Jim and his Staff.

The station staff were Jim, the boss, Frank his offsider, then Bill and an Aboriginal fellow called Percy Bedourie. Grog was banned but Jim knew that Bill and Percy had built a small illicit still, but chose to ignore it if it didn't interfere with their work. Percy walked with a slight limp and he told me that after sampling the still one night he went to bed and was scared witless when he saw a dreadful bunyip rising up at the end of the bed, so he shot it, and blew off his big toe. A few years later Jim retired and went to live with his daughter in Mt. Isa.

THE GIBB RIVER ROAD One of the top camping tour operators was Arthur Weston who ran Arthur's Safaris. Arthur loved being first and in 1978 he rang us at home one night to say, "Guess what, I have just driven the first coach across the top of the Kimberley on a new track they call the Gibb River Road", and of course we followed - in 1980. This eventuated in many adventures and encounters, such as this one.

Tim Bowden (who makes us smile by claiming to have the face of a friendly koala) wrote in his book *Penelope Bungles to Broome* - "We pulled off to what was Joe's Water Hole in 1982, since being renamed Jack's Water Hole, and the story of Ros's bush shower has gone down in family history. There she was, stark naked in a completely deserted wilderness, washing the Gibb River road dust off when our two boys Barnaby and Guy ran up shouting "Mummy, mummy, there's a tourist bus coming". There was too, full of adventurous seniors on a camping tour. But it was an unexpected sight in this isolated area".

Yes, it was the Sundowners. We set up camp and our crowd decided that evening to celebrate twenty years of Sundowner travel and arranged a party. Tim and Ros who both worked for the ABC came across and joined us. They taped the party, built a story around it, and it was later featured on an ABC program. He gave us a copy of the tape and I cringed at the sound of the singing. Although most were stone cold sober, it sounded for all the world like a crowd of elderly drunks. The following morning after Tim and Ros had left, we stayed on for an hour or more to swim and enjoy the water hole.

Tim also wrote "After Joe's Water Hole the corrugations simply got worse, a lot worse". Perfectly right, but he doesn't write about what happened next. Their Kombi broke down and after nearly two hours wait, and not another vehicle on the road, they were more than a little jumpy by the time we caught up. Craig was quite an expert on Kombies, having owned one and quickly reasoned that the excess vibrations had shaken the distributor points loose, which proved right and he fixed it in no time, to Tim's great relief. I think he was afraid the problem was something much worse.

Arthur Weston was an adventurous operator and a good friend, so I was sorry when I learnt he passed away in 1993.

17

SIMPSON DESERT CROSSING

The big news in 1982 was Argentina invading the Falkland Islands and the Poms kicking them out. Got Maggie Thatcher re-elected too.

We faced and overcame the usual hazards and were forced to increase prices, so the three-week Central Australia trip now cost $450.

Our regular Sundowners are hard to satisfy as they keep pressing us to tackle ever more difficult trips. Of course, we bring this upon ourselves by claiming a "go anywhere" coach and being willing to travel on obscure four-wheel drive tracks. In fact, we have seen four-wheel- drive people quite furious when, after battling along in four-wheel-drive they find a tourist coach parked at the end of the track. One fellow even abused us, saying "Didn't you see the sign, four-wheel-drive only"?

So, it was for years that people kept asking when we would take them across the Simpson Desert. Now, nobody in their right mind would tackle this without doing a lot of research, so at the end of 1982 Doreen and I decided to map the Simpson in our new Toyota HJ60 diesel station wagon.

Mid-summer (our only spare time) was not the recommended time to do this, but at least we wouldn't be worried by traffic.

At Birdsville we filled spare eskys with loads of frozen fruit juice from David Brooks cold store and headed into the desert with the air conditioner blasting away.

The tyres Toyota fitted in those days were far from satisfactory, being of heavy cross-rib design. These might have been good for hill climbing or maybe mud, but were absolutely unsuited to soft sand, and made the job much harder. A too-slow gear change caused a bog at one stage and being mad at myself, I jumped out and started shovelling sand, only to collapse.

I thought I was having a heart attack, but it was simply that you don't get straight out of air conditioning into extreme heat and expect to work flat out.

The heat was a real problem and that night we listened to the ABC Adelaide when they quoted Oodnadatta as being the hottest place in the State at 47 degrees C. As it didn't seem to cool down at night, our dry mouths could barely stand food and we existed on the Birdsville fruit juice. During daylight hours it was impossible to eat anyway as hordes of flies would descend on you and the food.

We were using maps of the desert provided by the oil rig boys at Santos that showed many of their tracks, as well as the usual "tourist" route. We spent much time selecting suitable routes for the coach, to avoid the worst of the sandhills. After the Simpson we followed the track beside the old telegraph line and explored Dalhousie Springs and Chambers Pillar area, to see if we could get coach access. Then it was time to catch up with our friends at Kings Creek Station, which was not much more than a bough shed at that stage and we helped in the construction of the water tanks and troughs for the camels.

With the coach we planned to travel west to east over the Simpson - the prevailing winds make it easier to run up the west side of the sandhills and hopefully have enough power to make it over the top and run downhill, so the return journey in the Toyota was to test our theory.

At Oodnadatta we met up with two nursing sisters who had finished their stint and wanted to cross the desert to spend time with their counterparts in Birdsville before heading home to Adelaide. The local cop forbade them to travel alone across the desert, so they asked if they could accompany us and the cop relented.

I reckon he was vindicated just the same. The girls really bogged their Nissan Patrol along the way and it took us ages to get them out. It was more than made up to us at Birdsville as the nursing sisters had arranged a party and of course we were invited.

The upshot of the exercise showed that it might be possible to take a coach across the desert, but necessary items would be -

1. A group of passengers prepared to act as slaves.
2. At least 2 out of 3 axles driving through diff locks (we had that).
3. Lots of power to shear through the sand (we had that too).
4. Be able to raise the coach on its air bags (can be arranged).
5. Automatic transmission. Don't take your foot off the accelerator when down shifting or it bogs immediately (yes, we had that too).
6. Specially made hydraulic jacks to lift the wheels (will modify panel beater's "Portopowers").
7. But a crucial item would be the tyres (must talk to Michelin).

Although I still had some reservations we scheduled a Simpson Desert trip the following year with selected passengers.

At Michelin they came up with the idea of using 15 inch-wide tyres called "super singles" on the front axle and 18 inch-wide tyres, called "wideys" on the drive axles. Then instead of running at 100psi pressure, drop this to 20psi in the sand. This could only be done at slow speeds and the "wideys" would bag out to a two-foot square footprint on the sand.

Of course, we had to check the legality of this set up with the DMR or RTA or whatever it was at that time. Although legal, no one would give us a piece of paper to that effect, which caused endless arguments with weighbridge attendants, although I loved the bloke in South Australia who asked what legal weight we could carry on those tyres. I told him, and he thanked me and said he would make a note of it as he had never seen them before.

Another time on one of our popular Mystery Tours we had been around Victoria, then cut up through central NSW, finally camping at Swans Crossing Forestry Camp inland from Kendall. We were stopped at the checking station north of Sydney where the operator insisted we were overweight on the wide tyres. I insisted he ring head office, but being Saturday afternoon, no staff there could give a decision.

Then he checked my logbook and asked where the hell was Swans Crossing, and why wasn't my book filled in coming from Queensland. I explained we were coming from Victoria (it is a requirement of Interstate Licence Plates that part of all tours must be interstate) and Craig had driven most of the previous days.

Where was Craig's logbook? In his luggage, which had been loaded first and all the luggage would have to be unloaded to get to it. Well, all coach tours have brochures, so let's see the brochure. No, I answered, this is a Mystery Tour. By this time, we had a stream of trucks behind us with irate drivers blowing their horns and shouting abuse.

The operator became truly rattled and said, "Get your bloody truck off my driveway and don't bother to come back". Everywhere we went those tyres had people scratching their heads.

1983 The year started with a Barker College tour of Tasmania. After twenty years of organizing tours, this would be the last trip for Ian Campbell as he was retiring. Of course, Ian would now have time to come along on his own but there was no way we would be prepared to handle a mob of kids without his essential backup.

There are some things I shall never forget, and there was one such incident on this trip.

Driving across northern Tasmania we crested a rise to look across a magnificent field of poppies, with the great bulk of Mt. Roland in the background. These of course are opium poppies grown for the production of morphine. It was a beautiful sight, and we stopped for photographs. While some of the boys were photographing, I turned to talk to the main group who wanted information about the growing and production processes, and not long after heard a scream of brakes as a car pulled up and a red-faced man jumped out in a fury and demanded to know who was in charge. I looked around and spotted some of the kids had got over the light fence and were in the poppy field photographing each other among the flowers.

I had no choice than to beg for mercy as this is about the greatest sin that can be committed in Tassie, but he wasn't satisfied and demanded to see my licence. He wrote down my details and intimated I would probably be wearing a ball and chain in Hobart Gaol for the rest of my natural life. Although looking suitably chastened, I didn't believe him, as he would get into as much trouble, if not more than me for having someone in his field, no signage, etc. etc. We heard no more about it, but I made sure it would never happen again.

Craig had been enthusiastic enough to go out with his brother and explore the Simpson Desert in his own four-wheel-drive, in his summer holidays, so it came as a bit of a shock when he told us he was leaving to work for a fellow known around the traps as Jock Strap.

I couldn't blame Craig, the job sounded enticing enough with a new four-wheel-drive coach and taking tours across the Simpson and driving up Cape York. Craig of course was being employed for his extensive experience in the outback plus his mechanical knowledge, but although all went well for a while, the not unexpected personality clash finally came between Craig and his boss. Craig walked out, and Jock Strap couldn't continue without him, the business was finished, and the coach sold to our friend Sid Melcham on Fraser Island.

Craig leaving only weeks before our Simpson Desert Tour created a problem as he was to drive our accompanying Landcruiser and be our backup mechanic, so we turned to Phil Biega.

Phil was a mate who had recently come out of his time as a diesel bus mechanic, was extremely capable and had a fascination about the outback, and even though his wife Karen was expecting their first baby, Phil signed on.

Jack Maddock and his wife Nita were regular passengers and they booked on this trip. At that time Jack was editor of *Truck and Bus* magazine and wrote up his experience of the trip. *Truck and Bus* have kindly allowed us to reproduce Jack's story. As well as *Truck and Bus* magazine, Jack contacted the *Sydney Morning Herald* and the story appeared in the 30th August, 1983 edition.

Jack named a couple of places in the desert, Kuncherinna and Poolawanna, these are just the sites of abandoned holes drilled by Santos some years before, although each has a disused airstrip.

Keith Knight was a regular Sundowner traveller, in fact it was a Sundowner romance when Keith met Helen on tour. He made movies of all his trips and bought a new camera to film the desert crossing. So, while others slaved, Keith as our official film maker captured our story and wondered if he might have a saleable product maybe for TV. It appears he dropped the camera early in the piece and when the film came out blank, Keith sat down and cried, and I think I did too.

We never asked any authority for permission to cross the desert, that is police or rangers, or whatever, assuming it was unnecessary. Today of course permission is required, and a fee has to be paid, then a vehicle inspection passed. As we were the first to drive a 40ft. highway coach across we would certainly be the last - that is until there is a bitumen highway.

When we first mooted the idea of trying to drive a tourist coach across the Simpson a lot of people considered it foolhardy, if not impossible, but having battled through countless bogs I had learnt one valuable lesson.

With a heavy vehicle, momentum is everything. Simply put, if you can build up enough momentum a vehicle like a tourist coach takes a lot of stopping, and in the following article Jack talks about the coach actually flying through the air. With that sort of momentum, maybe we should have fitted wings and flown across the desert.

**1983. Laying Marsden Matting in Simpson Desert.
Jack Orr carrying matting, Sgt. Bill Dickson in front of coach.**

Sundowner across the Simpson Desert TO BIRDSVILLE – THE HARD WAY

By Jack Maddock

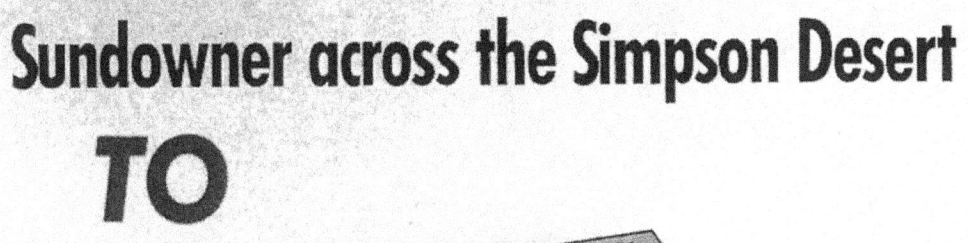

What's it like crossing the Simpson Desert in a tour coach?

I must have been asked that question several hundred times in the past few months. The short answer is: "Hard work."

Last August my wife Nita and I were among the 32 paying passengers who were on a conventional 12 metre Denning owned by Bill and Doreen Hand (Sundowner Coach Tours) of North Ryde, NSW, when they made history by becoming the first operators to take a coach load of tourists across the Simpson Desert. (See T&BT Oct. 1983.)

The Simpson Desert crossing was the second half of a Sundowner tour which started from Sydney on July 30 and proceeded via Broken Hill to other interesting and unusual places such as the Andamooka opal fields, Roxby Downs, Coober Pedy, and east from Kulgera on the SA/NT border to Chambers' Pillar (four-wheel-drive Land Cruisers were used on this sector), and on to Alice Springs via Rainbow Valley. From Alice Springs the itinerary covered trips to Hermannsburg and

Palm Valley, King's Canyon and King's Creek Station, then back down to Kulgera and east to Finke and New Crown for the commencement of the journey across the desert.

The historic crossing of the Simpson Desert was completed on August 18 and the party arrived back in Sydney on August 24. Bill Hand did all the driving across the desert; Doreen was responsible for the navigation and plotted a course over mainly unmapped tracks and abandoned oil rig supply roads; and Phil Biega of Chester Coaches, Chester Hill, NSW, was the mechanic. Bill is also a qualified mechanic, so the party had plenty of technical expertise at hand.

A share of the credit must also go to the coach which put in a mechanically faultless performance. It was purchased new by the Hands in 1980 and has a mid-mounted Detroit 8V71 engine coupled to an Allison HT740 automatic transmission and Eaton bogie drive with inter-axle lock.

The Hands' personal transport — a Toyota 4WD Land Cruiser — accompanied the party as back-up and (if necessary) emergency vehicle, and like the coach it turned in an impeccable performance. On the desert sector it was driven by some of the passengers. With Doreen as navigator it went ahead to check the route and road conditions and alert the coach party to any hazardous or difficult spots requiring extra care — or action with shovels!

The desert and its risks

The 89,600 sq km (56,000 sq mile) Simpson Desert sprawls across the border of South Australia and the Northern Territory and spills over into the far western corner of Queensland. It is sometimes called the 'dead heart of Australia' but this is really a misnomer; the thousands of parallel sand ridges stretching for hundreds of miles in a north-west, south-east direction give the impression of a wasteland when viewed from the air but there is plant and animal life throughout the region, admittedly not abundant nor sufficient to support human life.

It is, frankly, an inhospitable area and can deal with — in fact, has dealt with — the foolhardy and the ill-prepared in a silent and deadly fashion.

To say that the crossing of the Simpson held no fears for Bill and Doreen Hand would not be true. Although, in their 21 years of specialised outback tours they've been to some of the most remote places in Australia and have got into (and extricated themselves from) some incredibly difficult situations which have included literally hundreds of boggings in mud and sand, they were well aware that the Simpson exercise bristled with potential problems and very real hazards for the coach and its occupants.

They planned the trip very thoroughly; they made extensive inquiries from people familiar with the desert and adjacent country as to what conditions might and would be encountered. They followed this with a trip in December 1982 in their Toyota Land Cruiser, crisscrossing the desert looking for tracks which could be linked up and put together as a route from west to east. This survey occupied a fortnight.

In March last year, several months before the Simpson trip, Bill converted the coach to 'big single' tyres because these, in his opinion, would be better than conventional-sized duals on the bogie in areas where Sundowner operates. This proved to be a sound decision for coping with the conditions that are

Long sections of bulldust threatened the trip at first. It sent engine temperatures soaring and consumed excessive quantities of fuel.

(Right): There was no way the Denning could have crossed this sand ridge until many tonnes of sand were levelled off and Marsden matting laid ahead of the wheels.

encountered in the outback. For the Simpson crossing these wide profile tyres undoubtedly contributed to the success of the trip. The tyres were Michelin tubeless radials, 18SR22.5 on the rear and slightly narrower 15SR22.5 on the front.

Left: Fuelling at New Crown Station before beginning the run across the Simpson Desert.

Passengers briefed

Before the crossing was attempted Bill pointed out to the passengers that all-up weight and fuel range would be critical factors; to conserve fuel there would be no air-conditioning nor would there be the usual engine-driven air compressor assistance for blowing up the campers' air matresses each evening. They'd have to do it the hard way until Birdsville was reached!

Decision point would be Purni Bore, said Bill, just inside the western edge of the desert. If track conditions and fuel consumption deteriorated, the crossing would be abandoned and the party would head south for civilisation and safety via Macumba Station to Oodnadatta.

Extra water was carried both on the coach and in the Toyota and passengers were advised as to what quantities of food to provide for themselves (as is the style of Sundowner tours) so that they had adequate supplies in the event of the crossing taking longer than planned. The Toyota also carried additional jerrycans of fuel plus a spare 18SR22.5 tyre. As things turned out, none of the emergency supplies were needed.

From Kulgera and Finke (NT) we proceeded to New Crown Station where, by prior arrangement with the station management, the fuel tanks of the coach were topped up to 650 litres and the Toyota's to 150 litres.

From New Crown we headed generally south-east on a reasonably graded road. We paused briefly at Charlotte Waters where a few heaps of rubble are all that remain of the important repeater station that once relayed messages between Oodnadatta and Alice Springs on the old Overland Telegraph Line.

From there our route took us across the border into South Australia through flat country dotted with gidyea and mulga which gave way to gibber plains and huge clay pans with numerous tracks leading off in all directions without a single signpost. In summer one could imagine the sun glaring down on those blackened

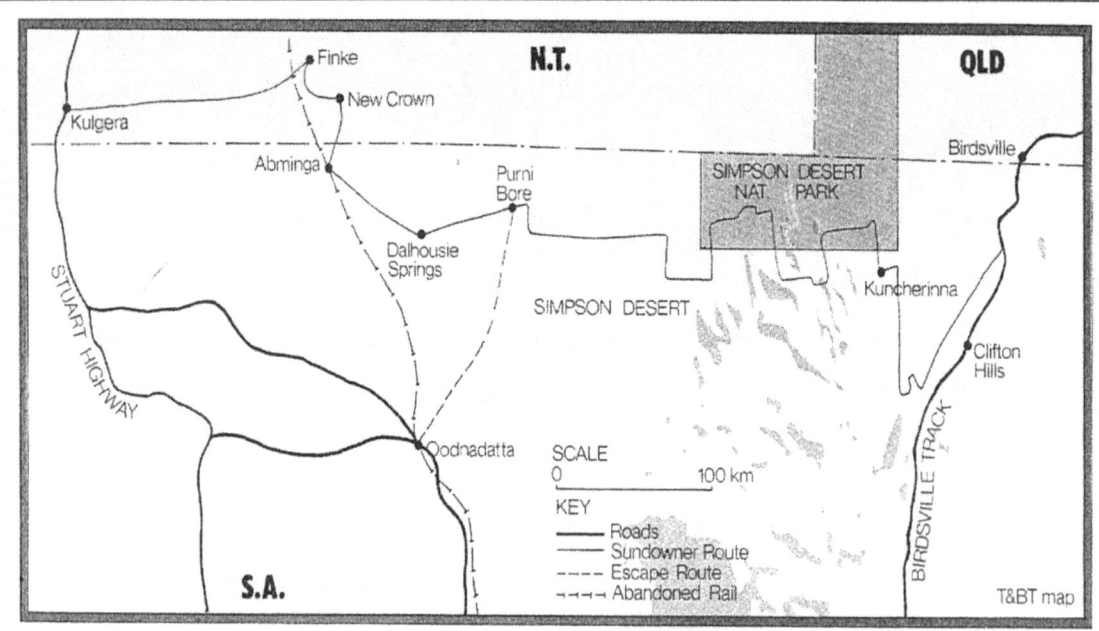

gibbers, and the gibbers glaring back at the sun!

It's no country for the inexperienced or unprepared traveller.

After opening and closing innumerable gates as we passed through Mt. Dare Station we came to Abminga, a small derelict railway settlement on the abandoned Marree-Alice Springs railway line. Steel overhead water tanks from which the tenders of steam locomotives were replenished are still standing, as is a coal loading stage and a steel-railed stock yard which was in near-perfect condition and would no doubt last for many more years. In contrast were the old railway station and train crew quarters where change-over crews rested; these and other railway premises are deteriorating due to the ravages of time and vandalism.

A signpost near the former railway level crossing pointed to Finke 87 km, New Crown 67, and Oodnadatta 210.

Before we left Abminga we took the precaution of loading some old railway sleepers aboard the coach for use in jacking, placing under bogged wheels and for firewood if need be because we thought there'd be little dead timber in the desert with which to make a fire for cooking. But we didn't have to chop the sleepers; we found adequate firewood at our camp sites but those sleepers came in for plenty of use under the wheels in the sandhills.

Bill and Doreen Hand confer on the route to be taken.

Warm springs and bulldust

From Abminga we proceeded along a graded single-track road to Blood's Creek. There were extensive areas of bulldust followed by hard, stony plains. Crispe Bore was flowing vigorously with very hot artesian water. We had to cross the bore drain about 1 km distant and although the sight of bullrushes caused doubts as to the firmness of the crossing it was found to have a stony bed which took the weight of the coach without trouble.

We camped that night at Dalhousie Springs, a region which has extensive areas of warm springs and artesian mounds spread over many square kilometres.

For quite a distance along our route next day there were bubbling hot springs for as far as the eye could see. Then the topography changed to undulating gibber country with flat-topped mesas in the distance.

Next we came to more long stretches of deep bulldust which made the 8V71 grunt somewhat and sent the Allison box down to 2nd and 1st for most of the time. It also put the head temperature needle very close to the red sector. It played havoc with the rate of fuel flow and gave warning that if these conditions persisted we might have to consider 'giving it away' and heading out of the area and down to Oodnadatta — and safety.

Fortunately, after a couple of hours, the deep talcum-powder bulldust country gave way to hard stone-strewn surfaces and the transmission was able to shift up, with corresponding improvement in engine temperature and fuel consumption.

Near the oddly-named Alka Selza Bore the track divided: the road to Oodnadatta turned off to the right and a sign pointed straight ahead to Birdsville. We still had a little way to go before 'decision point' — Purni Bore — was reached. And we

30 Truck & Bus Transportation

April, 1984

began to get a taste of what was to come: the sand ridges were appearing in increasing numbers. They weren't very high at this stage; they were fairly close together but didn't appear as though they would present any serious problems.

From Purni Bore the route plan was to follow tracks which for much of the time run up and over the sand ridges and at other times its direction was to be parallel with the ridges. The tracks through the ridges had been 'clayed' by oil exploration parties, using graders to skim off some of the sand on the crests and then 'top' the formation with clay obtained from nearby claypans to provide a firm surface.

The distance between sand ridges varied; sometimes it seemed that they were only a few hundred metres apart; at other times wide claypans and dry lakes separated them. On average I would say we crossed three sandhills per kilometre, many of them over 30 metres high.

Generally the lines of sandhills ran north-east/south-west and they had a much steeper slope on the leeward (easterly) side than on the western, which would make an east-west crossing very difficult. Where there were 'live' crests of sand, the lip which formed at the top dropped away sharply on the eastern side. In places there were 'saddles' in the crests, forming a sort of double-topped sandhill which required considerable extra digging to prevent the wheels of the coach from going down in the hollow and losing traction.

Most sand ridges were well

Right: The road ahead — typical scene in the Simpson Desert as the coach makes its way across to Birdsville.

Below: Debogging operation — one of many such scenes on the way across the Desert. Bill Hand uses a special jack with head inserted under the wheel rim to begin lifting one of the wheels.

Right: Bellied on a sandhill — forward section of the body (luggage bin area) and transmission are buried in the sand and the wheels are unable to obtain a grip.

Above: Sloshing through shallow lakes of water in the Goyder's Lagoon area. Fortunately, the moisture didn't penetrate far and the ground underneath was firm.

"We've made it!" Ceremonial picture-taking as the coach emerges from Goyder's Lagoon to join the Inside Track south of Birdsville. Sign in front of coach (low down) says: ROAD CLOSED.

Above: What's the plan of attack? The back-up Land Cruiser comes to a big drift across the track. Bill Hand and Phil Biega have a head-scratching session. There is much digging in store for the passengers.

Sundowner across the Simpson Desert

covered with spinifex, desert canegrass, saltbush and in many places with mulga and acacia.

First of many bogs

For a time Bill was able to use a 'charging' technique to get over the sand-covered crests. After unloading the passengers and lifting the body by about 25 centimetres by means of the air suspension to provide increased belly clearance, Bill would back-off and then bore up the slope and clear the top, sometimes just scraping the body on the soft sand.

Just as we were beginning to think that this was going to be the way to conquer the hundreds of sandhills that lay ahead, the desert had news for us: a big crest stopped the Denning and all efforts to reverse out of it failed as the wheels on the drive axles began to dig themselves in.

So, there was nothing else for it but to get the de-bogging gear out. Using a portapower-type jack with special shovel-shaped head designed by Phil Biega to fit under the wheel rim without distorting it, relays of male passengers pumped the jack and shovelled, and the womenfolk used buckets and bare hands to move sand so that sleepers could be put under the wheels when they had been jacked to the same height as (or were slightly higher than) the front axle. This meant that there had to be several lifts by the jack to gain the necessary height. The railway sleepers also came in handy forming a base for the jack in the soft sand.

After four and a half hours of digging and jacking and removing sand from under the mid-section of the body, the heavy coach came out of its first Simpson sand bog.

Learning from this 'stranding' on a big sand ridge the tactics were changed. Tyre pressures were reduced from 85 to 35 psi (586 to 241 kPa) to provide better traction; any ridge that looked as if it would cause trouble was reduced by shovels and buckets; and lengths of Marsden matting were laid under the wheels as the coach negotiated our 'modified' crests.

Soon afterward we removed so much material from one particular crest that when Bill charged up at considerable speed, expecting some resistance from the sand, the coach became airborne; all six wheels left the ground, causing much chaos among passengers' belongings in the racks, under the seats, in the 'fridge, etc.

To see a 12 metre coach in full flight is really quite an experience!

Later a too-slow approach to a crest that had been cut back proved 'fatal' and the result was a delay of two and a half hours while the bogie axles were jacked wheel-by-wheel, lifted in stages, packed with sleepers and Marsden matting, and sand cleared from under the engine, transmission and luggage bin area.

From time to time the characteristics of the sandhills would improve and Bill would go over them with an occasional 'thump' felt underneath indicating that the floor of the luggage compartment and the steel protecting plate under the transmission was taking some punishment. Then the coach and passengers would get a respite as the course changed and we travelled between the sandhills for a while.

Waterlogged desert!

When we reached Poolawanna, about 80 km west of Kuncherinna, where we decided to camp for the night, no sooner had the tents been erected than heavy clouds began to gather, and just as darkness fell rain driven by a strong wind made us wonder if we were really in the arid Simpson Desert!

Rain poured down for most of the night, accompanied by gusty winds. A large annexe had been erected along the door side of the coach to provide shelter while we cooked, ate, talked, etc. It also replenished the drinking water supply.

By morning the ground was sodden; the coach looked forlorn in a large lake of water — in the middle of the Simpson Desert! Bill decided we'd better stay put until the weather improved and the countryside dried out a little. He didn't fancy the task of tackling the clay-topped sandhills after rain.

He decided to run out the aerial for the short-wave radio and call up some of his friends on stations hundreds of kilometres around.

He talked to Tim Lander at King's Creek Station, Arthur Liddle at Angas Downs, "Fly" the Aborigine fencer working near Andado, Mike Steel at Innamincka, and David Brook at Cordillo Downs. He obtained a general picture of the extent of the rain and whether or not it was clearing. He then contacted VNZ at Port

Sundowner across the Simpson Desert

Augusta to obtain a weather forecast; in turn VNZ could be heard talking to Pandie Pandie, Clifton Hills and other stations regarding the general situation and condition of tracks in their areas. He told all of them that although we would be delayed waiting for an improvement in the weather, we were not worried and were holding at least four days supply of food and water. Although we were more than half-way across, we had used less than half our fuel.

Both Mike Steel and David Brook own aircraft and if the worst came to the worst the party was assured of a food drop or a lift out, but that would be very much a last resort. Yet it was part of the overall safety factor built into the tour program.

We sat it out until lunch time. The rain had ceased and an inspection on foot of the nearest sand ridge indicated reasonable dryness, so Bill decided to move on.

Unfortunately his earlier misgivings about clayed sandhills proved correct; although we had no trouble going up and over the top of the first two or three, the next one was very greasy on the downward side. The front tyres simply slithered all over the place, and there was no response from the steering, and the coach slid sideways off the track and came to rest in a somewhat ungainly and precarious pose. In fact it appeared momentarily as though it would fall on its side. The passengers were unable to get out because the bottom of the door was buried in the sand. The Toyota crew came back and dug the door free and then the passengers began the task of freeing the wheels from the wet sand and clay.

Once the wheels and bodywork were cleared and some Marsden matting laid down, the coach was cautiously driven ahead along the side of the clayed track until an opening could be found to get back onto the formed surface. With the coach safe and on an even keel once more it was decided to make camp right there and hope the rain would stay away. We had travelled a total of 10 km for the day!

Slow to dry out

There was no further rain on the following day but the clouds persisted and slowed the drying-out process. It was decided to move on but the first sand ridge stopped us. The coach bellied on it and we spent the next 2½ hours with shovels, buckets and bare hands clearing wet (and heavy) sand from around and under the coach.

By lunch time we had travelled only 30 km, so frequent were the ridges and so widespread was the sand on the crests. But we didn't bog again; our technique of knocking the tops off the ridges and laying Marsden matting ahead of the wheels, painstaking though it was, proved successful and saved hours of frustration and hard work in cramped conditions.

Although our progress across the desert had been somewhat slower than some of the passengers had anticipated we were steadily achieving our objective. The sandhill regions were drying out and in other places where the route was across wide pans with water in them from the recent rain the surface was sometimes soft but the moisture hadn't penetrated far and the ground was hard underneath. Anything that looked doubtful was skirted by driving around it on the firm sand.

The only matter of concern was: how much rain had fallen on the flat, clay country in the Goyder's Lagoon area, and would we be able to get through?

We put that question aside as we made camp that evening. There was no point in worrying about what *might* be ahead. Doreen Hand's philosophy and sensible advice throughout the trip was: meet each problem as it arises and don't worry about what the next one might be. And ... don't be in a hurry, just take things calmly.

That seemed to lower the blood pressure of the impatient and the impetuous ones in the party!

Emerging from the desert

On what we hoped would be — and in fact proved to be — our last day of the crossing, we'd been on the road for about 40 minutes when what appeared to be a 'friendly' crest not needing our ministrations with shovels and buckets turned out to be a little sharper than we thought and the coach bellied on it. So, once more it was a case of 'get out and get at it' but this was an easy one in comparison with the others; once we'd dug the sand away from under the luggage bin and transmission it was simply a matter of 'firing up' and driving away because the wheels hadn't gone down.

The crests were definitely more 'docile' now and most of them could be driven over without much fuss or at worst the bin and protection plate would take a bit of a thump now and then.

After about 90 minutes we left the last of the sandhills and began to head north-east for the 150 km run up via Goyder's Lagoon to Birdsville.

At first we drove through sandy/loamy country, arid but fairly well covered by vegetation and low scrub. Then, shortly after we entered Clifton Hills Station (19,000 sq km or 7,510,000 acres), one of the largest cattle stations in the world, we began to have some doubts about reaching Birdsville that day. Sections of the track were very slippery, obviously there had been fairly heavy rain through here and the clay-like nature of the soil caused considerable difficulty in steering. The vehicle simply went its own way at times; fortunately the countryside there is dead flat and no matter where we slid there was no risk of hitting anything (other than scrub or lignum) or dropping down into a drain or ditch because there were none.

While Bill wrestled with the wheel to keep the coach pointing in the right direction, we settled back and either read or snoozed; we couldn't see out of the windows because they'd gradually gone opaque as we sloshed through numerous shallow 'lakes'.

Then, at 11.38 am on Day 6 we knew we'd made it; we joined the Inside Track from Clifton Hills to Birdsville. A notice at the road junction told us that the road we'd

continued on page 58

Sundowner across the Simpson Desert

continued from page 35

just travelled was closed!

From here to Birdsville the big Denning seemed to sense that its hard work was over, and for the first time since leaving Purni Bore the transmission shifted up to top gear!

It was 2.30 pm when we reached that famous outpost town of Birdsville. A celebratory drink for all in the bar of the Birdsville pub was No. 1 priority, and then came hot showers — our first good wash since Dalhousie Springs five days previously — and the washing of clothes, thus restoring the social equilibrium.

From New Crown Station where we had taken on fuel six days ago we had travelled 860 kilometres across to Birdsville and the 8V71 had used 534 litres of distillate. That worked out at 1.6 kilometres to the litre of fuel or, in more readily recognisable language, 4.5 miles per gallon. In addition to the untouched reserves of fuel carried in the Toyota we still had 116 litres in the tank of the coach.

And ... as a result of careful planning and use we still had plenty of drinking water and food. Water for ablutions, teeth cleaning, etc., had been rationed to a little over a pint per person per day; there was no specific limit on drinking water although the exercise of commonsense and caution was recommended, because there was no water available between Purni Bore and Goyder's Lagoon on the route we followed.

The run home

From Birdsville the remainder of the journey back to Sydney was a relative breeze, although the rain which swamped us in the desert had inundated much of the top portion of South Australia, causing a few problems with soft ground and near-bogging in mud on our way through Cadelga, Cordillo Downs and Innamincka. But from there through the Moomba gas field to Murti Murti, Bollard's Lagoon, Cameron's Corner and Tibooburra there were only isolated soft spots, one of which had badly bogged a single-axle coach only a couple of days previously. That vehicle, incidentally, which we met at Innamincka and which was heading for Birdsville over the same track through Cordillo Downs where we'd experienced some anxious moments — and remember, we had bogie drive and wide profile tyres — had been sent into this type of country with little thought as to the conditions it would meet. One could only look with incredulity at this strictly highway-type coach and its neatly uniformed driver and wonder at the mental limitations of the company management that instigated this musi-comedy project!

The one concern that lingers with me after the trip is that some 'press-on' types of operator with conventional highway equipment may latch on to the Simpson as something they can add to their customers' entertainment and they'll plunge in without adequate and careful preparation that is absolutely fundamental if human life is to be safeguarded.

The responsibility for a large part of people travelling through one of the most inhospitable and arid areas of Australia — or in the world, for that matter — is something that can't be shrugged off.

You can't "gung-ho" your way across the Simpson Desert with a load of passengers!

Footnote: The coach came out of it virtually unscathed. The only damage, if it could be called that, was a couple of dents in the floor of the forward luggage compartment; these must have occurred when we hit the crests of some of the sandhills rather solidly and bumped our way over. There was no sign of bending or distortion of the bin side members nor, for that matter, of structural damage anywhere.

A front air bag blew out after hitting a sharp-edged hole in the road west of Tibooburra, but this was one which was nearly due for replacement and in 30 minutes Phil Biega had fitted a new bag. The wonder was that not a single bag blew when the coach landed so heavily after the 'flying' episode in the desert! ■

April, 1984

"The coach came out of it virtually unscathed"

— Jack Maddock, "Sundowner Across The Simpson Desert"
Truck and Bus, April, 1984

We don't recommend testing your Denning to this extreme, but it is nice to know that reliability is still our aim whatever your requirements — offroad or express highway work, you can be assured of long, reliable service.

When ordering your new coach ask Bill and Doreen Hand why they chose Denning, then contact Bob or Dick on (07) 345 1151, Glenn on (065) 52 6177 or (049) 97 6263. AH or Graeme on (03) 531 3087.

Denning
Landseer St., Acacia Ridge
Brisbane, Qld 4110
Telephone (07) 345 1151 Telex AA43022

1973. First New Zealand Tour.

1994. Arkaroola S.A.
Doreen flying in Ultralite with Doug Sprigg.

1988. Bogged on track to Gosses Bluff, Central Australia.

DOLPHINS Having heard about the dolphins at Monkey Mia we included this on our Gunbarrel South Tour in 1983 and were amazed to find a new bitumen road out to Denham. Back in 1974 we had driven out to Denham when the track was just dirt with the idea of driving to the most westerly point of Australia and at the time no one knew anything about Monkey Mia and its friendly dolphins.

The track was in poor condition, although not bad as far as a quarry where blocks called ashlars were cut out of material called coquina. There was a vast amount of this material made out of tens of millions of small shells, all welded together. The ashlar blocks made wonderful building material and were widely used around the area.

We finally reached the small fishing town of Denham and while we were there, school came out and the kids flocked around the coach asking where we had come from. They had a mixture of skin colours and spoke in something of a dialect of English. The storekeeper explained that they were descendants of British, Malay, Malacca, Chinese and Aboriginal pearl diving pioneers "who didn't care too much for the formalities of marriage". Eleven years later the town had become something of a tourist resort for fishermen and the gateway for the increasing numbers of people going through to Monkey Mia to see the "tame" dolphins.

At Monkey Mia we camped right on the beach and the dolphins came in close to the shore in the late afternoon and again early in the morning. Everybody swam with the dolphins and some people camped nearby gave us some fish to feed them.

Wilf and Hazel Mason were building a caravan park and the shower block had bore water that was so hard, soap was useless, and we used hair shampoo to get a lather. Over the years Monkey Mia became a top tourist destination, requiring Rangers to control and oversee the viewing of the dolphins and the caravan park became a Resort with first class facilities.

AMERICA'S CUP Probably the biggest story of 1983 was Australia winning the America's Cup and Alan Bond being our country's biggest hero.

We were camped in a beachside Caravan Park in Albany W.A. the night of the big race and some of our people elected to take caravans which had TV sets. Doreen went off to one of the caravans to watch TV but as I needed some sleep, went to bed in our tent. Sometime after midnight I awoke and decided to listen on the coach radio for an update and was amazed to hear Australia was leading.

Nearly all the caravans were lit with people watching TV, but I had no idea which caravan Doreen and the group had gathered. I sneaked around a number of vans peering in their windows. It was a warm night and people were lying around half naked watching their screens. I expected at any moment to be jumped upon and hauled off as a Peeping Tom when I finally found the right caravan.

The following day in Albany people went crazy celebrating, helped along no doubt by the pubs putting on free beer. Then Bob Hawke the Prime Minister proclaimed Alan Bond Australia's hero. Well, times do change.

FENCES Fences everywhere, all our favourite camp spots were gradually being fenced off, and on returning from Western Australia we were even finding this on the Nullabor. I could not find an unfenced camp spot and finally saw a possibility. There was a grove of trees though quite a distance off the road. As we got closer it was not a satisfactory location as the trees were too far apart and the ground became soft and puggy and was dragging on our wheels. I powered in a wide arc, expecting to bog at any moment and headed back towards the road.

I was aware of a car parked on the road, but just getting back to the bitumen was taking all my concentration. We made it back to find it was a Police Car with the cop leaning on the bonnet just staring at us. "Mate, will you tell me what the bloody hell you're doing?" he asked. I explained, and he took pity on us and said, "Follow me".

We drove on to where there was a gate. He opened the gate, showed us a camp spot and said, "The owner's a mate, I'll square off for you". Outback cops were usually pretty good blokes.

Roadside repair northern S.A. Manufacturing new gear drive using fibreglass.

1984/87 YULARA, KINGS CREEK, EDITH FALLS, CHARACTERS

1984 This year we realised many regular Sundowners had travelled more than 300 days on the road with us, so we formed a 300 Club, allowing them to travel on selected tours at cost price. We reckoned they had earned it.

One person, Dorothy Webb, who had recommended the Fiji Tour finished up travelling over 1000 days on the road with us, which I think is phenomenal when you consider that this is the equivalent of every day for nearly three years.

Also 1984 saw the opening of Yulara Village at Ayers Rock. To mark the opening, a Pioneers Reunion was arranged for people associated with the Rock tourism. I flew up to Alice Springs and drove out to the Rock in a borrowed car to join this most wonderful get together.

While having a couple of beers that night, someone remarked they had never seen me drink, and the rumour was that I was a Seventh Day Adventist. The truth was that I never drank and drove, and seldom drank on tour. This was in sharp contrast to most drivers who drank pretty heavily in those days, although Kevin Bryant and one or two others were non-drinkers.

I got talking to a white haired old chap called Bill McKinnon about the Rock and he said, "The last time I climbed it was 1932". What a jaw dropping statement, and I thought we were something of pioneers.

It turned out that Bill had been a Territory Trooper who used to take the Police Camel Patrol through this country in the early 1930s, and was one man who could certainly say he had seen some changes. Bill told me of how he was injured in the first Japanese raid on Darwin in 1942.

Then for those who remember the Petrov spy case in 1954, he was also involved. Petrov's wife, Evdokia was muscled aboard an aircraft in Sydney by two Russian bodyguards, thought to be K.G.B. Bill was in charge of the police party that met the plane in Darwin as it touched down on its way to Russia.

"The guards each had their hands inside their coats holding guns, and I cocked my gun and with my men we overpowered them. It left me with three loaded and cocked pistols, theirs and mine" Bill said.

Bill had climbed the Rock that day with his old mate Peter Severin from Curtin Springs. Bill was 82 and I don't know Peter's age at that time, but he was certainly no spring chicken. I was sad to hear Bill McKinnon passed away in May 1997 aged 94, and so another genuine link with our historical past has gone.

Yulara was an amazing place, as you would expect from something costing $160 million in 1984 dollars. The developers were proud of the fact that there was only one stop work on the entire project, and that predictably concerned beer. They refused to pay Alice Springs prices, and these were subsidised back to Adelaide prices. Tourists should be so lucky.

I still couldn't help feeling the mystique had gone - bitumen roads, the lavish reception with champagne, prawns, satay sticks and frozen desserts. The effort of just getting there had somehow created the elation of arriving at the Rock. I could see that we would have to remind people that they had travelled thousands of miles to see the wonders of nature and not spend all their time shopping.

KINGS CREEK With the road to Kings Canyon being upgraded, we now had this firmly on the itinerary and it was proving to be a highlight.

Tim Lander and Ian Conway had obtained the lease on a block of about half a million acres called Kings Creek, between Angas Downs and the Canyon and proposed constructing a tourist resort.

Ian was one of Arthur Liddle's nephews who used to spend his school holidays with the family at Angas Downs. Tim and Ian quickly ran out of money as the bills mounted up right from the start with things like the compulsory fencing and sinking of bores. They asked us to become financial partners to save their dream and we finished up pouring a good deal of money into the venture, largely because of our long friendship with Tim.

One day a German film crew arrived in Alice Springs to film outback Australia for a TV program. They were advised to go to Kings Creek and film camel catching. Helicopters were often used for spotting, and bull catchers (stripped down Toyotas with wrap around bars) for catching. Trail bikes drove the camels toward the bull catchers and one of the team would then leap off, grab the camel and try to pull it down as the rest joined in. They tied the camel's legs and loaded it onto a truck.

While the Germans were filming this routine from a helicopter, Johnnie Liddle was racing through the scrub on a trail bike when he crashed into a kangaroo. Johnnie somersaulted off the bike and landed upside down in a patch of spinifex. The German cameraman missed this action and begged Johnnie to repeat it, but to no avail.

Tim suggested he change places with the cameraman who could ride on the bull catcher while Tim rode on the skids of the chopper. From here he reasoned the pilot could drop him right on top of the camel. He was only joking - I think - because they never tried it, but you can never tell with Tim, he will have a go at anything.

On the tour side of the business, Kings Creek was very good, we camped on the Station and helicopter roundups of wild camels being a sideline, our passengers sometimes became involved.

Tim and Ian were both clever hard-working fellows, but as in so many partnerships, strains develop, and Tim finally walked out and started what became a successful contracting business in Alice Springs.

Doreen's mother died in 1987 after enjoying many years travelling with us. She loved Kings Creek and had high hopes about our involvement with it, so we buried her ashes at the foot of a big Desert Oak tree on Kings Creek.

An Aboriginal land claim was placed on the property and after some ten years and numerous court cases a large proportion of the property was given to the Aboriginal claimants. From our point of view our investment was a costly mistake.

In 2001 Doreen and I went for a bit of a drive and finished up in Alice Springs. We stayed with Tim and his family, and had a wonderful time catching up with old friends.

Angas Downs is now Aboriginal land and we drove out and spent some time with the Aboriginal people we knew there, but never went on to Kings Creek, as it is something we would just as soon forget.

EDITH FALLS Back in the early 60s our friend Paddy Ethell, who produced the *Inland Review* magazine did a trip up the track to Darwin looking for off-beat stories for his magazine.

He told us of a beautiful spot called Edith Falls, but said the track off the highway was dreadful and we had no hope of getting a coach along it. This of course was a red rag to a bull, and while Paddy's description was fair enough, we did drive in.

It was a magnificent circular pool, two or three hundred metres across with a waterfall cascading down a high rocky escarpment on the far side. Over the following twenty years we included it in our itineraries, and as we usually had it to ourselves, camped overnight.

On the 1984 tour we came to the Edith Falls turnoff and noticed the signpost was missing. made rather a big deal of explaining to the passengers how fortunate they were to be in the hands of such knowledgeable operators who didn't have to rely on sign posts, the track would be bad, but not beyond our capabilities. The track became almost impassable, there was no sign of tyre marks and deep washouts that would engulf a car. It seemed no one had used the track since the last wet season and we would have the place all to ourselves.

We slowly battled through, only to finally come out on a new bitumen road, a short distance from the Falls. There was a brand-new camping area, a fast food van, tents, caravans, and hordes of people. This new bitumen road left the highway further south and ran parallel to the old road - no wonder there was no signpost on the old road.

After enjoying the pool and not wanting to camp with this mob we found a bush camp off the new bitumen road. Driving out on the well signposted new bitumen road the following morning, it became obvious why there was such a mob at the Falls.

A few years later we camped at this same spot, sitting around enjoying the fire after dinner, when a Holden Ute came roaring into our camp. A young hippy looking fellow leapt out and read us the Riot Act. It appeared he was an advisor to the Jaywon Aboriginal Land Council and we were on newly declared Aboriginal Land. He told us to pull down tents, pack up and leave immediately.

Having no intention to move, I watched as his headlights, which he had kept on, getting dimmer as we argued. Finally, he went back to his car, maybe to get reinforcements, only to find it wouldn't start - flat battery. Would our people push start him? No, he was on soft sand and our people were too old and not fit enough for that. Well, could we move the coach closer and jump start him? Dreadfully inconvenient, but we will try. Finally, we started his car and in the meantime he had changed from being arrogant to being somewhat crestfallen, and we parted almost as mates, with him saying "O.K., but you won't do it again, will you?"

WE HAD OUR OWN CHARACTERS Ted Egan wrote many songs about characters in the outback, and some of our passengers had enough character to be song writing material.

Jack Orr would be a stand-out. We first met when Jack was touring the Top End in his own car and he so enjoyed the company of our Sundowners he booked on a Gunbarrel tour. He lived in Melbourne and loved telling of his exploits. As a young fellow he had ridden a bicycle right around Australia and had a diary to prove it.

When we were in Marble Bar, Western Australia, Jack said to me "You know I worked around here during the War, I was a sailor and some of us got on the grog one night in Pt. Hedland and I went to sleep in a railway carriage and woke up next day in Marble Bar. I never went much on the Navy anyway and spent the rest of the War working around here."

Knowing the railway was non-existent I wrote this off as another of Jack's tall stories, only to discover later that this line had been built in 1911 and ran until 1951. One day we were using a communal shower block and when Jack bent over to pick up the soap I saw two big oriental eyes looking at me. They were tattooed on the cheeks of his backside, maybe it was some sort of Navy thing?

Jack so enjoyed the trip that on returning to Sydney he immediately booked on the following one, but rather than returning to Melbourne, he considered staying on in Sydney. "I reckon staying at your place for the week is my best bet" he said and simply moved in.

He had a thing about making model windmills out of clothes pegs, and in no time every table in our house had been taken over with partly-constructed windmills waiting for the glue to dry. Jack used to present people with these windmills as a softening up process before imposing on them in some way, and I have seen his windmills all over Australia.

We often picked up old railway sleepers for camp fire wood before going into desert areas, and a couple that had been unused on the trip were still on board the coach, so I threw them out on the side of the driveway at home, thinking I would cut them up for our home fire.

Jack was a stocky little bloke and fancied himself with an axe, so I thought nothing of it when I saw him sharpening our axe. Then I watched him walk down the drive, swing the axe over his head and drive it through one of the old sleepers. A column of water shot up about 30ft. into the air and he stood there getting drenched with a shocked look on his face. He had buried the axe deep into the garden and cut right through our water main.

While he was a nice enough bloke, he was never far from creating some sort of strife. He made sure he was introduced to our friends wherever we went, then when touring in his own car later would make use of these friendships.

Freddie Teague in Hawker South Australia was a great old mate and he told me how Jack showed up on his doorstep one day and gave him a model windmill, saying "Remember me coming through with Bill and Doreen?" Jack then suggested the Teagues might like to put him up for the night, but Fred explained he had relatives staying and there was no room.

Fred said Jack must have slept in his car out the front, because as they sat down for breakfast, he walked in rubbing his hands asking what was for breakfast.

Jack also booked on the Simpson Desert Crossing trip and a friend in Melbourne sent us a copy of her local paper dated September 18, 1983. On the front page was a photograph of Jack with a set of buffalo horns in one hand, a spear in the other, and a water bottle around his neck.

It was a long article, but the interesting parts were –

> "Jack Orr, 67, arguably the west's last white tracker has decided to call it quits. Jack's nomadic life began 50 years ago when he left the big smoke in a bid to become the first man to ride a bicycle around Australia. He failed in 1930, 1932 and 1945, but finally made it in 1948, taking 20 months to complete the journey.

In between attempts he worked as a professional crocodile shooter. "You have to shoot them between the eyes, and when the water cleared of blood you jumped in and got 'em with your spear. Some of me mates got eaten because they went in too quick."

Jack worked as cattle drover, bounty hunter, and with a group that killed 70,000 donkeys up near the Kimberly Ranges. "I used to get two bob for the ears." He also helped build the dingo fence which crosses Central Australia.

His latest and last trek was the 800-mile crossing of the Simpson Desert in an 18-ton tourist bus in August. Jack was the tour guide. He and ex-racing car driver Bill Hans (sic) of Sydney took the first group of people across the arid waste land by bus. "It took seven days, and we were bogged many times in the soft sand. The sand moves so quickly and there's nothing out there, no trees. It was a mighty tough trip, but now I can say that I've beaten that hell hole."

Jack, single, wants the quiet life now, and wants to be cremated and have his ashes spread across the Simpson Desert."

I reckon that Jack Orr just couldn't help being a character.

On one trip we were driving up the highway planning to have lunch in Goulburn, having stopped for morning tea in Yass. It was a beautiful day, not much traffic and couldn't have been more pleasant. Then a Highway Patrol came up alongside, gave a blast of his siren and pulled-up ahead.

I stopped behind him and wondered what in blazes I had done wrong. Anyone who has had this experience would understand my feelings as the cop got out of his patrol car and ambled back to the coach. "Your name Bill Hand?" he asked, I nodded. "The boss asked me to radio your time of arrival in Goulburn, he's booking a table to take you and your wife out to lunch" he said.

In Goulburn I gave Bill Dickson a blast "Mate, don't ever do that to me again". Bill was another of our many characters and was Senior Sergeant in charge of the South Central Division of the Highway Patrol. He loved the outback, the camping life and the companionship of like- minded people. Typically, he was a tower of strength on our Simpson Desert Crossing.

Of course, some of our great characters were ladies - Norah was a lovely person, but a magnet to trouble. While in the surf at Cable Beach, Broome she was caught in a dumper and lost her false teeth. Try as we might we couldn't find them and reported the fact to the beachside kiosk. Norah was all for flying straight home, but we persuaded her to stay on, existing on soup and custard, and dunking her biscuits in hot tea. With her figure, Norah couldn't afford to lose much more weight, but she lasted the distance.

When we arrived home all the friends and rellies were waiting to greet us, including Norah's husband.

"My God, you look terrible," he said, "Put these in" handing her a set of false teeth. They had been handed in to the kiosk in Broome and they had posted them on to Norah's address in Sydney.

1985 Changes were coming thick and fast to the outback in the late 1980s and I must have been the only coach driver left not kitted-out in some sort of spiffy uniform. I felt on me it just looked pretentious. I dressed like the locals, check shirt, moleskins or jeans, elastic sided boots, that sort of thing.

It did have its downside sometimes, like asking for something at a Roadhouse and having the girl ask, "Who you are" and when I said I was the driver, she demanded to know why I didn't wear a uniform, so I probably missed out on a few free drinks by not being easily identified.

One big change in 1985 was being the last time we were welcomed into the Moomba Gas Complex.

It all began in 1976 when Les Pasley booked on a trip that took in the Cooper Creek country. Les was an executive with the Australian Gas Light Company and he told us he had a letter inviting him to tour the Santos Plant at Moomba as A.G.L. were to sign a contract to buy gas and build a pipeline to Sydney.

The Santos people gave Les the royal treatment, some of which rubbed-off on we Sundowners. We were lectured on the different types of gas, methane, ethane, butane, propane, etc. according to their number of hydrogen atoms.

All manner of interesting things were explained, like natural gas has no smell and A.G.L. would have to add rotten egg gas so people could smell and identify gas leaks. Then Santos put their gas through drying towers to eliminate water, but A.G.L. at the Sydney end would have to add moisture again to prevent leaks in their ancient seal joints all under Sydney.

We lunched in the canteen and were invited to use the showers and swimming pool, and they even stuck a Santos decal on the door of the coach to identify us as friendlies when using their private rig roads.

Of course, we pushed our luck and for the next ten years wrote ahead and booked and received similar treatment. People couldn't believe the free lunch in the canteen and I often cringed at the way they hit on the soft ice cream machine. The swimming pool was a great hit too.

All this changed in 1985 when Alan Bond bought a controlling interest in the company and was amazed to find it operated with little security and he appointed a security firm to oversee the operation. After being refused entry at the gatehouse, I gave the name of the works manager, trying to make out we were old mates and prevailed upon them to phone through. Next thing we were escorted in with an accompanying guard. It was explained that this was the last throw for old times' sake and could never be repeated.

We have learnt that nothing ever stays the same and sadly few things change for the better.

We had always worked on the principle of never keeping a coach for more than five years. Apart from appearances, it had always been an opportunity to incorporate the latest technology, but apart from costing nearly half a million dollars by the time we owned it, I couldn't think of a single mechanical improvement we could incorporate.

So, if not a new coach, we would totally strip the present vehicle and rebuild it with all new panels, and change it from a 1980 to a 1985 model in every way. It wasn't as much a money saving exercise as building on something absolutely proven and was in fact a very costly, if worthwhile move, and also it did wonders both for our and the Sundowners self-esteem.

1986 This was an easy year, the weather generally was kind, we both kept in good health, and the coach performed perfectly. Two great changes in the Top End were the wiping out of the great buffalo herds because of the B.Tec. Scheme and the explosion in crocodile numbers. Crocs are resilient critters as they were hunted intensely from 1945 till 1972 and their numbers plummeted during this period, but from then on, they were protected, and it is a rare river or waterhole in the Northern Territory that doesn't support a sign "Beware of Crocodiles".

I can't help but be in two minds about crocs as during the 60's and early 70's we swam in most of the Top End rivers and waterholes believing (and being told) that the crocs were on the verge of extinction.

Mudginberrie Station water hole was a favourite camp spot, on the right-hand side driving out to Terry Robinson's Border Store. Croc shooters had in earlier times set up camp here and considered it so safe that the Tarzan rope was still in place where they use to swing out to dive into the water.

The saltie or estuarine croc is the world's largest and most dangerous reptile, and is able to crush the bones of animals as large as buffalo in its jaws. I think it surprised everyone how quickly the crocs re-established after supposedly being on the point of extinction.

We were standing in a group near the waters' edge and I was carrying on about crocs and how they strike with amazing speed, driving themselves out of the water with their powerful tails, with jaws agape to snatch their prey. A young fellow laughed and said, "Well I'm not worried about that". I asked why, and he replied, "Don't you know I can run faster than you?" Well, he was probably right about that.

PROBLEMS IN THE SHOWERS Although we preferred the bush camps, it was necessary at many places to use official campgrounds. Some of these issued keys to open the amenities which created all sorts of problems as passengers would leave the keys in their night attire or toilet bags and forget to retrieve them until the luggage was packed away ready for departure next morning. It was easier to pay the fine than unload the coach.

I have some incidents of strange behaviour at the new camping area at Yulara:

One of our elderly Sundowner ladies returned from the shower block seething with indignation, her hair and clothing sopping wet. It appears a coach load of school girls had dragged their driver into the ladies' showers, stripped him naked and proceeded to throw buckets of water over him. Did the driver enjoy the exercise? Who knows, but to resist might raise a charge of manhandling under-age girls.

In the midst of this our passenger walked in and copped a misdirected bucket of water in the face. She sought out the lady teacher in charge and complained bitterly, only to be told that everyone involved was having the time of their lives, while she suffered some inconvenience, and where was her sense of humour.

On another occasion a tour company contracted to take an entire girls' school into the outback. With six coach loads of girls they created havoc wherever they stayed and after twenty-four hours at Yulara the ladies' showers and toilets were "stuffed" as one young girl explained to me. So, some 200 or so of them took over the male amenities. It was chaotic as we blokes were pushed and shoved around by young females in all stages of undress. It was an education to me to hear the language and cop the attitude of these school girls. One Barker College trip we were camped alongside a coach load of schoolgirls at Yulara and we heard giggling at the front of our tent and a voice whispered "Hey, are you asleep - can we come in?" For a moment I thought of pushing Doreen through the back of the tent and opening the front flap, but by then they had moved on. Just then Ian Campbell appeared with a long coat over his pyjamas and a beanie on his head looking like a minaret. He was waving his arms around as though swatting flies and shouting "Get out, all of you get out". There was a lot of whispering among the boys at breakfast, but I never did find out if the girls had any success.

Original camp at Kings Creek Station under Desert Oak trees.

1971. Doreen, Jan and Bill Trompp on top of Coronet Peak, New Zealand, wearing army surplus overcoats supplied by chairlift operators.
(Jan is the author of the Gunbarrel and Donohue Highway Diaries).

1988 AUSTRALIA'S BICENTENNIAL YEAR RULES & REGULATIONS
1989 CAPE YORK & THE GULF

Most of the big celebration events were in Sydney which of course we missed, although during our travels we caught up with many other activities around the country, one being the start of the Great Camel Race from Ayers Rock to the Gold Coast, with Queensland Premier Joh as the Starter.

Some work was done on the coach over our holidays - a new 475 horsepower V8 Detroit turbo, after-cooled engine fitted - the largest coach engine in Australia, and a unique roof mounted radiator. There were some initial bugs with such a big conversion, but the resulting performance, especially hill climbing and the saving in fuel made it worthwhile. Also new seat covers were fitted, and it looked like a brand-new coach.

Another must see in Longreach, opened by Queen Elizabeth in April 1988 was the Stockman's Hall of Fame. It really seemed all too modern for the old stockmens' heritage, with audio visuals and other clever exhibits. Nevertheless, it was a worthwhile enterprise and would be very popular.

It is an awful thing not to be at your own father's funeral, but that's what happened to me in August that year. We were completely out of touch in the Gulf country and by the time Doreen's brother Rod could contact us, it was too late to do anything. All thanks to Rod for making the arrangements in our absence. It brought up to us once again how much we have had to rely on back-up from family members to hold the fort when we have been out of touch in the outback.

Later in the year on the Gunbarrel South tour we parked near the open cut of the Sons of Gwalia mine in Western Australia and while everyone was taking photos a company car drove up and a smartly dressed fellow got out, came over and said, "Well fancy seeing you here Bill, remember me, Peter Carter."

Fact was Peter had changed more than somewhat from being a Barker College boy on a trip during the 60s. He explained he was the mine manager and would like to be our tour guide. With Peter on board controlling traffic on his mobile phone, we drove down the haul track to the bottom of the open cut, then through the processing plant with Peter giving a lecture on all things of interest.

The Sundowners could not have been more impressed with our "royal" treatment and when I was thanking him, he explained that the Central Australian trip had changed his life by creating an interest in geology which led to him studying in Australia and Canada and becoming a mine manger.

At the 1994 Barker College Reunion Ian Campbell gave me this letter –

"Dear Ian,

It was with both surprise and delight that I received your letter about the safari group reunion.

>As you anticipate it is most unlikely that I will be in Sydney at that time, so I will rely on you to remember me to Bill and Doreen and wish them a pleasant retirement on my behalf.
>
>The encounter at the Sons of Gwalia was one of those amazing coincidences that happen in our lives from time to time.
>
>It was nice to be able to do something in return for them as I had the fondest memories of the 1969 trip. (Signed) Peter Carter, Western Mining Corporation, Perth W.A."

Although we have bulging folders of thank you letters from past passengers, it is the Barker boys that I feel gained the most - and this is another typical one.

>"I remember with very warm feeling our two safari tours. The sights and sounds of the outback, the smells and the atmosphere of what is essentially Australian continue to live with me. I would venture to say that what I experienced contributed greatly to the feelings I now have toward Australia, geographically so far away. (Signed) John Pannell, Research Botanist, Wolfson College, Oxford, England."

At the Reunion we had three generations of Sundowners, with a couple who travelled in the early days, their son who came as a Barker boy, and his kids who were on our last Tasmanian tour.

Also, we were presented with an engraved silver tray with a thank you message from Barker College. The presentation was by a baldy-headed bloke who said he was on the first Barker trip, then he was joined by a young school boy who was on the very last trip. Not surprising really when you consider it was thirty years between the first Barker trip and the last.

RULES AND REGULATIONS After a couple of rather nasty bus/truck accidents, the powers that be rushed in new regulations.

They decreed we fit speed limiters and tachographs to record speed and driving hours as well as new style logbooks.

Some newspapers called coaches "Tin Coffins on Wheels" when the truth was that coaches were really the safest form of transport apart from airlines.

National Parks then decided to add to our paperwork by requiring we write ahead to obtain visitor permits and of course pay fees in advance.

Earlier laws decreed we couldn't send out travel brochures unless we were registered travel agents, which meant what we considered working capital be locked up in a trust account. All finances were audited before annual renewal.

We both had to pass Driving Accreditation courses and get little photos to display to the passengers confirming we knew how to drive - after nearly three million kilometers without one driving offence, I now had proof that I could drive. How simple life was when we started in business and how difficult it would be to start-up today.

Next, we had to have registered off-street parking and an approved maintenance area.

A friend had a five-acre property at Kellyville which he needed to sell quickly as he was moving to Queensland. The price he accepted was more than reasonable and we had our maintenance area by putting down a concrete slab and building a workshop onto the old house.

Along with our weekender, this meant we were probably the only people who owned three houses and continued to live in a tent.

I submitted the plans to the Department and they picked the fact that I hadn't shown the length of the frontage, so having not the faintest idea, said 80 metres. It was stamped, no one would ever look at it again and does anyone really care? It's just that every box had to be filled in.

Next, we had to have an accredited Office Manager. With our workload, this required Doreen attending Sydney University over a period of six months, with exams to pass at the end. Better Doreen than me, trying to absorb the detail of local bus operations, planning routes, fare structures, timetables, wages, industrial relations, duty rosters, costing charters, workshop managements etc. etc. She passed with "A"s in everything except Sales and Publicity where she only rated a "B". Fair enough I thought seeing we have never had to do any of this and left it all to our passengers.

It was a most impressive night at Sydney Uni. when Doreen, along with her classmates filed up one at a time to shake hands and receive their diplomas in Tourist Management.

It's quite understandable that the public expect certain standards to be met by people in business in the way I have detailed. That is vehicles tested for maintenance, tour operators tested for competency, weight restrictions and of course health of accredited drivers. While necessary, it is hard not to feel threatened by all this checking and testing and the medical test annually was a worry as it became similar to that of airline captains.

The eyesight test in particular was very thorough, and always a worry as the years roll by. One day I asked our mate Phil Biega how he went on a test and he said "The bloke said, can you read the bottom line? And I said "Yeah, made in China". I guess Phil doesn't need glasses. All these things I have listed are all very well, but someone has to pay because they all add to our costs, just as a new testing machine decided we were blowing a whisker too much exhaust smoke, necessitating a complete engine overhaul.

1989 CAPE YORK & THE GULF

We had been trying to find time to do a survey trip up the Cape when another possibility became available.

The *Noel Buxton* was an ex-lighthouse tender, about the ugliest old tub I have ever laid eyes on, but no doubt seaworthy and quite comfortable on board. Doreen and I joined a cruise from Cairns to Thursday Island, travelling mostly at night and by day exploring Lizard Island, the Cod Hole, tip of Cape York and many other places including islands on both the outward and return journeys.

With this experience we scheduled three tours incorporating the cruise. Unfortunately, after two tours the *Noel Buxton* was leased out for other duties and we were forced to charter a much newer and luxurious boat. While this was an excellent vessel, we felt things were getting too expensive and up-market and took it off our itineraries.

At this time there was a concerted push to publicise the tourism potential of many places in far North Queensland and the Gulf country. An organisation called Savannah Guides was started, whereby certain locals became trained and uniformed advisors to visitors to their area.

After we completed the Cairns/Thursday Island cruise we headed west to Mt. Surprise, camping in the excellent camping area alongside the Pub where the publican, Bruce Butler, arranged a barbeque dinner with the locals. Bruce was also a Savannah Guide and we were asking him about the Lava Tubes which we knew were in the area.

He explained he had permission from the Collins brothers who owned the local station to act as guide to people wanting to see these so-called Undara Lava Tubes.

Bruce drove ahead in his Suzuki four-wheel-drive and he had advised us the track was four-wheel-drive only and the coach would only get so far and then we would have a rather long walk.

At one point, Bruce came to a high old lava flow, his Suzuki gradually climbed to the top making rather hard work of it. At the top he stopped and called back that from this point we would have to walk. So, I locked the auto in low gear, engaged the diff locks and decided to give it a go. The coach made light work of it much to Bruce's amazement. Then we drove right through to the lava tubes, only ripping off a few tree branches with our air conditioner.

The section of the tubes we came to was known as Barker's Cave and was quite amazing. Thinking in terms of the Sydney Harbour Tunnel, it was at least as long and more than twice the diameter.

There are other lava tubes in Queensland, Victoria and we have seen them in Hawaii, but none of these could compare with the size of those at Undara.

A couple of years later Gerry Collins built a tourist village, then bulldozed roads through to the lava tubes and we were there for the official opening of the complex by the Queensland Premier, Wayne Goss.

There is a mounted photograph in the tourist village of John Craig of Buffalo Tours bringing in the first tourist coach party. Quite right, John did - after the roads had been bulldozed and the village set up, so good luck to Johnnie Craig (a real nice bloke).

Lawn Hill Gorge was another place we had heard about, but it too was on privately-owned land. In 1981 Doreen wrote to Lawn Hill Station enquiring about access and received quite a nice letter in reply. In one paragraph it said "The period May through to November each year is a period of intense cattle mustering and working, and subsequently we must limit the amount of traffic using our internal roads. You would however, be welcome to visit the gorge area, but the road is rough, passing over stony ridges, and is suitable only for four-wheel-drive vehicles with plenty of ground clearance".

In 1984 it became a declared National Park and the access road improved, although still narrow and requiring great care. Lawn Hill Gorge was indeed a spectacular place, all we had expected and more. So much so we included it twice in 1989 and many folks thought it the most beautiful place in Australia.

We found it gave us greater flexibility to set up camp at nearby Adel's Grove outside the National Park where we could have a fire and there was a small general store. Adel's Grove, or the Frenchman's Garden was commissioned by the Government in 1930 for a French Botanist, A. de Lestang (his initials ADEL becoming the name of the area) to experiment with the growing of tropical fruit trees.

Although most have not withstood the ravages of time, there are still a few exotics surviving along the river flat. The place was run by Barry Kubala, an ex-New Zealander and a

Savannah Guide, who allowed us much more room to spread out than could be expected in the National Park.

We believed, like most people that the only road in was via the Gregory Hotel on the main road, but Barry spoke of a more direct alternative route from Mt. Isa through Riversleigh Station, but it was quite rough and suitable for four-wheel-drive only. Well that sounded OK by us and we came to use it instead of retracing our steps.

In our retirement in 2000 we returned in our Landcruiser to spend time studying the famous fossil fields at Riversleigh and found the roads much improved due to the nearby Century Zinc Mine. We camped at Clive Campbell's beautiful tourist camp on the Gregory River, and accompanied his tours of the fossil fields. Clive was an old friend of many years standing and his family ran Campbell's Coaches in Mt. Isa.

**1995 Retirement. On the Silk Route - the Golden Road to Samarkand.
Lake of Heaven near Urumqi, Western China.**

1990-94 OUTSIDE JOB, SORE TOE, TASMANIA, LAST GOODBYES & RETIREMENT

The decade from 1980 to 1990 saw huge increases in prices, with a standard Denning coach rising from $120,000 to $320,000 and drivers' wages from $4.80 per hour to $10.50 per hour. However, during this period there was no increase in fares, typically Sydney to Brisbane was $42, the same as 10 years earlier.

One of the reasons - in 1980 an eccentric, Max Holman started V.I.P. Express and announced he would hold down fares and take over the market. It became a price war and it worked in as much as about a dozen express companies folded - Ambassador, Trailways, Roadranger, Bus 44, Aussie etc. Discounting meant there was no money for replacement vehicles, while those in use became increasingly unreliable.

In ten years the beautiful V.I.P. fleet was worn out and "Mad Maxie Holman" (as everyone knew him) was finished.

During all this mayhem one company continued to apparently prosper. Everyone agreed that it was due to management skills that Deluxe Coaches became the dominant operator throughout Australia with some one hundred and eighty coaches.

None of these operators actually owned their coaches as they were leased from the banks and it must always have been a balancing act between income and lease payments.

1990 brought another blow to the industry when Saddam Hussein invaded Kuwait, sending fuel prices up by as much as 45%. However Deluxe appeared to be going from strength to strength when suddenly they collapsed, and as drivers knew they would no longer get paid, coaches were left all over Australia.

We had a call from one of our old Barker boys - they keep popping up everywhere, now an executive at the Advance Bank. He had been handed the job of repossessing five tourist coaches, 1 in Darwin, 1 in Alice Springs and 3 in Brisbane as a result of the collapse of the big Deluxe coaches' operation.

The ANZ was holding a $1.7 million line of credit for Deluxe and seems to have panicked and foreclosed. The Commonwealth bank had 58 coaches on lease and were "furious at the ANZ decision", knowing the second-hand market would be flooded with coaches, sold at a loss.

The Advance boys were not exactly thrilled about if either, as they were money men not second-hand bus dealers and had no experience with this sort of thing and asked if we could handle the repossession for them.

This would be an interesting and nicely paying little job, but where would we find the time to grab coaches and drive them across the country? We asked Phil Biega if he would be interested - would he what! He jumped at the chance and was issued with an all-expenses credit card.

We arranged with Darryl Tutty, our old mate in Darwin to hold one coach in his bus depot, then George Sabbadin in Alice Springs did the same. George was our Mobil fuel supplier and an old school chum of Tim and Ian at Kings Creek.

Initially I anticipated having to put some work into the enterprise, but Phil carried out the whole thing like a precision military operation. This was another example of how very fortunate we have been over the years in being able to turn to so many capable and reliable friends when they have been needed.

Phil flew to Darwin, drove the coach down to Alice Springs, then with George's help employed a driver and brought both coaches back to Sydney. Then he flew to Brisbane, hired drivers to take two coaches back to Sydney, but on checking the third, found it was undriveable with a failed clutch. This upset the bank boys who thought the coach would have to be auctioned, as is, where is, in Brisbane. But Phil loves a challenge and contacted Joe Calabro at Surfside Coaches on the Gold Coast who we knew from Joe's days as an ex-Sydney bus operator. Yes, Joe had a rebuilt clutch assembly in stock and Phil worked into the night fitting it. He then surprised us all by driving it into Sydney a day later.

The Advance bank happily and promptly paid all bills, and Phil was pleased enough to suggest we offer our services when the next bus company failed. In our dealings with them, we found the Advance Bank to be a well-run organization, but the name no longer exists as they were taken over and integrated into the St. George Bank.

Now there's a coincidence, just as I was writing this, the news came through that the big King Bros. bus operation on the New South Wales north coast has gone into liquidation. It seems they have only mislaid about two hundred million dollars?

AUSTRALIAN NATIONAL PARKS

At the end of 1991 and early 1992 we were obliged to attend seminars in Kakadu and Uluru National Parks, so we would have sufficient knowledge to conduct tours. Permits were required by all tourist operators and attending the seminars was necessary for approval to be granted.

Mostly our study group appeared to be young people who worked in travel agencies. At Kakadu at least I kept a low profile and bit my lip on a number of occasions, but at Uluru I'm afraid I cracked as we had a young hippie-type instructor who used a combination of extreme prejudice laced with bad language.

He got the shock of his life, and he backed down when he found out a bit of my history and then of all things I was asked to give a talk about the early days at the Rock.

Yami Lester, the Uluru Chairman of Management was at the seminar, and sometimes accompanied us on walks around the Rock. We had many mutual friends going back over many years and as Yami was blind he found my shoulder the ideal height to hang onto while we walked.

The upshot was we finally earned certificates to prove we knew enough about Northern Territory National Parks to conduct tours.

While at the Rock we took advantage of the attractive off-season prices to stay at the ex-Sheraton, now Sails in the Desert Hotel. The new manager obviously under the misapprehension we were somehow important, took us under his wing. We could see he was the product of a management school as he went on to explain how hopeless the previous people had been. "We are changing that dumb name Yulara Resort back to Ayers Rock Resort, now that is a real brand name", then added "It wouldn't hurt to do the same with the Rock". From a purely commercial point of view he was probably right.

After the Kakadu lectures we felt we earned a few days break at Seven Spirit Bay on the Coburg Peninsula. We flew in a small plane from Darwin and enjoyed the Wilderness Lodge and surrounds. Once again taking advantage of the cheaper off-season prices, in fact there was only one other person staying, so the service was great with about ten staff to look after three of us.

LEAVE IT TO THE EXPERTS - TASMANIA
Why did I think Jacko needed help relining our brakes? The only thing I did was drop one of the damnably heavy brake drums on my toes. I crushed my right big toe just as I had my fingers years before, and although I have not lost the toe, it has never regained normal movement.

I hobbled around on my heel for a couple of weeks and couldn't bear putting my foot down on the accelerator for any length of time, so once again we turned to Phil Biega for help.

The 1992 Tasmania Tour I acted as navigator over Phil's shoulder. At one stage, probably tongue in cheek he remarked "You know every pothole on this Island, don't you". Just the same I think Phil was disappointed when I was able to drive the following tour.

A welcome change we noted in these later years was the excellent operation of the Bass Strait ferry.

On our earlier tours to Tassie the unions quite literally ran the ferry service, and service was not the correct word. It was only with the introduction of a new ship that the Government took control and broke the union control on their TT Line.

Typical of the bad-old days, we had a tour departing from Devenport to Melbourne, all the paper work correct, Doreen took the group on board to allocated cabins, suggested they have a shower while waiting for departure to avoid the crush later. I was kept on the dock with the coach waiting to drive on board and finally told, "Bad luck, no more space". I raced on board, found Doreen, then she had to find all the Sundowners, gather their gear and leave the ship. The attitude of the company was, bad luck, but you will get priority in two-days time.

This meant we had to spend another couple of days in Tasmania before we could get the coach and group back home, not a great problem for us, but if we had been running a more costly and accommodated tour, the cost and inconvenience would have been considerable.

On another occasion we berthed in Melbourne just as the union had a disagreement with management and they refused to dock the ship. We lined the rail to watch seemingly endless heated meetings on the wharf which went on for hours before we were finally allowed off.

The whole attitude today is so different, when it is service with a smile, in comparison to the often surly take it or leave it of the old days. Not that I ever enjoyed the journey and have always regarded any time spent on a ship like the time spent in jail, with always the added possibility of drowning.

On our last tour to Tassie in 1994 on the *Spirit of Tasmania* Doreen was thrilled to be invited onto the bridge to watch the berthing in Melbourne at the invitation of an old Sundowner who had been a Senior Skipper with the shipping line.

1994 TIME TO HANG UP OUR BOOTS
When to finally retire is not an easy decision, and running a business is not simple at any time, so while we were still in good health, we made the decision to retire at the end of 1994. We let it be known at the start of the year that this was our swansong, and were amazed as so many old Sundowners rushed to book seats for the final tours.

One of our regulars, Thelma Bridges, booked and came on every trip of this last year. Dorothy Webb worked out one more trip would assure her of the record of over one thousand days of Sundowner travel. It became a real tear jerker of a year, saying goodbyes to friends and colleagues all around Australia.

We first stayed at Arkaroola in 1970 when a mutual friend of Reg Sprigg recommended we include this fascinating property in our tours of the Flinders Ranges. It developed into a great friendship with Reg and his wife Griselda (see *Dune is a four-letter Word* by Griselda about these early days) and particularly with their schoolboy son Doug.

Douglas Sprigg was a remarkable young man who never ceased to amaze me with his knowledge on so many subjects. He obtained his flying licence the day he turned sixteen and over the years we flew with him in all manner of aircraft, and he allowed Doreen and I to take the controls of his Ultra Lite which was great fun.

We both drove four-wheel-drive ridge top tours with Doug and one young Sundowner couple so fell in love with Arkaroola they went back and worked there. Although we had grown used to last goodbyes in this final year, Doug's friendship had become something special and we shared quite a tearful parting.

Central Australia was the most difficult of farewells, and we managed to catch up with many old friends who demanded we return and spend some time with them in our retirement. We promised we would, and of course we have. Six years after making the promise we threw a few things in the back of the car and went for a drive, finishing up in Alice Springs, staying with Tim Lander and spending days reminiscing with old mates.

On the last Central Australia trip, we were invited to camp at Impolera, an outstation of Hermannsburg, by the Aboriginal owners, Herman and Mavis Malbunka. Mavis, who is Gus Williams' sister led walks around the property which had magnificent scenery and even had Gasses Bluff in the "backyard".

Birdsville was going ahead in leaps and bounds with a new amenities block and water and electricity to each site. No shortage of power these days with a real power station instead of the old water powered generator mounted on the bore head.

Blocks were being surveyed in a new estate they called Birdsville Heights, and the kids kept saying "Hey, Bill an Doreen, get a block and build a house an ya can run tours into the Simpson Desert".

I told Barnsie at the garage about this. He had a better idea and offered me a job. He needed an off-sider mechanic also "with motor bike experience". No shortage of work for us in Birdsville.

OUR VERY LAST TOUR

Our last tour for the year, in fact our last tour forever, was going to be so easy, only twenty-two days and sealed roads nearly all the way. It was listed as Kangaroo Island, including the Grampians, Mt. Eccles, Lake Mungo and Kinchega, all for the price of $1,450.

Doreen always added all sorts of interesting little side trips to itineraries, and so it came to pass that after leaving Colac and driving through Lavers Hill to join the Great Ocean Road we took a side trip to see Melba Gully State Park. It was an excellent morning tea location with an interesting walk track. The track out of the gully was rather steep so I put my foot down for the uphill grade, there was a loud bang, then the motor peak revved, and we slowly drifted backwards.

I locked the brakes, got out and rolled underneath, not knowing what to expect. I lay there absolutely amazed, the main tail shaft connecting the gearbox to the first differential had vanished, there was just a bit of jagged metal at the driving flange and then nothing.

Of all the places this could have happened, like in the middle of the Simpson Desert, not that this place wasn't relatively isolated as well.

I sent Sundowners down the road to find the tailshaft, but they returned empty-handed, so on crawling back underneath and looking carefully I found it sitting up inside the chassis rail. I unbolted the driving flange and was left with the tubular tail shaft with a broken, twisted rim at one end and the flange with similar damage where they rather vaguely fitted together.

Taking the bits, I got a lift back to the Road House at Lavers Hill. Meantime Doreen began organizing setting up camp in the bush as apparently, I had muttered something about "we won't see this fixed this side of Melbourne".

It was about 11.00am by the time I got to the Road House and the manager assured me the

R.A.C. bloke at Port Campbell would look after us. While devouring a meat pie I rang through and the R.A.C. bloke said it was a very unusual thing, but he could repair it OK. Then as a sort of afterthought he asked, "What sort of vehicle is it?" I replied, "A tourist coach". There was a dead silence, then he said, "Forget it, I wouldn't touch it". I pleaded, but he came back with "Public Transport vehicle, liability and all that stuff, no way".

Feeling dejected and defeated, I turned back to the Road House bloke and ordered another meat pie, as I seem to get awfully hungry when dejection sets in. He gave me a number at Apollo Bay, saying "Try this number'. The answer was "I'll get the boy to pick you up and bring you down here".

What a surprise at Apollo Bay, this fellow had a magnificent engineering shop. Using high tensile steel tube, he replaced the damaged portion, welded it beautifully, balanced it, and arranged for the "boy" to drive me back and help me fit it.

In the meantime, Doreen was arranging repacking the coach, for against all odds we were once again mobile and finished up driving into camp at Port Campbell before dark the same day. So much for an easy trip.

After about twenty-five years of staying at Ellson's Guest House on Kangaroo Island, Ivan Ellson arranged a wonderful farewell dinner and our passengers put on a fancy-dress pageant culminating in Doreen and I being presented with "Order of the Outback" medals. A night to remember!

COMING HOME TO A STREET PARTY

We had been using Ron Deane's depot as a departure point and I don't know what Ron made of the scene when we came home on the last trip.

Hundreds of people had arranged a street party with streamers, party hats, balloons and celebration cakes. The whole thing was overwhelming, and I honestly didn't know whether to laugh or cry.

We spoke to everybody and thanked them for sharing their lives with us and assuring them we would never have survived in business without their support and how they had left us with so many wonderful memories.

Many wished to continue with friendships made on tours and expressed a wish to get together from time to time and suggested day walks, picnics, luncheons, weekends or week-long stopovers on friends' properties, or other locations with hostel type accommodation. Doreen has been organizing on average half a dozen of these reunions each year ever since for people who travelled with us, going back nearly forty years.

We have formed life time friendships with not only hundreds of our old passengers, but of course mates all over Australia and in some cases overseas. We still send out hundreds of Christmas cards and receive the same amount in return.

With constant travel the better part of our lives, it seems to have become a bit of an obsession, particularly with Doreen, who is forever planning that we be somewhere else, and with the number of people we know, perhaps it is not surprising we seem to run into friends wherever we go.

The most extreme example however would have to be in a small town on the south coast of Turkey called Kas. We were booked into room 15 on the second floor of a small hotel, and Doreen had showered and was getting into bed when we both noticed the door handle slowing turning back and forth. I could hear whispering and scratching on the door lock.

Maybe I had had a couple of drinks, or fell back on belief that sudden violent attack is the best defence, so I eased off the safety catch, whipped the door open, and yelled in the best banzai tradition. The fellow bending down at the door lock fell over backwards crashing into a woman behind him who went down in a screaming heap.

The poor fellow on the floor looked up wide-eyed and said, "Bill Hand - what are you doing in our room?" It was a Sundowner couple, John and Sheila. They were with a coach group and booked into the room above us on the third floor, and had got out of the lift on the second floor by mistake.

When we came down for breakfast we were greeted by John and Sheila and the entire coach group who had been told of their adventures the night before. We had a few more laughs as we bid them farewell.

CLOSING THE BOOKS
Early in 1995 we sold the coach and most of the equipment, so we no longer required Kellyville. We met with various Kellyville neighbours as there was talk of big developments planned for the area and it was advised to hold onto the property. In 1997 Mirvac made us a most attractive offer subject to water supply being available. It took time, and the deal was finalized in 1999. This has improved our retirement fund and allowed Doreen to plan more travels.

These days when we meet and reminisce, people invariably ask 'Don't you miss the coach travelling." The answer of course is yes, and it is the good memories we remember most, looking forward to catching up with old mates, seeing passengers happy and enthusiastic with the sights and places we show them and probably most of all, just sitting and yarning around a camp fire under a sky full of brilliant stars.

I'll admit however, there are some things I don't miss, repairing flat tyres, fixing break-downs, or getting covered in thick, black greasy mud when digging out of a bog. As mentioned before, we have returned to many of our old haunts in our own car since our retirement and people ask what has changed. The simple answer is everything - technology has changed practically everything.

The isolation of outback towns due to horror stretches of road is pretty much a thing of the past, and a Mini-Minor could handle the Birdsville Track as easily as our Landcruiser.

Instead of powdered milk and canned food, everything from fresh vegetables and fruit to ice cream is available at every wayside stop, and I cannot help wondering at all the fuss about Telstra. In big towns like Alice Springs we used to book calls to Sydney and then sometimes wait around for hours to get through, only to barely understand any dialogue over the crackling. At Ayers Rock there was nothing, no phone of any sort. Phones all across the outback work as well as at home in Sydney, with instant dial tone. Even remote homesteads are on untimed local calls, often carried by solar-powered microwave towers.

Many outback pubs have become theme park caricatures with their walls lined with memorabilia to convince the patron he is still living in some long past era.

Not that I'm knocking any of these changes - I think it's great that people are getting out and really seeing Australia and I applaud those Grey Nomads with their G.P.S. and C.B. Radio-equipped motor homes who are enjoying travelling across the top of Australia during our Southern winters. Dangers have been minimised and so has adventure, but there is still so much to enjoy exploring Australia.

Just how privileged we have been living in one of the freest and most prosperous societies in the history of the human race. We were the first generation ever to be able to afford the time and money to travel freely across vast areas of mostly pristine countryside.

We sold adventure as much as travel, not scary, but adventure nevertheless, and unfortunately this is becoming less possible with insurance, restrictive legislation, modern communication and such basic things as fences and bitumen.

The freedoms we took for granted are fast disappearing and we were so lucky to have enjoyed that small window in time, when travelling the outback was still adventure.

But the strangest thing of all was that it all started with Doreen reading a book at school that made her absolutely determined to see Ayers Rock.

Let's hope that kids keep reading books that inspire them to go out with dreams to be fulfilled.

www.ingramcontent.com/pod-product-compliance
Lightning Source LLC
Chambersburg PA
CBHW081420300426
44110CB00016BA/2326